Handbook of
Compensation Management

Matthew J. DeLuca

PRENTICE HALL
Englewood Cliffs, New Jersey 07632

Prentice-Hall International (UK) Limited, *London*
Prentice-Hall of Australia Pty. Limited, *Sydney*
Prentice-Hall Canada, Inc., *Toronto*
Prentice-Hall Hispanoamericana, S.A., *Mexico*
Prentice-Hall of India Private Limited, *New Delhi*
Prentice-Hall of Japan, Inc., *Tokyo*
Simon & Schuster Asia Pte. Ltd., *Singapore*
Editora Prentice-Hall do Brasil, Ltda., *Rio de Janeiro*

©1993 *by*

PRENTICE HALL
Englewood Cliffs, NJ

10 9 8 7 6 5 4 3 2 1

Library of Congress Cataloging-in-Publication Data

DeLuca, Matthew J.
  Handbook of compensation management/Matthew J. DeLuca.
  p.   cm. Includes index.
  ISBN 0-13-159658-6
  1. Compensation management.   I. Title.
  HF5549.5.C67D45   1993
    658.3'22—dc20   93-13378
                                                     CIP

ISBN 0-13-159658-6

9 780131 596580   90000>

PRENTICE HALL
Career & Personal Development
Englewood Cliffs, NJ 07632
Simon & Schuster, A Paramount Communications Company

Printed in the United States of America

To Nanette for all her assistance

ACKNOWLEDGMENTS

Every book that gets published does so only with the assistance of a great team of people in a variety of capacities. This book is no exception.

First let me thank Nanette DeLuca for graphics and ongoing editorial assistance. If the concept made no sense, she was always the one to say so.

Then there is Brian Dunn from Towers Perrin. He kindly reviewed the concepts in their earliest stages and enlisted the support of Susan Rowland and Cheryl Zapolsky of the Towers Perrin staff.

Thanks go to Christine Steltz and Christopher Healy from Hewitt Associates for sharing their materials and allowing me to include them.

For salary surveys and forms, Rick Kravitz and Laura Kaiser of Panel Publications were most helpful, as were Len Adams, Maria Bruck, and Joan Paolucci.

For other advice in compensation I appreciate the time given by Bob Hanley from Canon USA. Vincent Lee, Ed Sullivan, and Gil Tucker were always there for a positive and encouraging word.

One more person who was extremely helpful in this project, as she has been in so many others, is Melva Diamante. She was a big help particularly in the area of job analysis. In fact, she is the person primarily responsible for the research and final version of Chapter 2, "How to Analyze Jobs to Determine Pay Rates." On the subject of software, I would like to thank the staff at CMI and AbraCadebra.

Last, thanks go to Ellen Schneid Coleman, Philip Ruppel, Ruth Mills, Sybil Grace of the Prentice Hall staff, and a special thank you to production editor Zsuzsa Neff for dealing with all the details of production. It has been quite a while since I first ran with Ellen Schneid Coleman's suggestions to my current editor, Sybil Grace, who has been most helpful in seeing this book through to its successful completion.

ABOUT THE AUTHOR

Matt DeLuca, SPHR, is president of the Management Resource Group, Inc., a human resources consulting, training and recruiting firm in New York City. A major focus of this firm is "nuts and bolts" consulting for clients in both the private and not-for-profit sectors. Services that the firm provides include the design of pay programs, salary surveys, and performance management systems and the installation of human resource information systems (HRIS).

Matt formerly served as vice-president and manager of human resources at the Bank of Tokyo for its New York facilities. Prior to that he was hired by Bank Hapoalim, an Israeli bank, to develop a personnel function for its United States operations. He started his career at Chemical Bank, where he served in a variety of human resource and training and development positions.

He has been an adjunct faculty member at New York University since 1981. In addition to courses for the Management Institute, he has made presentations to a variety of institutions and organizations throughout the United States. NYU has presented him the "Award for Teaching Excellence." Matt has also served on the graduate faculty of Polytechnic University and teaches on the undergraduate level for the College of Saint Elizabeth, and Mercy College.

He is frequently asked by a variety of professional associations, including the Society for Human Resource Management and the American Payroll Association, to make presentations at national conferences. His past board appointments include the New York Chapter of the American Institute of Banking and the New York Personnel Management Association.

Matt has published two books, *Cost Containment in Human Resources* and *The Personnel Recordkeeper* (currently in its sixth annual edition).

WHAT THIS BOOK WILL DO FOR YOU

One of the problems, paradoxes, and opportunities for the human resource profession is deciding whether human resources is a people function or an information function. More and more, "both" seems the appropriate answer; yet, for the HR professional to gain and maintain credibility depends on his/her ability to provide answers whenever required—for any function perceived to be a subset of personnel/human resource activities.

TO HAVE THE ANSWERS WHEN NEEDED

The experienced personnel/human resource professional doesn't worry about the unexpected question, but not because he/she knows the answer each and every time. Rather he/she is confident in knowing how to access a resource that will provide the opportunity to develop a complete and timely answer. We hope that *Handbook of Compensation Management* will become such a resource.

A ONE-STOP SOURCE

Early in the project, a senior compensation manager from a major global electronics firm, when told of the book proposal, acknowledged the total lack of a compensation book that would be a "one stop" volume for pay and other compensation issues. *Handbook of Compensation Management* intends to fill that void.

FOR THE PAY, WAGE AND SALARY, AND COMPENSATION ADMINISTRATOR

For those pay, wage and salary, and compensation professionals who need a comprehensive and up-to-date source, this *Handbook* is a ready reference for a timely inquiry on an appropriate subject.

FOR THE PERSON NEW TO THE FUNCTION

For the recent arrival, *Handbook of Compensation Management* will serve as a solid first work or "primer" (that is, a book covering all the basics of a subject in a thorough manner). We hope it will soon become dog-eared as it is frequently consulted as a "quick learn."

FOR THE SEASONED PAY PROFESSIONAL

For the seasoned compensation professional—regardless of title—the *Handbook* will serve to address specific issues that may require in-depth consideration. For recent developments such as skill-based pay, the impact of the ADA and the role of budgets in the pay program, the *Handbook* provides relevant information. At the same time, due to changing circumstances, the absence of need for a variety of pay issues on an ongoing basis for the majority of topics provided between the covers of this book will nonetheless allow the seasoned pro to update his/her knowledge in a specific subject area whenever it becomes important.

FOR THE PERSONNEL/HUMAN RESOURCE GENERALIST

Handbook of Compensation Management may also serve as a reference for the intermediate generalist. The book will serve as a "hole plugger" that will enable him/her to refer to specific topics in which there has been little or no opportunity to gain experience. The *Handbook* will make one knowledgeable after a brief amount of time.

HOW THIS BOOK IS ORGANIZED: AN ACTION-ORIENTED, BIG-PICTURE ORIENTATION WITH A DETAILED STRUCTURE AND EXAMPLES

The text is balanced with graphical displays as well as usable forms to acquaint the reader with a variety of informational tools. This will enable the reader to not only find the answer to a specific question but to also determine an appropriate course of action.

In addition to basic frequently discussed issues of pay, this *Handbook* addresses other topics that are normally beyond the scope of the subject but an integral part of understanding the complete picture. The additional understanding that will come when integrating the discussion of pay with compensation policy issues, the business plan, and payroll will prove invaluable.

Handbook of Compensation Management provides answers to questions and problems like these:

- What impact does the Americans with Disabilities Act (ADA) have on job descriptions?
- What pay problems should you be sensitive to that a simple audit procedure will eliminate?
- What is the real answer that management wants when it asks for "headcount" numbers?
- How to select a payday and frequency to maximize staff morale.
- How to design a staff budget linked to the rest of the business plan.
- How to determine the staff needed to complete the implementation of the pay program and what their role should be.
- How to conduct effective job analyses that will lead to complete job descriptions and cost-effective job evaluation by enlisting line support.
- How to develop a more effective pay program while living with the one already in place.
- How to conduct successful salary surveys—without doing all the work yourself.
- What training considerations must be given for the implementation of any pay program?
- How to develop a complete and practical approach to effective audit activities.
- What steps to take to turn the performance appraisal process into a performance management system.
- Is there an alternative approach to staff-related expenses that will lead to a greater return for the organization?
- How to ensure that incentives will deliver.
- What are the ongoing requirements that provide linkage between payroll and the organization's pay program that are essential to an organization's effectiveness?
- Whether (and to what extent) the pay function should be automated.
- How to develop a practical approach for building an automated system (HRIS) once the decision is made to go ahead.

The tables, lists, forms, case studies, and narrative, in an easy-to-read format, will give you the timely information you need to design programs, plan projects, and determine the answers to management questions essential to building and sustaining your personal credibility.

CONTENTS

FOREWORD

"Unequal Pay Widespread in U.S." read the headline from a recent *New York Times* article.* The article disclosed widening salary gaps not only between high school and college graduates but also between men and women and between minorities and non-minorities. The article went on to cite increasing pay disparities among workers regardless of race or gender, because of the growing importance of certain skills in the workplace and the declining role of unions. Other influences, such as an organization's continuing ability to meet its payroll, growing reliance on other forms of compensation, and marketplace factors were also mentioned for having significant impact on pay levels. Unfortunately, the impression left by the article is that pay should be considered only from its "paycheck" aspect. Benefit elements, though a major portion of payroll cost, were never discussed at all.

What is significant about this article is that its very presence is one more sign of the growing importance of pay and the subject of compensation as a business topic. As organizations shift priorities to meet the challenges of changing conditions, these changes affect the workforce and the organization's ability to pay its employees.

The issue of pay is in fact too frequently missing from the strategic plans of organizations. They may fail to give sufficient time and attention to compensation issues, including the basic determination upon which pay levels will be decided.

On what basis should pay-level decisions be made? The question has received a variety of muddled answers for a lot of different reasons. For several years a person's pay has been considered by many to be nothing more than an entitlement. Additionally, concerns regarding discrimination and the union movement have not only diffused considerations of pay levels but also eliminated the need to address pay as an opportunity for reward. Now, however, agreement is growing that decisions regarding pay should be determined only after a deliberate process addressing the organization's current and future ability to pay. Only then should an organization move on to consider pay as the basis for rewarding its employees.

Some issues that will have a major impact on the wage and salary area from now through the end of the century include demographics, global competition, and technology.

* The *New York Times* 8/14/90 pp. D1, D8 by Louis Uchitelle.

DEMOGRAPHICS

During the 1990s the demographic characteristics of the workforce, not only in the United States but throughout the world, will continue to change as workers start to grow older in greater numbers. Fewer entry-level workers will be available. There will be greater numbers of minorities and women in the workforce both in terms of actual numbers and in percentages that will increase due to heavier proportions of them entering the workforce for the first time.

Immigration also is considered a major issue as the United States prepares for the challenges of the 1990s. The Department of Labor predicts the greatest influx of immigrants since the mass movement of people to this country early in the twentieth century.

There will be other complications as employers continue to encounter "graduates" from the school system who seem unable to meet requirements of the job that earlier graduates had no problem fulfilling. Added to this pressure will be the variety of values that each of these employees bring to work with them. For some, pay will not be the major consideration that it will be for others, who will be as interested as their predecessors in using their employment as an opportunity to obtain wealth that would be unimaginable otherwise.

GLOBAL COMPETITION

Organizations in the United States have realized throughout the 1970s and 1980s that the United States no longer possesses a monopoly in technology. The United States is also not the sole determinant of global economic policy. Quality and product are two words that don't necessarily mean U.S. leadership throughout the world as they did in the 1950s and 1960s.

To meet the realities of the new world, organizations headquartered in the United States must be able to compete effectively. The cost and quality of products and services must match or surpass those produced elsewhere, or the product itself must be uniquely attractive to the customer regardless of location. If goods and services cannot be produced effectively here in the United States, then each corporation will increasingly think in terms of the location where it will be more appropriate to produce them.

The United States has already witnessed this happening on a more and more frequent basis. Insurance carriers based in Hartford, Connecticut use workers in Ireland and Jamaica to process claims. Automobile manufacturers headquartered in Detroit employ workers in Mexico. Garment companies located in New York City use factories in Hong Kong. This is not something that is unique to the United States. The Japanese, in their efforts to continue their economic miracle, pursue a similar course as the wages of Japanese workers become increasingly less competitive. They, too, search for these same markets in the continuing quest for the cheapest and highest quality labor. In fact, the scramble for talented workers throughout the world is increasing as evidenced by the fact that five Japanese automobile manufacturers currently have plants in the United States and have become the third largest automobile manufacturer in the United States, replacing Chrysler.

TECHNOLOGY

Increasingly, the life span of new technology is growing shorter, accompanied by rapidly changing systems. Accordingly demand for skills rapidly changes and the supply and the demand for workers who are able to provide those skills switches accordingly. No longer is a skill something to be acquired and developed and maintained throughout one's professional life. Such books as *Career Veer** heralded the arrival of the requirement that any employee who is going to continue to be attractive in the workplace should plan on having at least three careers throughout his/her professional life. Otherwise, that worker is all the more likely to become obsolete and lose the ability to attract wages that will sustain personal prosperity.

THE GROWING IMPORTANCE OF THE WORKER

The Japanese have been instrumental in destroying the approach to work that had been in place since the early twentieth century, when Frederick W. Taylor established the standard which defined the worker as an extension of the machine and the ideal worker as one who would perform in a totally machinelike manner (*Principles of Scientific Management*. NY: Harper & Row, 1911). As Japanese manufacturers attempted to rebuild their companies after World War II, they believed that the Taylor approach was no longer appropriate. They chose instead to encourage workers to play an active, meaningful role in the production process. The idea has strong American roots in the person of W. Edwards Deming**—someone who had little influence until his ideas were accepted by the Japanese.

---

* Houze, William C. *Career Veer*, New York; McGraw-Hill 1985.
** P 447 *Effective Behavior in Organizations,* Fourth Edition, by Allan R. Cohen, Stephen L. Fink, Herman Gadon, and Robin D. Willits; Irwin, Homewood Ill. 1988.

SO WHAT DOES ALL OF THE ABOVE HAVE TO DO WITH A WAGE AND SALARY HANDBOOK?

Because of all the factors and influences mentioned above, the personnel/human resources function has become a stronger force in organizations in the private, not-for-profit, and public sectors. With that increasing visibility, the "directly relevant" business-related issues have taken on increasing importance. Of primary importance are all the facets of compensation, including executive compensation, benefits, and wage and salary administration.

To attract the right people has always been the most important aspect of any personnel program. Retention and motivation have always followed closely behind. Attracting great workers continues to be a major compensation challenge as the demand for star performers continues to be greater than the supply. Needless to say, retaining and motivating them becomes increasingly important as well. In fact, any organization that becomes complacent with its current staff will soon find that the "magic" the organization originally used to pull this team together is now fading. The organization now faces the challenge of keeping its team together, while others are trying to pull them away. With decreasing organizational loyalty (and frequently downright skepticism displayed toward those who still choose to show it), the current workforce becomes increasingly difficult to retain and motivate due to the complexities of values and interests that the new workforce brings with them.

The basis for paying each worker then becomes crucial. To have a strong wage and salary administration function becomes all the more important so that the organization is positioned to pay the most effective wage: a wage arrived at after a decision making process with timely, accurate input from the wage and salary administration professional that provides the leadership of the organization with the information it needs to make those pay decisions and changes to that system whenever required, as quickly as possible. It must also possess the ability to continue to review its positioning as the factors described above continue to change as quickly as they are identified.

The wage and salary administration function then becomes all the more important as the area responsible for reading the market externally and for providing relevant and timely analysis of internal conditions.

PAY AS MOTIVATOR

Organizational psychologists have made efforts to determine the role compensation pays in the motivation process. For years all books on compensation have included a discussion that states early on that pay serves to attract, retain, and motivate employees. This continues to be a given, but it has become increasingly apparent that the whole concept of pay is a complicated one. When, as some compensation experts insist, all forms of pay (including benefits and perquisites) are elements of the compensation "package," then the pay issue become even more complex.

THE ROLE OF WAGE AND SALARY ADMINISTRATION

Wage and salary administration is the field of human resources that specifically addresses the implementation of an organization's compensation program. Wage and salary administration is responsible for the execution of the intent as well as the details of the program developed by the management team. The term is not in favor with many professionals in the field today but in searching for a better term for the person who is responsible for the issues discussed in this book we could find no better—especially because we feel that in going forward during these most challenging times, it is particularly important to make informed decisions with serious consideration given to past experience. Using the term "Wage and Salary Administration" we feel will be a constant reminder to do so.

At its inception, the wage and salary administration function is responsible for establishing the framework and the mechanics to ensure swift, accurate implementation. As the program gets underway, the wage and salary administration function is responsible for executing decisions and for monitoring actions to ensure compliance both with internal policies and procedures and with various legal entities.

Additionally, the function is responsible for keeping the organization current in its pay program by continuously monitoring internal conditions and external market factors. The wage and salary administration professional should be alert to changing conditions as they occur and should warn others in the organization of the need to alter current practices whenever the need is identified.

In *Managing Compensation,** J. Gary Berg mentioned "(t)he mental set of the compensation administrator is crucial to the success of the compensation program. . . . The compensation administrator's first step in establishing a valid compensation program is to assume a healthy mental set."

We trust that this book will provide the technical support to complement that healthy mental set and the result will be a truly effective and successful wage and salary administration professional.

---

* J. Gary Berg. *Managing Compensation* New York: Amacom 1976.

chapter one _____

ESTABLISHING A WAGE AND SALARY PROGRAM

An organization's compensation program encompasses the sum total of all payments—direct and indirect—made to its employees. These payments include the following five major categories:

- Base pay
- Short-term incentives (one year or less)
- Long-term incentives (more than one year)
- Benefits
- Perquisites

The Wage and Salary Administration function is a key element in any compensation program. Wage and salary administration is responsible for all direct cash payments to employees. These include base pay, incentives, cash awards, commissions, and shift differentials.

Most often, the major responsibility of the wage and salary administration program is to take care of direct base pay, commonly called wages for hourly employees (usually blue-collar and nonexempt), and salary for exempt employees and middle managers in both blue- and white-collar settings and includes "nonexempt" and "exempt" employees in white collar environments. As discussed, any incentive and bonus arrangements that are primarily cash in nature are to be included in any discussion of the subject as well.

Noncash benefits and perquisites—the two other aspects of the compensation package—are not the responsibility of the wage and salary function, with the exception of the "total compensation mix," which is calculated to determine the total cost of the compensation package. (For a brief discussion of benefit and perquisites aspects, see Chapter 10.)

The terms *exempt* and *nonexempt* refer to the terms used in the Fair Labor Standards Act of 1938 (FLSA) to define the categories of employees that are entitled to overtime wages. Briefly, categories classified as nonexempt are entitled to overtime compensation at a rate of time and one half their regular hourly rate for all hours in excess of forty per week. Any employees classified as exempt are not legally protected in the same way and are entitled to overtime compensation if, and only if, the employer wishes to pay it. (For more detailed discussions of FLSA status determination, see Chapters 10 and 11.)

When the United States had more of a manufacturing economy, the lines between wage earners and salaried staff were clearer and better defined. Now, in our service economy, more and more people are being paid on a periodic basis rather than hourly. Even though the workers may be nonexempt because of the work they perform, they will still be considered salaried workers because they are not on a time clock and not paid by the hour.

For executives, there is usually a separate and distinct program and that falls under the rubric of executive compensation. For senior-level employees, the base pay portion is usually a smaller portion of the total compensation package, which includes benefits and incentives (both short- and long-term) and often places heavy emphasis on perquisites. At that level, other parts of the compensation package, rather than "cash in hand" become more important because of the needs of the executive and the demands of the organization. In fact, the more effective the total compensation program for the executive, the more certain that he/she will realize that its components are inextricably intertwined. To accomplish this, the organization will spend a lot of effort considering timing, component mix, and payout formulas; the executive will be particularly mindful of tax consequences.

When commencing a project to develop a wage and salary administration program, the logical starting point is the present. By using the current situation as your reference point, you will develop much needed insights into the organization's traditions and values which will enable you to function effectively and develop a wage and salary administration program that truly fits the organization. Study the experiences from which the organization has emerged so that past successes can be repeated and past mistakes avoided. Review recent outstanding salary actions, promotions, reclassifications, and job description requests to give you an understanding of the organization's needs and, perhaps, suggestions about what to do to get ready for the future.

Exhibit 1-1 shows the steps necessary for developing an effective wage and salary program.

BUILDING A WAGE AND SALARY PROGRAM

In the wage and salary administration function—as in any other function—there are two aspects of responsibility. The first aspect is to provide solutions to internal "customers"—those staff members who approach the unit for assistance in a specific matter. These customers seek answers to their problems and look for a quick solution that will not make more problems for themselves. They may not be mindful of the organization's interest in building a new (or revamped), wage and salary administration program and may not be concerned, even if they know. When these interruptions occur it is essential for you to give attention to that particular issue or concern and work towards a solution. This "maintenance" aspect of the function is crucial to the success of any new program that is developed because the services provided during the operational phase of the project will be helpful in developing the credibility of the staff. As the program is developed and moves forward, it is important not to antagonize or frustrate those who come forward now for assistance. They will remember how they were treated, and that will influence their attitudes toward the wage and salary administration function. (For greater insight into implementing change, refer to Chapter 12.)

These "interruptions" are opportunities to gain insight each time they appear; to not give them the attention they deserve will create difficulties as this project moves forward. Do not overlook an opportunity to increase knowledge of the organization, its pay practices, and those of its managers and supervisors, an important group of staff members that the wage and salary administration program is being designed to support and assist. It would not be effective for the unit to shut down until this project is completed. At the same time, added insights gained from these interruptions may make the overall project longer to complete. The process, however, is as valuable as the completion of the project itself.

The second aspect of the function consists of the projects or programs alluded to above. In many ways, the wage and salary administration function operates as a set of wagon wheels (see Exhibit 1-2). While the goal of the entire

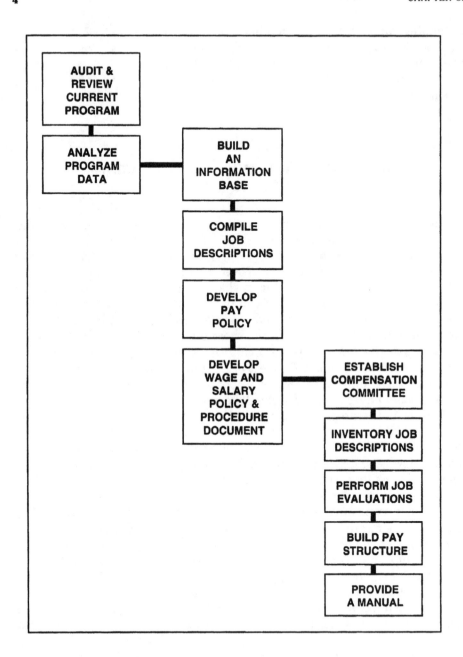

Exhibit 1-1
Wage and Salary Program Development Steps

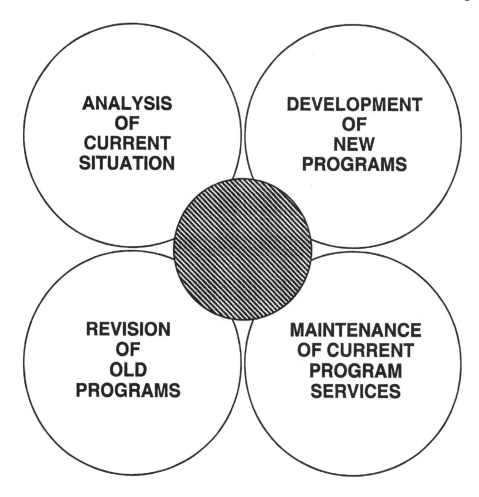

Exhibit 1-2
Wage and Salary Administration "Wheels"

unit (the wagon, in the analogy) is to go forward, it is the independent turning of the wheels that give the wagon motion.

Any ongoing wage and salary administration project (such as revamping the performance appraisal system or the introduction of an incentive program) should include an analysis of the current state of affairs in the organization, consideration/development of new programs, and revision of existing programs. Each of these elements (wheels) may each be progressing at its own pace, and if there are the resources to do so, they may all be spinning at different rates concurrently. Even if a project ends later than anticipated, it is better to continue a "business as usual . . . only better" attitude. The outcome of the project will then be far more likely to succeed because staff members will have developed a credibility for the wage and salary administration unit through their daily routines. Staff members throughout the organization will be more likely to see the benefit to them of the recently introduced wage and salary administration program and to anticipate its benefits—and that is the primary objective of the program.

AUDITING AND REVIEWING THE CURRENT WAGE AND SALARY PROGRAM

When any organization starts, it often commences as a small entity with only a few essential staff members. Initially, salaries and wages are determined by the entrepreneurs who have taken the risk to start the business. As for the rest of the organization, as strapped as any start-up is for cash, they will pay salaries at a sufficient level to attract the employees that they want and they will pay based on their experience, intuition, negotiation skills, and ability to pay. As the organization establishes itself in the marketplace, functions will be formally established and systems developed to support the growing organization. There comes a point when the organization's founders no longer have the time to make all the administrative decisions directly; they grow more dependent on the staff members they have hired to help them to build the infrastructure. These are the people on whom the responsibility falls to systematize each of the major areas. One of those areas usually is personnel/human resources, and the wage and salary administration function is frequently a responsibility of that area.

(The one exception is the new organization that is the subsidiary of an ongoing concern. Frequently, that subsidiary will adapt the policies and procedures of some other unit from within the organization already in existence, if possible—whether appropriate or not.)

Usually, when the decision is made to design a wage and salary administration program, people are already on board and are being paid in a manner that the employees consider equitable or they would not be there. In this situation, the first step in the development of any wage and salary administration program is to take stock of the policies and procedures currently in place. In order for you to take a systematic approach to the analysis of the organization, a 'Wage and Salary Administration Program Review' Worksheet has been provided in Appendix A. The worksheet lists issues to consider and information needed before determining the direction to take when either designing new programs or revising existing ones.

BUILDING AN INFORMATION BASE

With all the information gathered on the review worksheet, you now have a "portrait" of the organization's existing wage and salary function; now it is appropriate to go forward. The next steps may be considered independently and may progress at different speeds to put the independent-yet-linked elements of the wage and salary administration program together.

There are actually two distinct, major elements of the information base upon which the program is to be developed. The first is the installation of practices that will allow immediately for the accumulation, storage, and retrieval of data to allow for effective implementation of current pay demands while the formal pay program is being developed.

When building the data required for the establishment of a sound information base, two things happen. First, the professional establishes a systematic approach, using the organization's current resources to ensure that he/she understands how the organization is accustomed to dealing with pay issues. This process allows the professional to determine the resources available (equipment, priorities, and competence of staff in issues regarding pay matters) that will prove invaluable in determining any new program. Second, without calling any of the processes "new," the pay professional will have the opportunity to test and retest a variety of procedures and practices before installing the new program. This process includes work-flow analysis to determine whether "re-engineering" may be useful in allowing the pay process to function more effectively. Inputs, processes, outputs (calculations and reports), and storage arrangements should be all considered as well as the communication element.

The second element required to build the information base is the compilation of job descriptions. This process allows the professional to perform immediately at a level required by the organization. This second element of the information base is separate and distinct from the determination of whether the organization is committed to the job description process in the development of the pay program (a subject that will receive further attention later in this chapter).

JOB DESCRIPTION COMPILATION

As mentioned previously, the second major aspect in the building of the information base is the compilation of job descriptions. Here the pay professional should standardize and complete the job descriptions that were found to be lacking or missing during the initial audit and review. This exercise should be undertaken (to whatever extent practical) in an effort to determine the organization's rationale for its current pay levels. Even if senior managers of the organization determine that job descriptions are not required and question their utility (particularly if they have any recent works by Tom Peters), the organization's job descriptions will serve as an anchor for the pay professional. They will provide a comprehensive understanding of the organization and will serve as the initial basis for job evaluation. Keep in mind that this process may be strictly for the pay professional, particularly if the organization has hostility for any reason toward job descriptions. At the same time it is important to know the organization's commitment or lack of a commitment to the job description process. If senior management does not have that commitment, organizational ownership will be missing if the process is forced on the organization by the pay professional when the pay policy is actually installed.

Current Issues and Concerns

There are several circumstances that warrant immediate attention. They are to be considered "windows of opportunity," that is, they are "snapshot" situations that allow you the chance to gain important insight into the organization, its values, practices, and needs, and the perceptions of its staff. They are often day-to-day matters that present problems to the line person who needs help now. These situations are to be seen as part of the new system that is being developed and as opportunities for taking a one-step-at-a-time approach while providing new direction, leadership, and expertise. Among the situations that provide opportunities to grow as a member of the organization and increase professional credibility are the following:

- A job description may be required for a new position that a line manager wishes to fill. Recruitment needs a job description to start the process and/or the position needs to be priced.
- A supervisor wishes to promote an employee and seeks your advice regarding title and amount of increase.

- An employee is annoyed that he/she isn't receiving overtime pay.
- A group of employees has complained to their supervisor that they are being paid less than their colleagues in the marketplace.
- A senior manager complains that the organization is not attracting the best employees.
- A salary increase recommendation is submitted for an employee whose title appears to be quite high for his/her current salary level.

Planning for the Future

To build an inventory of job descriptions, start the process of compiling a "complete" set of job descriptions. There are three approaches to consider:

- *Hiring outside support.* This can include either a consultant, a part time employee, or a student intern.
- *Creating an in-house project team.* This option can create an opportunity for the organization to increase the number of staff members possessing job description skills and to develop standardized job descriptions throughout the organization in "one fell swoop" while gaining a greater organizational buy-in for this laborious process.
- *Doing it yourself.* This is a golden opportunity to get to know a lot of people throughout the organization, but the task may be arduous, if not impossible to complete. The first effort is tough enough, but to maintain the inventory of job descriptions and keep them current is an even more formidable task in all but the smallest and most static organizations.

Defining the Job Description Process

One aspect of the job description portion of the project is the question of what philosophy to take when building the library (inventory) of job descriptions. Many organizations and senior members of management envision a job description project like any other project—it has a beginning, a middle, and an end. The end of the project probably comes with the presentation of a large, unwieldy, already out-of-date volume (usually an oversized three-ring binder with reinforced rear panel and lots of dividers).

At the same time that the congratulations go around, the perception also permeates the organization that the project has been completed so now everyone can move on to something else. The tome gets plopped on a high and musty shelf and is only remembered on special occasions (such as whenever there is an allusion to the last job description project). That scenario also signifies the organization's commitment and understanding of the value of job descriptions.

Then there is the other view: the job description project is a never ending process. Job descriptions are updated regularly, new ones are added, and obsolete ones dropped. Job descriptions are constantly being reviewed for accuracy and improved wherever possible because they are constantly being used for:

- Recruitment
- Transfers
- Promotions
- Performance Management
- Career Planning
- Staff Planning
- Training and Development
- Wage and Salary Administration Research

Job descriptions are reviewed whenever there is turnover of a position or when a promotion is contemplated. Supervisors and managers are encouraged to refer to them on a regular basis and to adjust and amend as appropriate.

In this rapidly changing workplace environment, job descriptions are changing to keep pace. Up-to-date job descriptions are tools that make change as orderly and effective as possible. Job descriptions are discussed in detail later in this chapter as well as in Chapter 3.

DETERMINING THE ORGANIZATION'S PAY POLICY

Determine the organization's philosophy toward the payment of its staff members. Even if not formally stated, by virtue of what the organization does and when and how it pays its employees, an attitude is projected. This organizational pay philosophy takes several different issues into consideration. Information gathered on the Wage and Salary Administration Program Review Worksheet (Appendix A) addresses these issues and calls for specific information regarding the existing pay environment. Do not confine this information to a question-and-answer format; discuss pertinent issues with senior management. Exhibit 1-3 provides a number of questions you can use to stimulate discussion regarding pay policy.

After reviewing all the information, discuss with senior management the current state of the organization's pay policy and the direction(s) the organization should take going forward. Bits of the pay policy may have evolved without a clear, cohesive pay philosophy. By bringing together all the various elements, you can present a complete picture to management, thus allowing an actual pay policy philosophy to emerge.

DEVELOPING WAGE AND SALARY ADMINISTRATION PROGRAM POLICIES AND PROCEDURES

From the information gathered from job descriptions, pay policy review, the review worksheet, and discussions with senior management, you can now begin developing a set of wage and salary administration policies and procedures.

Developing a Draft Document

Your first step is to draft a package of statements that provides an overview of the program for the senior members of management to consider. These statements should be considered a working document and a departure point for determining the mission and objectives of the wage and salary administration program. A sample Wage and Salary Administration Policy and Procedures—Draft Document is provided in Appendix B. As every organization is unique, you must choose those statements and topics in the sample that apply to the particular organization for which you are drafting the procedures and practices.

The procedures portion of the draft document will provide an overview of the major elements of the wage and salary administration program. The job description, job evaluation, grade, range, budget matters, and pay increase processes will each be briefly described. If the decision is made to establish a salary (wage) committee, its mission and composition will be defined as well. Last, there should be a statement of disclosure that the organization will use to explain the level of openness it wishes to pursue.

Does the organization wish to pay its staff "above", "at", or "below" similar organizations in the same market(s)? Would it consider paying the highest going rates for some jobs, "par" for others, and "sub-par" for yet other jobs?

What market(s) does the organization consider itself in? Do they differ as to positions, functions, or organizational performance?

Where does the organization prefer to obtain its employees? Does it prefer "trained" employees or will the organization train its own?

Does the organization prefer to promote from within, hire from outside, or some combination of both?

What is(are) the profile(s) of the ideal organization employee(s)?

What is the perception of management regarding the function of base pay?

Will pay be tied to performance? What role do benefits, incentives, and perquisites play?

Does equity have a function in the compensation mix?

How much should employees be told about their or others' salaries and other payments? What are supervisors and managers told?

On what basis should pay raises be considered?

Are pay raises granted on a "bulk" basis, with managers responsible for breaking down the increases within their department?

Are increases automatically processed if within budget, or are individual approvals required for each?

Exhibit 1-3
Questions to Stimulate Discussion Regarding
Pay Policy

Creating a Compensation Committee

Another decision to be made is whether the organization wishes to establish a standing compensation committee to review and approve various salary actions and other matters. If the organizational commitment is there, the committee could be a valuable part of the wage and salary administration program. It can enable the role and function of the wage and salary administration unit to be understood by a representative body of the organization, which will help to communicate issues effectively.

On the other hand, the committee might become a bottleneck that could delay actions and set up barriers to sound wage and salary decisions. It all depends on the values of the organization and the skills of the people serving on the committee.

In spite of the risk, a compensation committee is a route that should be considered as an opportunity for a more effective wage and salary administration program. The first task of any compensation committee will be to help to determine the details of the wage and salary program.

PROVIDING AN INVENTORY OF JOB DESCRIPTIONS TO USE IN THE JOB EVALUATION PROCESS

If senior management supports the use of job descriptions, the next step in the process is to create an inventory of job descriptions. The job descriptions will be used as the basis for job evaluation. (Job analysis and the job description process are discussed at length in Chapters 2 and 3.) The issue is important when discussing the development of wage and salary policies and procedures because it is the approach that is taken toward job descriptions by the organization that must be established before the inventory process can begin.

The first policy question you must address is: Will there be job descriptions in the organization? Only when senior management confirms its commitment to have job descriptions should the project proceed. Creating an inventory of job descriptions is a major, labor-intensive commitment, and the organization must realize this to ensure that the wage and salary administration unit is making the best use of its time in accordance with the wishes and priorities of the organization.

While the use of job descriptions can create problems—they can be too limiting and they create a lot of paperwork—the advantages far outweigh the disadvantages. Some of these advantages are:

- Helps to define the job for recruiting, performance planning, pay, transfer, promotion, training, staff planning, and career purposes.
- Uses a standard format that allows for consistent application.
- Gives employees a definition of their job in writing.
- Provides a reliable source when comparing jobs salary surveys in other organizations.
- Helps organization to move swiftly to increase or replace staff due to increased business or turnover.
- Helps those responsible for work flow to perform a systematic analysis of each organization's work process from start to finish.
- Helps each wage and salary professional grow in his/her knowledge of the organization by writing/reviewing job descriptions and discussing the results with managers.

The second policy question is a bit more difficult to deal with: What is the organization's approach to the process? As previously discussed, the organization can mandate that the wage and salary administration unit put together a book of job descriptions and report when the job has been completed, or the organization can make the commitment to set as its goal the updating of job descriptions as an ongoing process.

This is easier to choose than to do. If the organization prefers the second choice, then it must communicate that on a regular basis to all levels so that the organization sees job descriptions as part of an organization-wide effort to put an effective wage and salary Administration program into practice.

The third policy question regarding job descriptions is: What is the process by which job descriptions will be approved? A practical approach is to give first approval of the job description to the incumbent, second approval to his/her supervisor, and third approval to the manager of the line unit. Final review is reserved for the manager of the wage and salary Administration unit.

Evaluating Jobs Based on Job Descriptions for Pay Purposes

A primary purpose for having job descriptions is to evaluate each job in the organization for pay purposes. Job evaluation allows the organization to establish a hierarchy of jobs and to determine internal and external equity. It also helps to ensure that the organization is meeting the statutory requirement of providing equal pay for equal work.

Job evaluations can be performed by wage and salary administration professionals, managers and supervisors, or job-holders. The choice depends on the extent to which organization-wide understanding and acceptance is an objective. A compensation committee, if created, could be an effective body for job evaluations. An invitation could be extended to the manager of the unit who has the job to include his/her expertise and to provide an opportunity to build consensus for the program.

Usually different methods are used for different job families. Examples of different job families include: manufacturing, production, office/clerical, managerial, sales, technical, and executive jobs. A strong argument in favor of multiple methods is that each job family has different work characteristics and unique compensable factors.

DETERMINING THE APPROPRIATE METHOD OF JOB EVALUATION

The job evaluation process determines the relative worth of each position (job) in the organization by establishing a hierarchy of positions. This is essential to determining the price the organization is willing to pay for each of the positions that it fills. There are two approaches to evaluating jobs, quantitative and qualitative. There are five methods of job evaluation, three qualitative and two quantitative. Exhibit 1-4 summarizes the key steps required for each of the five methods.

Qualitative Methods of Job Evaluation

The three qualitative methods of job evaluation are ranking, classification, and market pricing.

Ranking

This is the simplest, fastest, and easiest method, but it is also the crudest. It does not work well if the organization has more than twenty-five positions. The problem is inherent in the method.

There are two ways to perform the ranking exercise, simple ranking or paired comparison. Simple ranking by alternate listing may be used to establish the hierarchy. In this procedure, the highest position is alternated with the lowest. Exhibit 1-5 provides a sample job ranking form. Then the second highest

QUALITATIVE METHODS	QUALITATIVE METHODS

RANKING PROCESS

1. Determine jobs and units to be included.
2. Conduct job analysis and prepare job descriptions.
3. Select evaluators.
4. Define contribution/value.
5. Rank either by alternate listing or paired comparison.
6. Merge unit rankings.

CLASSIFICATION PROCESS

1. Determine jobs and units to be included.
2. Conduct job analysis and prepare job descriptions.
3. Select evaluators.
4. Define classes.
5. Identify and establish benchmark jobs in the structure.
6. Apply system to all other (non-benchmark) jobs.

MARKET PRICING PROCESS

1. Determine jobs and units to be included.
2. Conduct job analysis and prepare job descriptions.
3. Select benchmark (key) jobs to enable comparisons.
4. Identify organizations to initiate surveys with.
5. Identify off-the-shelf surveys that will provide relevant pricing for comparable jobs.
6. Conduct the survey.
7. Perform an analysis of results.
8. Apply the scale to all other (non-benchmark/non-surveyed) jobs.

POINT PLAN PROCESS

1. Determine jobs and units to be included.
2. Conduct job analysis and prepare job descriptions.
3. Choose compensable factors.
4. Derive factor weights (only two ways: by committee or statistically).
5. Prepare evaluation manual.
6. Identify and establish benchmark jobs in the structure.
7. Apply process to all other (non-benchmark) jobs.

FACTOR COMPARISON PROCESS

1. Determine jobs and units to be included.
2. Perform job analysis and prepare job descriptions.
3. Select benchmark (key) jobs to enable comparisons.
4. Rank benchmark jobs on each factor.
5. Allocate benchmark salaries (wages) across factors.
6. Compare factor and salary (wage) allocation ranks.
7. Construct the job comparison scale.
8. Apply the scale to all other (non-benchmark) jobs.

Exhibit 1-4
Methods of Job Evaluation

Ranking Structure		
Jobs		**Rank**
Number	**Title**	**Most Valued**

Exhibit 1-5
Sample Job Ranking Form

alternates with the second lowest and the process continues, one high and one low, until the process is completed in the middle range. When paired comparisons are used, each job is compared to each of the other jobs and the result is a process that compares all possible jobs against each other. For twenty-five jobs that process will require three hundred comparisons, or $[(n)\,(n-1)]/2$.

Classification

The classification method is a qualitative method that involves slotting job descriptions into a series of classes or grades covering a range of jobs. In practice, the job descriptions are compared to standard class descriptions and to each other. It is a difficult exercise if there are jobs from several occupations or if all jobs are covered by one plan. This process is used by the United States Office of Personnel Management for its General Schedule (GS) system, and the result is the book Dictionary of Occupational Titles.

Market pricing

This method of job evaluation is initially seen as the most readily available, yet should also be considered the most elusive. In this approach, the process commences with market pricing by taking a pulse of the marketplace using salary surveys. (See Chapter 9 for a discussion of wage and salary surveys.) After this has been done, all the other jobs are priced either directly or indirectly by existing marketplace pay levels and pay relationships.

The most difficult aspect of this approach is determining the market for the jobs that are being priced. Not only are there many different approaches to be taken in defining the market but also within the particular defined market (markets within markets) and in different markets for different jobs. For example, an organization located in Chicago may have a national sales organization. It recruits nationally and therefore must compete nationally for sales talent. At the same time the secretaries and the computer operators in the Chicago facilities, while obtained from the local marketplace, require competitive salary levels for a segment of the marketplace that competes for those same secretaries and computer operators. That segment may not be in sales organizations or have the same technology. Meanwhile the organization is competing for computer operators that are in organizations that use the same technology in their systems area but not necessarily in the same industry.

The most important step in this approach is to determine the market. The market for each position may be determined by several factors, including geographic location, market performance, organization level, organization function, and line of business.

When using the marketplace as a barometer, the question is whether to pay at (match), below lag, or above (lead) the market for each position. A key point to remember is that there is no need to determine one approach for every position in every unit.

Quantitative Methods of Job Evaluation

Point plan

This is sometimes called the point factor plan. This approach assigns points to a group of compensable factors (usually four or five in number). A scale is created for levels within each factor, then each job is then rated in each factor, and finally each of the jobs evaluated is then "slotted" into the hierarchy by number of points. In this approach it may be helpful to identify benchmark jobs and then peg other jobs by comparison to the benchmark positions.

There are three major difficulties with the point evaluation approach to job evaluation and they all center around the matrix developed. It is difficult to select relevant factors, assign appropriate point values, and define differences in the degrees themselves.

Factor comparison

In factor comparison, job evaluation is based on two criteria: compensable factors and wages for a select set of jobs. More complex than both the ranking and classification methods, it is the approach utilized by Hay Associates, a consulting firm. The process starts with job analysis but requires an analysis according to a standard format that considers the job in light of compensable factors that are found in all jobs, usually four or five in number (although the Hay system uses three factors: know-how, problem solving, and accountability). Examples may include mental requirements, skill requirements, physical factors, responsibility, and working conditions. In this system, benchmark jobs are crucial since they serve as reference points for all the other jobs. Their criteria for selection is the same as that used for survey data:

- Job content for each job is well-known and agreed upon;
- job content changes very little over time;
- current pay rates are generally acceptable and differentials among the jobs are relatively stable;

- the benchmark jobs when taken together represent the entire range of each compensable factor; and,
- each of the jobs are accepted in the external market as a benchmark job.

The approach is difficult to explain to employees, and as jobs change so do the relationships; new comparisons must be continuously considered. Because of these ongoing changes, this approach is hard to maintain.

Frequently market and point factor or factor comparison approaches are combined to provide a comparative approach to the process. This method provides additional opportunities to test data in comparison to internal and external wage and salary levels to ensure the accuracy of the data obtained.

BUILDING THE PAY STRUCTURE

After the organization's jobs have been evaluated, the next step in the process is to build the pay structure. This is a two-step process that includes designing pay ranges and developing grades. A pay range is required to determine the actual pay rate for each job. It is a range and not a specific price to allow for contingencies and the particular characteristics of each of the persons occupying each job—unless of course there are reasons to establish a specific price (for example, if the price for the position has been collectively bargained and is defined in a union contract). Grades are then determined to establish groupings of different jobs that are considered substantially similar for pay purposes. Last, care must be taken that the organization's current pay practices are equitable both internally and externally.

Designing Pay Ranges

In situations where there is no collective bargaining agreement that has set pay rates, it is necessary to have a range or spread that an employer is willing to pay for a job because of the differences that people bring with them to a job and the differences in ability and performance from different employees on the job. There should be a level below which the organization will not pay—a difficult concept for some in management to accept, especially if there is a person willing to take less. Just as important, there must be a maximum level because the particular job in question is not, in the judgment of the employer, worth more than that price under any circumstances.

If any problem arises from discussion on ranges it is usually because ranges should be seen as instruments that allow the organization to peg prices in an orderly, consistent, systematic manner. If the ranges do not meet the requirements of the organization, they should be adjusted to reflect the concerns of the organization. This is much more practical and effective than a set of ranges with many exceptions, because the exceptions are living proof that the ranges are not accomplishing what they should.

Ranges should be revised periodically to accommodate salary actions and to remain competitive. Revising them once a year in periods of low inflation should be adequate. Twice a year may be necessary during periods of severe inflation.

Setting midpoints, minimums, and maximums

The midpoint is the key pay level in the determination of each range and is the point at which the organization is meeting the market in either a lead, lag, or match role. The minimums and the maximums are established by decreasing or increasing that level from 10 percent to 50 percent, with a spread of 20 percent to 30 percent the most common. Thus, if 100 percent is considered the midpoint and 20 percent is determined to be the spread, then the range would be from 80 percent to 120 percent of what was determined to be the midpoint (or market price) level.

The term *compa-ratio* is frequently used when providing the pay level for a particular incumbent and the designation is given in decimals. So, if a position is paying a midpoint salary of $30,000 and the range is ±20 percent, then the minimum of the range for the position will be pegged at $24,000 and the maximum will be $36,000. The compa-ratio at $30,000 will be 1.00; at $24,000 it will be .80; and, at the maximum it will be 1.20.

Determining overlap between ranges

There should be a degree of overlap between ranges to accommodate movement from one range to the next but also to allow for continuing salary growth while staying in the same range. A large overlap between ranges will be an indication of very little difference in the value of jobs in adjoining grades, while a small overlap will indicate the opposite.

Developing Grades (Classes)

Designing ranges is not a science and not difficult to do. If the reason for the grades is kept in mind—they are to provide a systemic ranking consistent with the organization's hierarchy in relevant worth of positions—and if similarly weighted jobs are grouped in the same range, then all the jobs considered to be roughly equivalent in value (even if unrelated) will be placed in the same range, designated by the same grade. Jobs of different value will be placed in different ranges. The number of grades depends upon the variety of jobs and organizational traditions as well as the hierarchical spread of the organization. Career paths also help to determine the number of ranges.

Broad-banding has been used with more frequency of late in the determination of ranges. Briefly, broad-banding is an attempt by organizations to reduce the number of ranges in the structure as they try to become flatter. At the same time, organizations attempt to increase the size of the ranges to change the perception that a promotion requires a move to a higher range. Instead, organizations using broad-banding are attempting to demonstrate to employees that two increasingly popular organizational trends—job enlargement and skill-based pay—are going to be accommodated with fewer ranges by increasing the spread in each range.

Determining Internal and External Equity

Every organization is unique and therefore must determine the extent to which external factors are relevant in the organization's job hierarchy. For some positions the organization may wish to pay at a higher level than other organizations in the marketplace. For other positions the determinations may be identical. Every determination of pay level should be one in which both internal and external data are considered, with the unique needs of the organization being the final determinant.

CREATING A WAGE AND SALARY BUDGET

If the organization currently has an ongoing budget process, the details will have been discovered during the program review (see Appendix A, Wage and Salary Administration Program Review). Armed with all the data regarding job descriptions, salary (wage) ranges, and classes you are now in a position to participate in the budget process—forecasting both salary costs and staffing needs for the next fiscal period. You will also be establishing procedures for auditing and reviewing the program, comparing actual results to budgeted figures, and monitoring compliance with policies and procedures.

If the organization does not have a budget program as part of its day-to-day operations, introduce one for wage and salary administration. For details regarding establishing budgets and for the audit and review of the function, refer to Chapters 4 and 5.

Implementing an Ongoing System of Standardized Procedures to Keep Program Current

Attention must be given to the development and implementation of an ongoing system of regular procedures that includes:

- utilization of procedures for monthly salary actions;
- job description updates at each promotion, transfer, termination (if the position vacated is to be filled in each of those circumstances); and,
- the generation of management reports including monthly "salary plan to actual" comparisons and periodic reviews to ensure compliance with internal guidelines.

PROVIDING A MANUAL FOR THE PROGRAM TO ENSURE ORGANIZATION-WIDE UNDERSTANDING AND COMPLIANCE

In addition to preparing the draft document of policies and procedures for senior managers described earlier (see Appendix B), you should also provide a manual to supervisors and managers. This will ensure that they understand the mechanics of the wage and salary administration program so that they can effectively process salary actions for the members of their own staffs. Also, the more they know about the system, the more they will buy into its processes and the overall program.

Include the following information in the manual. It may, in fact, be the final wording of the policies and procedures you have established (see Appendix B):

- Statement of policy and its relationship to organization objectives
- Steps required for processing salary actions

- Discussion of an audit element to guarantee organization-wide coordination of implementation
- Explanation of the job classification system and the wage and salary structure
- Mission and role of the wage and salary administration unit
- Legal ramifications

PROMOTING ORGANIZATION-WIDE COMMUNICATION AND SUPPORT TO ENSURE PROGRAM EFFECTIVENESS

An integral part of the program will be communication. For a wage and salary administration program to be effective, the support of the entire organization is required from the program's inception. Constant communication is one major way to accomplish this objective. This can be achieved in the following ways:

Discuss the Organization's Goals with Senior Management on an Ongoing Basis

In the course of discussions and in obtaining information for the Draft Document (Appendix B), the elements of the organization's philosophy and pay strategy will be blocked out. As these elements come together, continue to refine your understanding of the organization's point of view and goals. As a result of this exercise, the openness of the level of information is experienced first-hand. There is no better way to test the open-door policy of an organization than to try to share information.

Develop Relationships with Employees by Keeping Them Informed

It is necessary to develop a broad base of support for the wage and salary administration program in the organization's efforts to attract, retain, and motivate staff.

With a concentrated effort including a series of line management/supervisory training sessions and on-site visits, you can maintain a hands-on approach to the organization. Orientation presentations enable new employees to develop a positive relationship with and understanding of the wage and salary administration practices and programs. Whether introducing new policies or programs, redefining existing procedures, or seeking information and feedback, brochures and newsletters are valuable communication vehicles.

Train All Employees to Understand Pay Practices

The wage and salary administration program needs to consider ways to train all members of the organization to understand the organization's pay practices. This responsibility assumes a fundamental understanding by all wage and salary staff members.

Promote the concept of the internal customer

Any discussion of program implementation involving the wage and salary administration program should commence with the consideration of the role of the staff members of the wage and salary administration unit as providers of service to their internal customers. This service should be provided to all employees regardless of level. This approach sets a tone that makes interruptions a way of life and finding solutions to employee concerns regarding wage and salary matters a goal.

From this perspective, the development of a training element for the wage and salary administration program becomes a fundamental and essential element. If the program and the unit are to be effective, every employee should know what the unit does and what the program entails so that they know where to go whenever they have any questions or concerns on this topic.

Encourage participation and support from lower-level employees

Employees at all levels of the organization should have a fundamental understanding of the organization's approach to pay. Even if the organization decides that the entire matter is to be confidential, then in that environment employees should be told that is the organization's approach and an explanation of the approach should be made. To ignore the issue with lower-level employees is a lost opportunity to obtain a buy-in from this segment of the workforce.

Training approaches include briefings to newly hired employees, policy statements included in the staff handbook, orientation sessions, and encouragement to supervisors and managers to discuss pay matters at staff meetings. Even in a highly secretive environment, pay matters should be discussed in a manner consistent with the organization's policy toward pay.

The other aspect of training for lower-level employees is to enable them to feel that the environment encourages discussions of pay to stimulate consideration for further management action. This is not to say that the organization should stimulate discussions of pay in order to create an ongoing complaint system.

In every occupation, in every walk of life, there are many people who feel that they are not being paid fairly. This is a fact of life. It is also a fact of life that no matter who the employee is, he/she will always be able to find someone working somewhere who feels that he/she is being paid at a higher level for similar work. This extends to government workers, entertainers, and professional athletes. Major league baseball players at the high end of their pay scale, for instance, frequently compare their salary levels to those of executives of major corporations.

The object of listening to employee discussions of pay is to create an opportunity for them to voice their opinions internally as a barometer of pay issues and concerns. The other point is that there may be validity to what is being said as well as opportunities for resolution before unwanted defections occur.

These pay discussions should not be extraordinary opportunities to discuss work-related issues but rather should become part of an environmental fabric that encourages dialogue between supervisors and employees throughout the organization.

Develop an ongoing dialogue with managers and supervisors

There are two major reasons to train managers and supervisors in the policies and practices of the wage and salary administration function.

First, and most important, managers and supervisors are needed to support the program. In fact, a dialogue should be developed and maintained to ensure the effectiveness and successful utilization of the program.

Second, managers and supervisors need to know what is expected of them in carrying out the policies and practices. They particularly need to know where to go for help and what the program and the unit are expected to do for them in executing their own duties and responsibilities.

Possible training instruments for this staff level include:

- An orientation module for newly hired employees at the supervisory or management level
- A training module for newly promoted managers and supervisors
- A policies and procedures manual to refer to at their work stations
- A list of people to call within the wage and salary administration unit for questions and concerns
- Periodic meetings and guest appearances at staff meetings
- Performance appraisal training sessions
- Budget training programs for managers, supervisors, and subordinates who may have responsibility for completing the forms
- Written self-instruction guidelines for salary actions, performance appraisals, and budget procedures

Keep executive management informed of "big picture" issues

Executive management should be considered part of the training process. Here the emphasis should be on "big picture" issues that warrant their attention. Particularly significant survey results, a periodic profile of the employee population by a variety of categories, comparison of salaries by gender, or initiation of a new program are suitable topics—in addition to the periodic discussions of the performance appraisal process and budget discussions. Discussing these topics is helpful in developing executive sensitivity to the issues of wage and salary administration.

Develop Relationships Outside the Organization to Promote Staff Growth

The development and enhancement of the wage and salary administration staff should continue with peers, consultants and other vendors, and academic resources.

AUDITING AND REVIEWING THE PROGRAM ON A REGULAR BASIS TO ENSURE EFFECTIVENESS

An ongoing evaluation of the wage and salary administration program should be included as an essential part of the wage and salary administration program as it is being implemented to ensure control and ongoing effectiveness. (For a detailed discussion of this topic refer to Chapter 5.) Major issues that the audit and review element should include are the following:

Internal equity

A major concern to be addressed on an ongoing basis in the administration of any wage and salary program is the issue of internal equity. As with the administration of any program in an organization, ongoing maintenance and review ensures that when staff members receive promotions and salary increases and when the internal value of jobs changes, these decisions and salary actions do not compromise the integrity of the job structure.

External equity

It is crucial that the wage and salary administration unit be constantly apprised of the marketplace and its dynamics. This ensures that there is a realistic understanding of what is occurring in other relevant situations—organizational, geographic, and demographic—in the external market that may affect pay levels in the organization.

Legal compliance

Monitor each policy and procedure, salary action, hire, FLSA determination, performance appraisal, promotion, transfer, and termination to ensure compliance with federal, state, and local laws. Periodically review aggregates of data to determine whether the organization is engaging in sound business and legal practice with pay-related decisions made on a unit and organizational basis.

Timeliness and accuracy

Conduct an audit trail exercise for hires, promotions, performance appraisals, salary actions, and any other pay-related matter to ensure that staff members are acting within the scope of their authority in implementing decisions. Consider dates on all documents from the start to finish of processes to determine their timeliness and identify ways to do them better.

Security

Pay attention to security issues to ensure that access is totally controlled at all times and that there are up-to-date procedures to protect access and unauthorized changes anywhere in the wage and salary administration system.

SUMMARY

The design of the wage and salary administration program is a particularly important project for any organization. It is inconceivable for any organization to be without one, because to do so is inordinately more time consuming. Each time a question is raised, the answer will have to be developed on an ad hoc basis. The time required to design and implement the program, therefore, will be well spent. Not only will the organization be building its team but, in the process it will also be building a process that, if well constructed, will effectively support the organization's mission and goals.

HOW TO ANALYZE JOBS TO DETERMINE PAY RATES

Job analysis plays a crucial role in managing the personnel/human resources function. As organizations experience change through growth, reorganization, or restructuring, jobs must often be more clearly defined or redefined. Job analysis is your primary tool for determining the value of a job in the organization and establishing the pay rate appropriate to this job.

An initial step in job analysis is to define what is meant by a job. The smallest element of activity that employees are asked to perform is called a *task*. Word processing, filing, calculations, and answering the telephone are all tasks. A group of logically connected activities are combined into a *position*. When different individuals occupy different positions but perform the same group of tasks, this is called a *job*. For example, the tasks mentioned above (word processing, filing, calculations, answering the telephone) constitute the job of secretary; there are several people, each occupying an individual secretarial position. Since their duties are the same, the title for all the positions is the same.

When some jobs are grouped with others because of similarities in skills, they are called *job families*. A hierarchy is established within families. For

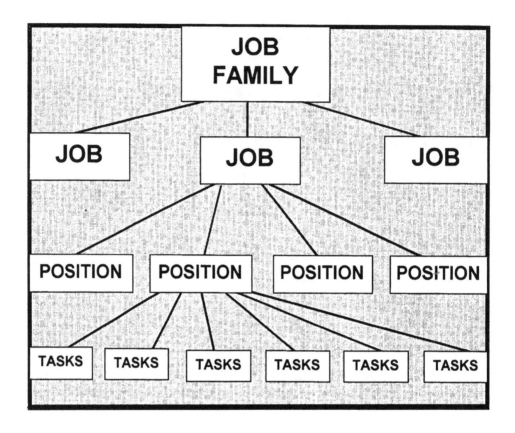

Exhibit 2-1
The Job–Task Relationship

example, there may be a job family that includes the typist/word processor, first-level secretary, second-level secretary, administrative secretary, administrative assistant, and perhaps customer service assistant. Exhibit 2-1 illustrates the job–task relationship.

COLLECTING, DOCUMENTING, AND ANALYZING DATA
FOR JOB ANALYSIS

Job analysis is the systematic process of describing the purpose of a job along with its component activities. To create this description, you collect and record data that will lead to an accurate identification of the responsibilities and duties of the job, as well as the conditions under which the job is performed. Also included in this description are the qualifications and requirements of the incumbent.

Job analysis may be broken down into a three-step process that includes gathering, documenting, and analyzing data that describe the characteristics of a job from three separate perspectives—content, requirements, and context.

Collecting Data for Job Analysis

The first step in data collection is breaking down the job content into easily understandable individual segments, and then gathering information on each segment. These job segments include:

- the specific activities that have to be performed
- the responsibilities and accountabilities of the incumbent; and
- the expected results, mission, or outcome of the activities performed.

The next step is to collect data on the skills, abilities, knowledge, and education that comprise the requirements needed to successfully execute the job's activities.

You must also obtain data regarding the context of the job within the organization. Consider where the job is positioned in the organization's structure and its relationship to others in the organization.

As part of determining the context of the job under consideration, also take into account the environment within which the job's activities are performed. This includes:

- the physical conditions of the work area where the job is located
- any physical demands that may be required
- work location
- nature and extent of supervision provided to incumbent
- visibility of the job in the organization
- the job's relationship to other jobs in the unit

Documenting Data for Job Analysis

Next, you need to document the data collected. These data will serve as the essential foundation for the completion of the job description and the exercise of job evaluation. The resulting documentation will also be used by other personnel/human resources areas for such functions as developing selection criteria and establishing performance standards.

Documentation serves another purpose: to provide the organization with information in the event that it has to justify its pay and other employment practices in the light of the Fair Labor Standards Act (FLSA) and equal employment opportunity laws and regulations.

Analyzing Data for Job Analysis

Now, thoroughly review and analyze the data collected and provide an accurate summary for your final report. Present this report according to the standard structure and format established by the organization. This analysis of the job content, job requirements, and the job context provides information necessary to evaluate the job's worth both inside the organization and in relationship to the marketplace in order to determine the appropriate pay level. The most common report format that emanates from the job analysis process is the job description. (For a detailed discussion of job descriptions see Chapter 3.)

HOW TO SELECT A JOB ANALYST

If you are selecting a job analyst rather than doing the job yourself, consider three major factors. They are on-the-job experience, professional expertise, and instruments available for carrying out specific tasks.

Using On-the-Job Experience as a Criterion for Selection

When taking into account on-the-job experience, the incumbent is the first candidate to consider. After all, who understands the job better? However, you may encounter problems with this choice. First, if incumbents are expected to perform their own job analysis, then all employees will need to be trained in how to analyze a job. Second, incumbents have a vested interest in increasing the relative weight of their positions, and that bias will be difficult to eliminate. Last, the writing style and communication skills of each of the incumbents may vary, and that will affect the quality of the job analysis that is produced.

The supervisor is another person who may be entrusted with the task of performing job analysis for the members of the staff under his/her authority. Part of the problem here, as with the incumbent, is training all supervisors (with their varied backgrounds and educational and conceptual levels) to standardize the quality of analysis throughout the organization. Another problem to confront when asking supervisors for their support for this labor-intensive project is a likely unwillingness to take this task upon themselves.

Using Professional Expertise as a Criterion for Selection

Any professional from the wage and salary administration unit is a definite possibility for the assignment. There is a bias to consider, however. People performing job analysis from this perspective may emphasize the job evaluation aspects of the job they are analyzing and, as a result, may ignore or give less attention to other aspects of the analysis merely because they have little or no value for the compensable aspects of the job being analyzed. Even with this problem, it may be preferable to go this route and have the analysis performed by those who are well versed in the process. This may be the definitive reason to consider the wage and salary professional for the assignment. The wage and salary perspective may be a small price to pay in exchange for getting the project completed in the first place.

Personnel/human resources professionals may also be considered for the position of job analyst. Their backgrounds and sensitivity for the assignment make them prime candidates for the task. The only problem is that if only personnel/human resources staff members are working on the project for the organization, it may be more than they can handle. When the project is completed, the rest of the organization may have a variety of reasons against accepting the results because they never had the chance to buy into the effort.

In addition to staff professionals, outside consultants are also available to perform job analyses. There are only two problems with this choice: the cost will be quite high, and these people are not as familiar with the organization and its positions as its staff members are. The quality of the work will usually be excellent, because the major consulting firms have a reputation for being extremely selective when attracting people to their organizations. The second reason to expect excellent work is the fact that consultants feel that assignments like these invariably lead to other proposals; the consultant and his/her firm have a vested interest in putting forth their best effort in hopes of further assignments.

Using Instruments in Job Analysis to Increase Objectivity

There are various instruments available that perform job analysis and may be considered an alternative to using people, such as stopwatches, videotapes, measuring devices, or production line records. Data obtained in this manner, through devices or instrumentation, may be graded manually or with automation. A big advantage to this approach is that the computation and analytical aspects are removed from the participants in the project and the scores come directly from the instruments. One problem may be that the instrument selected is not as complete as any of the "human" alternatives. Although not as frequently used by themselves as human job analysts, instruments certainly are an alternative to consider instead of the other approaches described above, either alone or in combination with methods.

Keep in mind that there are advantages and disadvantages to each of the approaches described. You might want to consider a combination of any or all of the alternatives. This combination approach should provide an opportunity to take advantage of the best of each alternative while minimizing the negative aspects of the individual approaches.

Five Essential Skills of the Job Analyst

Regardless of who is responsible for job analysis, the following five skills are essential:

Oral communication skills

The person must be able to ask questions in a face-to-face meeting in a logical, structured manner that will elicit the required data. The completeness of the data will allow the analyst to prepare an accurate analysis of any job that he/she has been assigned to.

When discussing oral communication skills, the listening aspects of those skills are particularly important when a job is being analyzed. The better the listening skills of the job analyst, the more accurate and complete the final analysis will be.

Oral communication skills also will be necessary at another level. When the time comes to discuss the written analysis, it will frequently be necessary for the job analyst to address the issues and answer the questions that may arise at any meeting he/she may be asked to attend.

Written communication skills

It is not nearly enough for the job analyst to be proficient in oral communication skills. He/she must be able to put together the documentation required to complete the job analysis project. Only the person with good written communication skills will be up to the task of providing a document that is complete, succinct, understandable, and accurate.

A discerning mind

The job analyst must be able to separate major from minor activities, rank responsibilities by level of importance, and include ancillary activities that provide an important dimension while ignoring incidental aspects of little consequence or value.

Strong intellectual curiosity

The effective job analyst is the one who is curious about the environment in which he/she works. He/she explores issues and pursues questions until a solution or explanation is unearthed.

Adequate training

In spite of opinions to the contrary, no one is born a job analyst. It is, however, likely that most persons doing analyses have never had any training—even if they have been responsible for job analyses at one time or another during their careers. It is quite common that the person was drafted into service with little or no formal training.

Like any other skill that needs to be acquired, job analysis training ought to be considered an integral part of the job analysis process. The training ought to include practice reviews and write-ups. If interviewing is a part of the job analysis process then it should also be included. There should also be a follow-up and review aspect to the project to determine the effectiveness of the training.

HOW TO USE JOB ANALYSIS FOR FUNCTIONS OTHER THAN WAGE AND SALARY ADMINISTRATION

As we have discussed, job analysis plays a critical role in the design and management of an organization's wage and salary administration program. It also plays a vital role in almost all the other aspects of personnel/human resources management.

Many of the human resources functions use information derived from job analysis as a starting point. Exhibit 2-2 identifies the personnel/human resources functions that utilize information derived from job analysis.

Using Job Analysis in Personnel/Human Resources Planning

Job analysis plays a significant role in personnel/human resources planning because it helps to identify the jobs, skills, and the competency requirements for both short-term and long-term planning. With this information, the organization is able to evaluate the resources and skills it currently possesses, determine skills gaps, and identify the staffing and training and development strategies to ensure a competent workforce.

Job information is also essential in redesigning and restructuring jobs to meet an organization's business strategy. Furthermore, an understanding of the content and requirements of existing jobs helps the organization to build career paths and provide career opportunities for its employees.

Using Job Analysis for Recruitment and Staffing

In order for the recruitment and staffing functions to be effective, the personnel/human resources professional charged with the responsibility must have sufficient understanding of the jobs they are trying to fill. In fact, it is difficult to consider a job search being conducted without a job analysis in place. Job analysis is the starting point for understanding job content; the skills, knowledge, and abilities that the job requires; and what makes these qualifications essential. This information becomes the primary input for developing job-relevant selection criteria. A personnel/human resources professional's success in matching the job with the candidate is greatly enhanced when there are clearly established job-related selection criteria.

Using Job Analysis for Performance Management

Key staff members must have an understanding of job content and the amount of time it takes to perform an activity and its expected outcome to define performance criteria and standards for each job in the organization. Only after clarifying and communicating the job's objectives, performance standards,

Exhibit 2-2
HR Functions that Use Information Derived
from Job Analysis

and expectations to the employee can a manager effectively evaluate an employee's performance.

Using Job Analysis for Employee Training and Development

Job analysis enables the personnel/human resources professional responsible for the training and development functions to identify the skills or competence levels that are required in the organization. Once this information has been gathered, training and development needs may be assessed and training programs designed and implemented.

Complying with the Law to Ensure Fair Employment Practices

There are various federal and state laws that govern employment practices.

The Fair Labor Standards Act of 1938 requires that job analysis be performed to support exempt and nonexempt determinations.

The federal Equal Employment Opportunity (EEO) laws prohibit discrimination in employment based on race, color, religion, national origin, sex, disability, and age. The term "employment" in EEO legislation is construed broadly to include such activities as selecting, hiring, promoting, compensating, training, terminating, transferring, and demoting employees. In order to ensure nondiscrimination under EEO laws, employers have to base employment decisions on job-relevant criteria. It is through job analysis that these job-relevant criteria are determined.

The Equal Pay Act of 1963 protects employees from discrimination in wages on the basis of sex. Its basic requirement is "equal pay for equal work." Employers cannot pay lower wages to employees of one sex than they pay to employees of the opposite sex for equal work on jobs requiring equal skill, effort, and responsibility performed under similar working conditions. Job analysis is needed to accurately define a job's skill and competence requirements and its working conditions.

The Americans With Disability Act (ADA) adds a new challenge for job analysts. The ADA prohibits employers with fifteen or more workers from discriminating against a qualified individual because of disability with regard to job application procedures, hiring, discharge, compensation, advancement, job training, and other terms, conditions, and privileges of employment. Since the information derived from job analysis is used to establish standards for selecting, compensating, evaluating, promoting, and terminating employees, job analysis will be a vital instrument to ensure compliance with ADA regulations.

The person responsible for analyzing any job must be aware of what employment practices are vulnerable to legal challenges and what policies and procedures can minimalize such risks. (For additional information see Chapters 1 and 11.)

PLANNING THE JOB ANALYSIS PROCESS

There are three major steps in the job analysis process as shown in Exhibit 2-3. They are: planning the process, collecting the data, and documenting the findings.

In preparing for the job analysis process, there are a number of questions you must answer:

- "For what purpose is the job being analyzed?"
- "Will there be other purposes for which the results will be used?"
- "What job analysis method will be selected?"

The job analysis plan should identify:

- the method to be used
- the specific tasks to be completed
- the sources of job information
- the individuals responsible for conducting the analysis
- the required resources

As discussed, in the wage and salary administration function, job analysis is an essential first step in determining the pay levels for jobs. Since job analysis provides essential information for the wage and salary program, its format and content should be consistent with the requirements of the pay system. It is, therefore, important to determine what specific job information is needed.

As part of the wage and salary program, for instance, job evaluation may have to be conducted to determine a job's worth in the organization and to ensure internal pay equity. The job evaluation method might require a specific format and criteria or dimensions for analyzing the jobs, such as:

PLAN THE PROCESS

- Objectives

- Wage and salary administration program requirements

- Methods/approaches/ time/resources

COLLECT THE DATA

- Sources: incumbents
            supervisors
            job analyst

- Methods: questionnaire
            interviews
            observations

ANALYZE THE DATA

- Group activities

- Rank activities

- Review results with management

Exhibit 2-3
Steps in the Job Analysis Program

- accountability
- responsibilities
- use of judgement and problem solving
- skill requirements
- mental and physical demands
- working conditions

The dimensions will then be used to compare jobs with each other. If the job evaluation process requires the analysis of a job in terms of these specific dimensions, the job analysis process has to be designed to meet the prescribed format and provide these dimensions.

The method of job analysis must be consistent with the wage and salary administration program that it is expected to support. Some wage and salary administration programs, for example, stress the importance of identifying not only the tasks performed but also the expected outcomes or results. In these instances, the method and format of the job analysis will utilize data that deal with results or outcomes.

In addition to the requirements of an organization's wage and salary administration program, the objectives of job analysis, and the choice of the analysis method, you must consider the number and variety of jobs to be analyzed and the amount of time and resources (labor, automation) available.

How to Use the Functional Job Analysis (FJA) Method

There are a number of job analysis methods. One of the most popular is the **functional job analysis method** (FJA) described below.

The approach was given a lot of attention in the early fifties by Sidney A. Fine, Ph.D. when he was with the United States Employment Service and was used as the basis for the classification system of the third edition of the *Dictionary of Occupational Titles of the United States Employment Service, 1965*. For further discussion of the classification system as a tool for job pricing see page 18.

Functional Job Analysis focuses on:

- the elements of a job, that is, tasks as they affect data, people, and things; and
- the skills and competencies required to perform these tasks.

Scales are the frame of reference used in this approach to indicate the degree of an incumbent's involvement with things, data, and people, and the scales are based on the premise that:

- in the execution of their jobs, workers are always involved in an interaction with three elements-regardless of job-namely; things, data, and people;
- workers are also required to utilize physical, mental and interpersonal skills in the execution of their jobs;
- the execution of any job activity reflects a hierarchy of skill levels;
- all jobs involve performing activities on more than one skill level; and,
- selecting the three highest activities or functions (one from each scale) very accurately describes what workers do in their jobs.

It was these premises and their practical application in the *Dictionary* mentioned above, that allowed the project staff to classify specific content and skill requirements for more than 22,000 job "definitions" (in the latest edition over 30,000) and with minor adjustments they have been used ever since.

A Task Orientation

In this approach, the emphasis is on the tasks to be performed rather than the title assigned to the job titles are considered unreliable. From research it was determined that the same tasks showed up repeatedly in different jobs and task elements could therefore be determined to be the basis for job relationships. The tasks were then presented in a cause and effect relationship. (For example, the cashier pays out the correct amount of cash so that no discrepancies will occur.)

The Scales Themselves-A Brief Explanation

The data-function scale describes the worker's involvement with information and ideas in the performance of a task.

The people-function scale describes the worker's involvement in the performance of a task that requires communication and interaction with other people such as customers, clients, and co-workers.

The things-function scale describes the worker's involvement in the performance of a task with tangibles-for example, machines, tools, equipment, and work aids.

In using the scales one must be careful to note that the things-data-people arrangement is crucial since data is central to the execution of any job. One must be mindful too that while related, each of the three elements is unique in the role required in the execution of any task. Even though data functions tend to vary independently of things and people, as the things and people functions get more complex, so does the data function.

Gradations within the scales are meaningful but usually not between them. Thus a medium weight level for the *people function* or the *data function* is not necessarrily equivalent to a medium weight level for the *things function*. For further explanation consult the notes provided with the following Chart.

Exhibit 2-4 *A Summary Chart of Worker Function Scales* was developed by Sidney Fine, who continues to be an authority on functional job analysis and frequently gives workshops on the topic. It illustrates the hierarchy of functions that is used.

It also shows the three functions and the levels that have been determined for each of them. In the table, the greatest weight is assigned to level 7 and the least weight to level 1.

In the FJA scale, each of the functions is defined and assigned a level (as shown in Exhibit 2-4). If you are to determine a task level in the data function portion of the scale, then the function that relates to the used of data needs to be examined further. For example: In the data function section of the table, the tasks "computing" and "compiling" are two different functions that are assigned to level 3. To distinguish these functions within a level, alphabetic characters are attached to the numbers. Notice that in level 3, computing is at 3A and compiling is at 3B.

To illustrate the use of the FJA scale assume that you are determining each position's function as it relates to data. Assume also that the position requires the incumbent to primarily copy or post data to a log. This function would then fall under level 2, as indicated by the word "copying." However, if the position involves analysis of data as well as using information for problem solving, then the function will be as level 6 on the scale because "synthesizing" accurately describes the level of the function.

There are two common criticisms of the functional job analysis approach. The first is that the job description "essays" do not adequately describe the jobs in question and second that the method does not directly relate to the specific behaviors required for each job within any one organization. These comments notwithstanding, FJA is a useful technique to employ when building a human resource information system that has meaninful job analysis as one of its cornerstones.

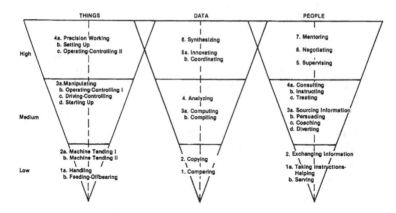

SUMMARY CHART OF WORKER FUNCTION SCALES

NOTES:

1. Each hierarchy is independent of the other. It would be incorrect to read the functions across the three hierarchies as related because they appear to be on the same level. The definitive relationship among functions is within each hierarchy, not across hierarchies. Some broad exceptions are made in the next note.

2. Data is central since a worker can be assigned even higher data functions although Things and People functions remain at the lowest level of their respective scales. This is not so for Things and People functions. When a Things function is at the third level, e.g., Precision Working, the Data function is likely to be at least Compiling or Computing. When a People function is at the fourth level, e.g., Consulting, the Data function is likely to be at least Analyzing and possibly Innovating or Coordinating. Similarly for Supervising and Negotiating. Mentoring in some instances can call for Synthesizing.

3. Each function in its hierarchy is defined to include the lower numbered functions. This is more or less the way it was found to occur in reality. It was most clear-cut for Things and Data and only a rough approximation in the case of People.

4. The lettered functions are separate functions on the same level, separately defined. The empirical evidence did not support a hierarchial distinction.

5. The hyphenated functions, Taking Instructions-Helping, Operating-Controlling, etc. are single functions.

6. The Things hierarchy consists of two intertwined scales: Handling, Manipulating, Precision working is a scale for tasks involving hands and hand tools; the remainder of the functions apply to tasks involving machines, equipment, vehicles.

Exhibit 2-4
Functional Job Analysis Hierachy

Reprinted here with permission from Sidney A. Fine, Ph.D. *Functional Job Analysis Scales,* revised edition, 1989

How to Use the Position Analysis Questionnaire

The second most commonly used job analysis method for wage and salary administration is the position analysis questionnaire (PAQ). Unlike FJA which focuses on job elements, PAQ focuses on the behavior required to perform a job. This approach provides a great deal of insight into the behaviors that enable an incumbent to succeed on the job. A sample position analysis questionnaire is provided in Appendix C.

The PAQ has been described as an attempt to identify six job dimensions:

- information sources critical to job performance
- information processing and decision making critical to job performance
- physical activity and dexterity required by the job
- interpersonal relationships required by the job
- physical working conditions and the reactions of individuals to the conditions
- other job characteristics, such as work schedule and work responsibility.

Both FJA and PAQ provide tools for conducting a comprehensive job analysis. Since there are a number of tested job analysis tools and models, it may be practical for you to select one "off the shelf" that meets the organization's needs. It is also possible to select features from different methods in order to design an instrument tailored to meet the organization's specific needs.

COLLECTING DATA FOR THE JOB ANALYSIS PROGRAM

Collecting information about a job is the second key step in the job analysis process. As stated earlier, information concerning jobs may be obtained from incumbents, supervisors, and other management employees in the same unit or department.

These sources of information may be referred to as "job content experts." Tools such as questionnaires, interviews, and observation are used to facilitate the data collection process.

How to Select Job Content Experts

The selection of job content experts depends on a number of considerations. It is clearly preferable to obtain information from all the incumbents, their supervisors, and the supervisors' supervisor. However, there may not be sufficient time and resources to do this. If there are several incumbents in the job to be analyzed, select a few representatives to act as job content experts.

Before selecting these job content experts, the incumbents should be classified or grouped according to such factors as length of employment, sex, ethnic background, and education. The job content experts can then be randomly selected from each group. This way you can ensure that they represent the different groups of incumbents. Whenever possible, it is useful to obtain information from both the incumbents and their supervisors.

Before collecting information, meet with the potential job content experts to explain the process and its objectives. This is important in order to allay fears or anxiety that may accompany the job analysis process.

Using Questionnaires, Interviews, and Observation in Job Analysis

There are several tools that a job analyst can use in collecting job data. The three most commonly used are questionnaires, interviews, and observations.

Questionnaires

The questionnaire provides a systematic and structured tool for collecting information about a job. Before designing the questionnaire, the wage and salary professional should speak with the job content experts and observe some examples of tasks performed on the job to obtain pertinent information.

The questionnaire may include open-ended questions where the job content expert is asked to explain or elaborate on some specific aspects of the job. Some examples of questions that incumbents may be asked are:

- What activities take up most of your work day? Describe each one briefly.
- How do you decide which task has to be performed first?
- What steps do you take to complete. . .?
- What responsibilities do you have?

Another type of questionnaire would ask the respondent to list the activities or duties performed on the job, their expected outcome, and the amount of time spent on each of these activities.

The questionnaire may also be designed as a checklist where activities are listed and briefly described and the job content expert selects the activities that are performed on the job. In addition, the respondent may be asked to indicate the frequency that an activity is performed and to rate the activity's importance. The job content experts can show the frequency and importance of activities in a variety of ways. They may describe each activity in the checklist by:

- using a rating scale of 1 through 5 to show critical nature of the activity or frequency;
- indicating agreement or disagreement with each statement about activities performed (that is, "strongly disagree" through "strongly agree"); or
- using terms such as "always," "seldom," and "never" to indicate the frequency of occurrence of an activity.

The checklist may also include questions concerning job requirements and the job context. An example of a checklist questionnaire is shown in Exhibit 2-5.

Each approach to designing a questionnaire has its advantages and disadvantages. For instance, it is possible for you to obtain more information by asking open-ended questions. However, since the job content experts are allowed to elaborate on their answers, it will take more time and effort on your part to sort and analyze the information. The checklist type of questionnaire takes time to prepare initially. However, at the end of the process, information collected through a checklist is structured and can be easily sorted and analyzed.

In selecting or designing a questionnaire, it is critical that the instrument selected be easily understood by the employees who will be asked to complete it. It must serve as a useful tool in the gathering of the data required, and should be able to be completed in a timely and accurate manner.

Interviews

You may conduct face-to-face interviews in lieu of the questionnaire to collect information about jobs. The type of questions you choose for the questionnaire may provide the "script" for an interview.

A structured interview will provide consistency of approach and ensure that all the required information is obtained. It has the advantage of allowing the interviewer to obtain clarification as needed, on information provided. The exchange that takes place during an interview allows a good interviewer to probe further into the job content. If there are several jobs to be analyzed, however, the interview process may not be the most efficient method to use because it is time consuming and could be expensive to conduct.

The interview method is, however, an excellent supplement to questionnaires. You could interview the job content experts to clarify or verify some of

Prepare the attached questionnaire as follows:

1. In the first column, answer the question: "To what extent is each activity a part of the job?"

        Y   for **yes, this is part of the job.**

        N   for **no, this is not part of the job.**

2. In the second column, rate the activity's importance:

        4   **Critical.** One of the most important things done. Major impact on overall effectiveness on the job.

        3   **Important.** Among the more noteworthy parts of the job. Considerable impact on overall job performance.

        2   **Minor.** Of relative little importance. Little impact on overall job performance.

        1   **Trivial.** Part of the job but has almost nothing to do with overall performance effectiveness.

3. In the last column, rate the activity's frequency:

        4   **High.** Much more time is spent doing this activity than other parts of the job.

        3   **Moderate.** A bit more time is spent doing this than other parts of the job.

        2   **Low.** A bit less time is spent doing this than other parts of the job.

        1   **Infrequent.** Much less time is spent doing this than other parts of the job.

Exhibit 2-5
Sample Job Analysis Checklist

DATE: POSITION: PREPARED BY:		DEPARTMENT/SECTION: INCUMBENT:		

Job Activities:			Importance	Frequency
1. Types (using typewriter) plain text copy and/or prepared lists of primarily non-numerical material.	Y	N	1 2 3 4	1 2 3 4
2. Word processes text by means of a dedicated word processor or computer.				
3. Composes correspondence, reports or memoranda.	Y	N	1 2 3 4	1 2 3 4
4. Writes instructional or procedural materials.	Y	N	1 2 3 4	1 2 3 4
5. Reads, interprets, and acts upon written messages/requests from other departments or from outside the organization.	Y	N	1 2 3 4	1 2 3 4
6. Prepares routine summaries or reports, based on information at hand, following standard operating procedure.	Y	N	1 2 3 4	1 2 3 4
7. Selects and/or gathers specific data, information, or desired items, according to standard operating procedures.	Y	N	1 2 3 4	1 2 3 4
8. Compiles numerical or statistical data for tables, charts, summaries or for other uses.	Y	N	1 2 3 4	1 2 3 4
9. Greets and meets face to face with customers.	Y	N	1 2 3 4	1 2 3 4
10. Answers questions and gives information concerning bills and other problems, face-to-face or over the telephone.	Y	N	1 2 3 4	1 2 3 4
11. Records and resolves customer calls and written inquiries.	Y	N	1 2 3 4	1 2 3 4
12. Determines and verifies total payments received against appropriate forms or report.	Y	N	1 2 3 4	1 2 3 4
13. Reconciles and adjusts accounts.	Y	N	1 2 3 4	1 2 3 4
14. Keys data into a computer terminal ("PC") and/or mainframe.	Y	N	1 2 3 4	1 2 3 4
15. Performs and/or checks simple arithmetic calculations manually.	Y	N	1 2 3 4	1 2 3 4
16. Determines where errors occurred in a series of calculations and which calculations were affected by the error(s),	Y	N	1 2 3 4	1 2 3 4
17. Collects and distributes mail, packages and other materials.	Y	N	1 2 3 4	1 2 3 4

Exhibit 2-5 (continued)
Sample Job Analysis Checklist

their responses to the questionnaire, to fill in gaps, or to resolve inconsistencies in their responses.

Observations

Direct observations can generate information that would ordinarily be difficult to obtain through questionnaires or interviews, and they offer a number of advantages. They enable you to determine the amount of time spent to perform an activity, the frequency of an activity's occurrence, the context of the job, and the interactions between the incumbent and other individuals. In addition, observation may be the only effective way to understand the operation of equipment or the process involved in a complex technical task. However, if observation is the only method used for collecting job data, it may be a very time consuming and expensive method, especially if there are several jobs to be analyzed in a short period of time.

In conjunction with questionnaires, observation enables you to increase your understanding of the job being analyzed. It is apparent that a comprehensive view of the job may be obtained by using a variety of tools. While questionnaires could be the basic data collection method, they may be supplemented with interviews and observation.

ANALYZING THE JOB DATA

After the job information has been collected, the data must be analyzed through a series of activities. This analysis phase is the "value added" portion of the exercise, where you evaluate all the information collected from the various sources to provide a concise, accurate, and coherent report. Exhibit 2-6 provides a sample Job Content Analysis.

Ranking the Activities by Frequency and Criticality

The activities could be ranked according to the frequency of their occurrence by using the scores obtained in the questionnaire. Using the rates or scores assigned by the job content experts for each activity, identify the activities that have high frequency and criticality and eliminate those with relatively low frequency and criticality.

JOB CONTENT ANALYSIS		
Date: March 10, 199x	**Prepared By: K.B. Smith, Analyst**	
Position: Senior Typist	**Incumbent: S.L.Jones**	

TASK	ACTIVITIES	REQUIREMENTS (Knowledge/skills/ability)
Types/ Word Process and Data Entry	Types (using a typewriter) plain text copy and/or prepared lists of primarily non-numerical material. Word processes text by means of a dedicated word processor or computer. Keys data into a computer terminal (PC) and/or Mainframe.	Typing accurately, Word Processing (specific software), Knowledge of Automated Data Entry
Writes Reports, Instructions, etc.	Composes correspondence, reports or memoranda. Writes instructional or procedural materials. Prepares routine summaries or reports, based on information at hand, following standard operating procedures.	Written communication skills
Respond to Customer Needs	Reads, interprets, and acts upon written messages/requests from other departments or outside organization. Greets and meets face-to-face with customers.	Verbal Communication Skills Problem Solving Analytical Skills

Exhibit 2-6
Job Content Analysis

Grouping Activities into Major Tasks

The result of the ranking and grouping of activities is used to identify the major or essential components of the job, which in turn will be used to evaluate its worth to the organization.

Listing the Requirements of the Job

Using the information provided by the job content experts, list the requirements for each group of activities as shown in the job content analysis.

Defining the Job Context from Data Collected

This analysis may be performed manually or as part of the Human Resource Information System (HRIS). There are computerized statistical packages that can assist you in grouping and ranking the activities or tasks. There is also automated job analysis software available in the market. One example is Identifying Criteria for Success, developed by Development Dimensions International (DDI), a management consulting firm based in Pittsburgh, Pennsylvania.

Reviewing the Completed Job Analysis

Review the completed job analysis with the supervisors responsible for the job analyzed. This will ensure accuracy of job information as well as management's acceptance of the job analysis results. The analysis of the job content, requirements, and context will be used to prepare the job description, evaluate the job, and determine its pay rate.

SUMMARY

Job analysis is an activity that is required not only to perform all the activities of wage and salary administration effectively but also for a variety of other organizational needs.

To accomplish the task initially requires a strong commitment from the organization to obtain the data and to select the method but also to provide the necessary resources and training to undertake and maintain the project.

Employers will be more effective in dealing with the challenges presented by current federal, state, and local laws and regulations. More important however, job analysis properly done will also mean a more productive workplace, because the organization, through its commitment to pay for the job and not the person, will have developed credibility through the process. This credibility will demonstrate a real commitment to its employees based on objective data that are applied in an objective, consistent way.

Job analysis is one major effort that, although time consuming and labor intensive, will be worthwhile in the organization's attempts to meet its business objectives with the help of its committed workforce. As the cornerstone of job descriptions and job evaluations, job analyses assure the integrity of the organization's pay policy.

chapter three ————————————————————————

CREATING JOB DESCRIPTIONS TO FACILITATE WAGE AND SALARY EVALUATIONS

In Chapter 2, job analysis was discussed as the first step towards evaluating each job in your organization. The evaluation process cannot proceed efficiently and accurately until the second step, job description, is complete. At this point, you must apply the information gathered in the job analysis process to complete a job description. A job description is a critical tool for determining the worth of each job in your organization, and, if pay increases are tied to performance, for establishing standards of performance.

Job evaluation is a difficult and not very scientific process; good job descriptions lead to accurate job evaluations. The absence of job descriptions makes the evaluation process very difficult. The following summarizes this three-step progression from job analysis to job description to job evaluation:

- Step 1: Job Analysis—A study of tasks, employee skills, time and situation factors (such as technology, physical aspects, data exchange, interactions) which are required to complete a job; provides information to define and evaluate jobs.

- Step 2: Job Description—Complete explanation of responsibilities of grouped set of tasks to complete a function to be performed by one person; identifies reason for job and skills, knowledge, abilities required for effective execution.

- Step 3: Job Evaluation—Determination of the relative value of a job within the organization; assigns jobs to hierarchy of pay grades or other index of job value; most concerned with the criteria of internal equity.

For this discussion, the term *job* is used to describe a group of positions that are basically identical in their duties. The term *position* is used to refer to a collection of tasks performed by a single incumbent.

Job descriptions by their very nature are written in position terms, and without any reference to the incumbent. The point of the job description is to evaluate the position regardless of who the incumbent is. It is the job that is to be evaluated and priced, not the incumbent. That is not to say that it is incorrect when determining the pay rate or salary to consider the incumbent's personal characteristics, experience, or other attributes in the process of arriving at a figure. However, that is not the intent of the exercise here.

DETERMINING WHEN TO PREPARE
A JOB DESCRIPTION

Just as job analysis can be used for many purposes, job descriptions may be used for the same purposes described in Exhibit 2-4 in Chapter 2. For wage and salary administration purposes, there are several times that a job description should be considered to either review an already existing position or to define a new position.

When a new position is proposed

Here, of course, there will be no incumbent to draw upon for information, but there is the subject matter expert who is proposing the job. Usually this will be the person who has determined that the job is needed and is making the proposal. Review the description to determine the job's value to the organization and price it according to the procedures and policy of the organization.

When the decision is made to recruit candidates for either a new or open position

Whenever the decision is made to commence a search to fill a position, the basis upon which to conduct the search is an accurate, current job description. This document is an invaluable tool in assisting the recruiter to screen candidates. The job description also serves another purpose: it is a marketing tool for the candidate and for any outside sources the organization wishes to use. An accurate job description not only encourages appropriate candidates to apply, it also helps to screen out those who are not suitable candidates and will not ultimately be considered for the job.

Last, try to make it a matter of policy that all requisitions for staff include an updated job description. Only if the supervisor or manager has reviewed the duties of the position before commencing the search will he/she and you know whether the job has had any changes and therefore is due for reevaluation. Making these determinations up front, before the actual search begins, increases the likelihood that an appropriate candidate will be found and ultimately selected and that the price established will be right for the job.

When a person is being promoted

Review and update job descriptions whenever a person is being promoted, regardless of whether the incumbent is remaining at the same workstation. If he/she is going to stay at the same location, provide a current description for the new job so that an evaluation can be undertaken. If the person being promoted is moving, then both the "new" position and the "old" position should be reviewed for accuracy (assuming, of course, that the promoted person is being replaced).

When performance is being reviewed

At the start and at the end of the performance period, review the duties of a person's job to ensure a complete understanding of the details and scope of the position and how it relates to performance. Additionally, if the job is undergoing change, if the technology is being replaced, or if there is any question about changes in priorities and performance, raise these issues as soon as they surface during the performance period. Another reason for reviewing the job descriptions, at least at the beginning and end of the performance measurement period, is to build into the organization and its management an automatic review process. This assures that all job descriptions are reviewed at least once during each performance appraisal cycle (usually a year).

When completing a salary survey

Even if position descriptions are up to date, it never hurts to reconsider them for benchmark jobs to ensure that the fit is sufficient to warrant comparisons with the same or similar title in the market being surveyed. The reason for the review may come, in fact, from a reading of the descriptions provided by the originator of the survey.

When required for reorganization, downsizing, or restructuring

Whenever a restructuring, downsizing, or reorganization occurs, job descriptions should be reviewed in each area affected by the management action to determine impact from a job standpoint. The primary question "To what extent will the positions in this unit be affected?" is an effective starting point.

When required for benchmark purposes

Job descriptions included in outside surveys should be reviewed for accuracy. Even if no salary surveys occur that include an important, pivotal position, periodic reviews should be conducted to determine whether the job needs a reevaluation. There is no formula for determining an appropriate time framework in which to conduct these reviews; it depends on the volatility of the job and the industry of the organization.

DETERMINING WHO SHOULD PREPARE
THE JOB DESCRIPTION

Writing job descriptions is perceived by most people as a very difficult task. For others, however, it is one of the more positive aspects of a job. Writing job descriptions is a prime opportunity to get to know many aspects of the business and many successful people in the organization under positive and important circumstances.

The purpose in having a wage and salary professional, rather than each incumbent, prepare his/her own job description is that a trained person will more likely be effective in obtaining accurate information that includes all the aspects of a particular job. It will also ensure that a standard format will be followed, which will enhance the job evaluation process.

Taking the responsibility away from an incumbent will probably make him/her relieved for not being responsible for writing the description. It is a win-win-win situation. The person responsible for writing the job description wins the knowledge gained from one more job understood. The incumbent wins from the recognition and the opportunity to reflect on his/her own function and status in the organization. The organization wins from accurate portrayals of the tasks being performed so that it may pay appropriately and therefore compete in the marketplace successfully.

If there are other purposes for creating job descriptions (for example, for training or career development purposes), it will be more appropriate for someone with that perspective and expertise to create the job description for those purposes. One of the problems that often occurs with job descriptions, as with performance appraisals, is that they are frequently considered catch-all solutions. In the process of trying to be so many things for so many different purposes, a focused perspective is sometimes compromised.

HOW TO FILL OUT THE JOB DESCRIPTION FORM

The first component of a job description is the reason for doing one. In your case, the purpose is to determine both the value that the organization places on the job and the price the external marketplace is willing to pay. If the person with the "need to know" understood the job, then there would be no need for the job description. The job description in its final form should be understandable to the person who would not be able to carry out his/her responsibility without knowledge of what elements constitute the job. The components of the job description should then be so comprehensive that they incorporate the essential elements of the job so that the reader will be able to use the job description for his/her purposes.

Job Summary

Exhibit 3-1 provides a sample job description form. At the top of the job description form, for administrative purposes, provide the following items of data:

- **Job Title**—This term refers to a group of positions with basically identical tasks. This title should be functional and should describe the title as it may be used across organizational lines in the marketplace.
- **Organizational Title**—If the organization uses separate titles internally to help define the hierarchy of the organization, include these

JOB DESCRIPTION		
JOB TITLE:	SALARY GRADE:	JOB CODE:
ORGANIZATION TITLE:	EXEMPT / NONEXEMPT	
DEPARTMENT/LOCATION:	EEO-1 CATEGORY:	
NAME OF INCUMBENT:	SUPERVISOR:	
APPROVED ON (date):	APPROVED ON (date):	
JOB ANALYST:	DATE COMPLETED:	

PURPOSE OF JOB:

JOB RESPONSIBILITIES:

Exhibit 3-1
Sample Job Description Form

titles here. Common organizational titles include vice-president, assistant vice-president, and director.

- **Department**—This is the location of the job within the organization.
- **Date**—This is the date the job description was completed.
- **Job Code**—This is the code number assigned by the organization to the job.
- **EEO-1/AAP Categories**—These are the Equal Employment Opportunity/Affirmative Action Program categories in which the position is located.
- **Exempt/Nonexempt designation**—This is the FLSA determination for overtime purposes (for a more detailed explanation see Chapter 10).
- **Name of Incumbent and Approval of Incumbent/Date**—Include the name of the incumbent along with his/her initials to confirm that the position provided has been reviewed and approved for accuracy.
- **Name of Job Analyst**—If there are any questions about the job description or if it needs revision at a later date, the job analyst who wrote it can be contacted.
- **Name of Supervisor and Approval of Supervisor/Date**—Provide the supervisor's name and approval as with the incumbent to indicate that the person responsible for the position has attested to the accuracy of the description.

Below the administrative details, such as position title, grade, date of job description completion, and approvals, there will be a brief statement of the job's purpose. This may either be given in terms of process (activities) or results. Even though the process approach is most commonly used, the result approach may be more effective. The title sometimes given to this section is "position charter."

The position's purpose or mission should describe the end result for the job so that the reader can immediately understand where the job fits in meeting the organization's objectives. This section should describe what aspect of the organization's objectives this position is expected to accomplish or what would not get accomplished without this position. Another way to describe the mission statement is "what the incumbent is being paid to achieve." The statement should be brief and not exceed three or four sentences unless it has more than one main purpose.

Job Responsibilities

This is the narrative portion of the job description form. It provides the reader with detailed information on what he/she needs to know to determine the nature and scope of the job. The following five components should be included in this section of the form.

General framework. Include a brief statement of each major function of the job. Describe the specific training and experience required to perform the responsibilities of the job effectively.

Environment. It would be useful to include an organizational chart to show reporting relationships one level up and down from the position being described, along with the positions on the same reporting level. Describe the levels and functional job titles of the other positions reporting to the same position. Also describe the subordinate positions reporting to the position being described.

Degree of autonomy. Include in the body of the text a description of what the incumbent in the position can accomplish on his/her own and what issues must be brought to the attention of his/her supervisor.

Role of the job in meeting organization objectives. Also include in the body of the text a brief description of how the job's mission is related to or affects the organization's objectives.

Quantitative dimensions. Provide a list of all the quantitative dimensions of the job, such as size of budget, revenue and expense figures, staff numbers, and any other figures that will give shape to the level of responsibility of the position.

STEPS IN THE JOB DESCRIPTION PROCESS

As previously discussed, the job description process, from start to finish, is one of several steps in the job evaluation process. Developing an accurate job description also involves several steps. Exhibit 3-2 illustrates the progression of steps in the job description process.

Determine the Method of Collecting Data

The first step in preparing a job description is determining the method for collecting the data from which the job description will be prepared. The

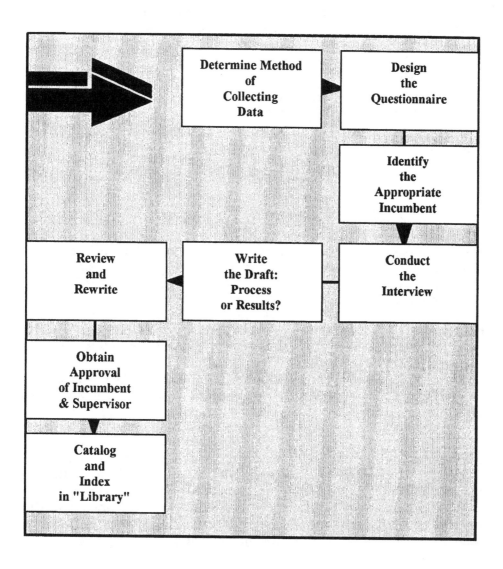

Exhibit 3-2
Job Description Process

time frame, type of job, organizational requirements, and available staff to complete the job descriptions will dictate the most feasible choice or combination of sources of information. The following lists possible methods:

- Observation
- Interview
- Review of output (reports generated, products or services provided) and input (raw material, sources of work activity)
- Diaries or logs
- Questionnaires
- Review of film or tapes of actual performance
- Direct participation (incumbent prepares job description)

The most common method for gathering data from which to prepare the job description is a combination of the observation and the interview methods. Although it requires a great deal of effort for each job, it also provides a direct understanding of the job because of the contact with the incumbent and the opportunity to see him/her actually performing the task.

There is another approach that allows for the same first-hand look but is less labor intensive: the inclusion of a questionnaire in the interview/observation approach. When a questionnaire is submitted to the incumbent for whom a job description is to be prepared in advance of the interview, several objectives are accomplished.

Using the questionnaire prepares the incumbent with the announcement of a forthcoming interview and provides a questionnaire he/she is expected to complete. The questionnaire serves as a preliminary interview by asking questions in a structured format. The job analyst then meets with the incumbent at his/her work site after the completed questionnaire has been reviewed. Interview questions are prepared in advance from the written answers already obtained. This approach, by allowing the analyst to "preview" the job through the questionnaire, puts less of a training demand on the analyst and reduces (but does not eliminate) note taking by the analyst during the interview. This two-step approach clearly signals to the incumbent that the organization is putting serious effort into its job description project.

Identify the Appropriate Incumbent

There are several sources of information from which to draw information to write a job description. They include:

- the incumbent
- the supervisor
- a subject matter expert
- a job analyst
- an instrument or machine (a camera, for example)

The most common and arguably the best source for the research required to write an accurate and complete job description is the incumbent. Whether an expert or a neophyte, the incumbent's performance is an accurate portrayal of that job. However, if the incumbent is deemed to be too inexperienced to perform the group of tasks that has been assigned to him/her, then even though the person is performing some aspects of the job, he/she is not performing the job in question. The person certainly is performing a job, but whether that is the job that requires the job description is the question that should be raised instead.

This point addresses the issue of the incumbent as the subject matter expert. The problem with every job description is the question of whether the incumbent is actually performing the responsibilities and tasks as they are portrayed. The higher and more responsible the position the more latitude allowed. Consider for a moment whether it is easier to determine the tasks of a word processor or of the chief executive officer.

This is a major reason why, regardless of position, the work being performed is determined by the person responsible for accomplishing the tasks. No one is better at determining what tasks they are performing, and the duties and responsibilities of the position, and the knowledge, skills, and abilities required to perform the job.

Having you, the wage and salary professional, go to incumbents sends an organizational message of recognition to all the staff that they are important. If job descriptions are being prepared and the incumbents participate in the process, they will then have a stake in the project undertaken.

The person who provides the data from which the job description is to be written should be articulate and knowledgeable about the job he/she is describing. That person should have held the position for a sufficient amount of time to be knowledgeable about it, and also about any subtleties and cyclical aspects relating to the position. A rule of thumb is that for an incumbent to be a credible source for the job description, the person should have been at the position for at least one full cycle so that he/she may understand the environment in which the position is located and be able to share his/her findings with the job analyst.

Obtain Data for Job Descriptions Through Interviews

The interview continues to be a very popular tool from which to develop a job description. It is also an effective method from which to perform an observation of the person functioning in the position, if the interview is conducted at the incumbent's workstation.

The incumbent's workstation may not be the most effective place from which to conduct a meeting to discuss the incumbent's job. The interruptions that may occur will certainly provide an opportunity for actual observation of the person in action. However, the location may cause other problems because of the eavesdropping, lost trains of thought, and wasted time.

Nevertheless, it is not a good idea to ask the incumbent to come to your office to discuss the job. By conducting the interview at his/her location, deference is given to the incumbent. It is the incumbent's job that is being discussed and you are the one requesting the information. If you prefer not to conduct the interview at the incumbent's workstation, give the interviewee an opportunity to choose a place for the meeting.

In order to obtain as much data as possible, the more quickly rapport is established, the more successful the meeting will be. By agreeing to meet with the incumbent at the site of his/her choice, preferably in his/her work location (but not at the workstation, except if the incumbent has his/her own office or enclosed area and agrees to provide uninterrupted time), the incumbent will be likely to share more aspects and details of his/her position in familiar surroundings.

Conducting the interview at the incumbent's work location gives the interviewer the opportunity to observe the environment in which the incumbent works. The more you are able to observe first-hand, the more the incumbent will be able to put a "real feel" into the job description.

The interview should be structured and may follow a designated format based on the following four steps.

Set a friendly tone and restate the purpose of the meeting. Mention the purpose of the meeting at the start of the interview to ensure that the incumbent remembers the reason for the session. Clearly state that the incumbent's input is critical and emphasize the importance of his/her role in this process.

Additionally, state soon after the meeting commences that the job description that will be prepared will be accurate and it will be the incumbent who will take responsibility for its accuracy. The preparer will report his/her own findings, but the incumbent needs to be aware that after the job description receives the incumbent's approval, the job description will be passed on to his/

her supervisor to ensure that the supervisor concurs with the accuracy of the job description as well.

Establish control of the meeting. Once rapport and a friendly tone have been established, take control of the meeting. The meeting belongs to you, but at the same time you need the incumbent. Carefully establish both confidence and dependency and set an appropriate pace.

Ask the questions. This is the key to the session. You must be able to use the questions to stimulate the incumbent to speak openly, freely, and succinctly while being focused on the task at hand. Take written notes during this part of the meeting to convey to the incumbent the importance of what he/she is saying and to ensure that what you're hearing is accurate. A tape recorder may be used for the session but it requires trust on the part of the interviewee. The trust demonstrated at this meeting will be a reflection of the incumbent's attitude toward the organization in which he/she is working.

One cautious note about using a tape reorder: you must be careful that the presence of the recorder doesn't restrict the incumbent's openness about discussing his/her job, not because of organizational concerns, but just because of the incumbent's own exposure or lack of exposure to recording devices.

Exhibit 3-3 provides a list of sample questions for a structured interview. In addition, consider giving the incumbent a questionnaire before the interview; this is discussed in the next section.

Close the meeting. The closing should be brief and should include thanks and a promise that you will not share the draft of the job description with anyone prior to the incumbent's review. Additionally, let the incumbent know the date at which the first draft will be completed and available to the incumbent for his/her review. Then, to ensure credibility, give the incumbent the job description for his/her comments and review as promised.

How to Use Questionnaires to Enhance the Interview Process

Exhibit 3-4 is an example of a questionnaire that may be used to obtain data for the job description. As you will see after reviewing it, the questionnaire is based on a structured interview.

Ideally, a questionnaire should not be used alone in completing the job description but, if necessary, it may serve the purpose. If an interview is used in conjunction with a questionnaire, it is important for you to review the completed form at length before any meeting with the incumbent. If sufficient

What would you, the incumbent, say the organization hopes to accomplish through your position?

How does this position fit into the organization?

Whom do you report to?

Who else reports to the same person?

Who reports to you? What are their titles and functions?

What is your functional title? Please provide an organizational chart.

What are your most frequent contacts within and outside the organization?

What dimensions are part of this position? (budget, revenue generated by the unit, staff size, other statistics)

Do you have any output goals? What are they?

Do you have any cost limits? What are they?

Do you have any role in establishing quality standards? If so, what is your role?

What reports do you generate? What is the frequency of reports?

To whom are these reports directed? For what purpose?

Where do you get your source material and information?

Whom do you go to for help?

Exhibit 3-3
The Structured Interview: Sample Questions

How frequently do you report to your supervisor? With what problems?

What are the principal rules, regulations, precedents, or personal control within which the job operates?

Is the supervision you receive direct or advisory?

Where is the biggest challenge? The most autonomy?

What problems are referred to senior staff members or are resolved consultation with others?

Give a brief sketch of each of your major responsibilities/activities and describe the proportion of responsibilities that each takes as a percentage of your time (perhaps on a daily basis).

Describe a typical day.

Is any specialization required?

What would you look for as a replacement? (education, skills, background, experience)

How can your performance be measured in terms of your effectiveness in achieving objectives?

Are you able to complete your tasks on your own? What, if any, help is required from others?

Have you done any special projects? What were they? For whom and for what purpose?

What are the basic challenges of the job?

What are the job's biggest problems?

What training and experience is needed for this job?

Exhibit 3-3 (continued)
The Structured Interview: Sample Questions

JOB DESCRIPTION

epartment _____ Org. Unit _____ Cost   Analyst _____ Approved _____
                                                          Center No. ____   (Init & Date)

	Name	Org. Title	Functional Title
cumbent			
eports to			

Position Charter

ive a brief, specific statement of the basic function of your job. Why does the job exist? What organizational
ojectives must be accomplished by this job? Please limit this statement to one or two sentences.

Dimensions

Nature and Scope of Position

To whom does your superior report? (Title and Function)

Other positions reporting directly to your superior. (Title and Function)

If applicable, briefly describe the nature and objective of each department managed by your position.
Include the titles and functions of your supporting staff.

What specific work experience, training, and/or education are necessary to do your job well?
What aspects of technical/specialized experience are most important?

What are your most frequent contacts inside and outside the organization?

Exhibit 3-4
Sample Job Description Questionnaire:
Senior Position

JOB DESCRIPTION   page 2

F. Does your job involve travel? If so, describe the purpose and extent.

G. What types of problems must be solved in your job? (Give specific examples.)

H. What specific policies, procedures and/or principles do you follow in solving problems? What type of guidance do you receive from your superior in solving problems? What type of problems do you refer to a higher authority?

I. What is the job's greatest challenge?

---

4. Principal Accountabilities

List the principal accountabilities of your position. Each accountability listed should be an ''end result'' or objective that this position is designed to accomplish. Objectives should be general in nature and not specific targets for this particular year. This section should contain 4 to 7 statements listed in descending order of importance.

---

5. Other Important Facts Not Already Covered (For example, does this position have membership on any standing organizational committee?)

Exhibit 3-4 (continued)
Sample Job Description Questionnaire:
Senior Position

effort is not given to the completed questionnaire prior to the meeting, the person responsible for completing the job description may suffer in four ways:

- First, the completed questionnaire is a real opportunity for the person responsible for completing the job description to determine the level of interest in the incumbent and to obtain a solid understanding of his/her communication skills and perspective before conducting the interview. If the questionnaire is not completed as promised, it is a signal that there may be a problem for some reason with this project.
- Second, if you do not use the research that is readily available for the meeting, you will not be as prepared for the interview as you should be.
- Third, the incumbent will quickly notice that the questionnaire he/she had made the effort to complete has not been taken into consideration and reviewed prior to the meeting and so will question the credibility of the person responsible for preparing the job description and of the project itself.
- Fourth, if the questionnaire is reviewed only after the meeting, it is probable that the person responsible for preparing the job description will have questions which will necessitate one more contact but that might have been answered at the first meeting.

Ask Incumbent to Review the Document for Accuracy

After the job description interview has been conducted, there are a few more steps to the process to obtain a buy-in from both the incumbent and his/her supervisor and ensure accuracy of the job description.

The first step is to give the job description back to the incumbent for his/her revisions and alterations. If another meeting is required, then it should be held promptly so that established deadlines will be met.

Rewrite the Document Based on the Incumbent's Comments

After the job description and the comments provided by the incumbent have been reviewed, the preparer will take the job description and rewrite the document to ensure the agreement of the incumbent.

Obtain Necessary Approval for the Document

After the rewrite, return the job description to the incumbent for his/her signoff. After the incumbent attests to the accuracy of the job description, it can be submitted to his/her supervisor for approval.

If there is a committee responsible for the review and evaluation of all job descriptions, the recently prepared job description is then submitted to the committee for the review and approval of the committees members. Exhibits 3-5 and 3-6, on the following pages, provide two completed sample job descriptions.

Provide a Database Library

Whether the wage and salary administration function is on an automated or manual HRIS, approved job descriptions should be cataloged and indexed by title, date, job code, EEO classification, and grade in a central location.

The indexing will provide you easy access whenever job descriptions are to be referred to, thus increasing the possibility that the job description effort will result in a "living library" of current, accurate, and useful job descriptions.

JOB TITLE: *Senior Collection Clerk*   DEPT NAME: *Patient Billing/Accounts*

DEPT. #   *AR 567*   WAGE SCALE:

ORIGINAL (DATE) REVISION 1 (DATE) REVISION 2 (D ATE)

PREPARED BY: *bgw* 12/1/92

DEPT. APPROVAL   *syo'n 1/15/93*

PERSONNEL/HR   *rvp* 3/1/93

OVERTIME: ~~EXEMPT/~~   EXEMPT/   EXEMPT/
                 NONEXEMPT   NONEXEMPT   NONEXEMPT

REPORTS TO: *Supervisor*

MAIN FUNCTION: (Summarize responsibilities in 1-2 sentences)

Resolve outstanding Commercial Insurance/Self-Pay balances using intense telephone collection techniques and follow-up letters to guarantors, third party insurances and government agencies. Answer all inquiries regarding billing and payments.

DUTIES AND RESPONSIBILITIES:

1. Organizes and analyses accounts to determine action to be pursued for the resolution of account balances.

2. Initiates intense telephone and correspondence to follow-up to insurance carriers and patients securing promise dates of payment.

3. Receives and conducts a high volume of system generated collection calls to guarantors via an automated dialing system.

4. Explains insurance benefits and payment responsibilities to patients. Establishes payment arrangements with responsible parties and follows-up to ensure compliance.

5. Reviews problem accounts with supervisor and develops a plan of action.

6. Evaluates patient financial status on their ability to pay, referring accounts to the Financial Evaluation program or initiating write-off.

7. Identifies and prepares uncollectible balances for agency referrals.

8. Effectively communicates with patients, guarantors, insurance carriers, outside agencies, physicians, administrators and other hospital personnel to expedite account resolution.

9. Resolves all incoming telephone calls and correspondence from patients or insurance companies.

Exhibit 3-5
Sample Job Description A

10. *Establishes and maintains an internal follow-up procedure for system generated reports.*

11. *Prepares and maintains required logs/reports accurately and submits them within established time frames.*

12. *Completes all forms thoroughly, accurately and legibly. Attaches back-up documentation. Initiates timely refunds.*

13. *Reviews account demographic and financial information for accuracy and updates the on-line computerized system in compliance with operational procedures to effect updating of account records.*

14. *Notifies Supervisor of system problems by providing relevant support documentation.*

15. *Performs operational duties of varying types as need arises.*

KNOWLEDGE REQUIRED: (Minimum education or equivalent experiences; licensure)

- *2 to 5 years clerical experience or B.A. with 1-2 years experience preferably in healthcare environment with knowledge of third party insurance, reimbursements, billing and collection.*
- *Previous public contact experience.*
- *Excellent communication skills with command of English grammar.*
- *Ability to handle difficult interactions and produce accurate work under pressure.*
- *Familiarity with computerized operations.*
- *Good organizational skills.*
- *Ability to work independently.*
- *Ability to perform in-depth collection processes and determine confidentiality of information.*

CONTACTS: (Patients, employees, agencies, etc.)

- *Patients/guarantors.*
- *Insurance carriers.*
- *Other center personnel.*
- *Government agencies.*
- *Attorneys.*

PHYSICAL DEMANDS: (Types and frequency of physical effort, e.g. lifting, visual concentration)

Extended visual concentration on CRT and detail reports. Repeated daily access to physical patient records in file room approx. 750 feet down hall on same floor. Periodic use of file cart to obtain/return files.

WORKING CONDITIONS: (Summarize, include disagreeable conditions/potential hazards)

Main floor windowless office; outside area has waiting room and receptionist shared with other functions; office equipped with CRT, automatic telephone system; built-in workstation and filing cabinets.

Exhibit 3-5 (continued)
Sample Job Description A

JOB TITLE: *Secretary I*   DEPT NAME: *Domestic Sales*

DEPT. # S-105   WAGE SCALE:

ORIGINAL (DATE) REVISION 1 (DATE) REVISION 2 (DATE)

PREPARED BY: *NFD 1/2/93*

DEPT. APPROVAL *RBL 2/5/92*

PERSONNEL/HR *GH 4/20/92*

OVERTIME:	~~EXEMPT~~/ NONEXEMPT	EXEMPT/ NONEXEMPT	EXEMPT/ NONEXEMPT

REPORTS TO: *Administrative Coordinator*

MAIN FUNCTION: *(Summarize responsibilities in one or two sentences)*

Under close supervision provides secretarial and general office assistance.

DUTIES AND RESPONSIBILITIES:

1. Types correspondence, reports, etc. from longhand draft following required formats.

2. Answers and screens telephone calls. Takes messages. Greets and screens visitors and directs them to appropriate staff. Provides general information to callers and visitors, directing nonroutine questions to appropriate staff. Receives, reviews, and distributes mail.

3. Maintains supervisors' calendar, makes appointments, schedules meetings, and arranges for meeting rooms.

4. Prepares requisitions for supplies, equipment, repairs, etc. and obtains appropriate signatures.

5. Organizes and maintains a filing system.

6. Uses copy machine as requested.

7. Performs other related duties as requested.

Exhibit 3-6
Sample Job Description B

DUTIES AND RESPONSIBILITIES, con't.

KNOWLEDGE REQUIRED: (minimum education or equivalent experiences; licensure)

High School diploma or equivalent. Type 40 WPM. 0 - 1 year office experience. Ability to read and write English.

CONTACTS: (employees, public, agencies etc.)

Routine contact of a nonsensitive nature. Contacts may vary: sales personnel, employees, customers, clients, vendors.

PHYSICAL DEMANDS: (types and frequency of physical demands, e.g. lifting, visual concentration)

Daily pushing of mail cart to deliver mail to staff members within department; must use elevator to reach second-floor staff. Periodic receiving and storing supplies in supply closet on same floor.

WORKING CONDITIONS: (summarize, include disagreeable conditions or potential hazards.)

Reception area within plant-filled lobby. Can be objectionable to person with low tolerance or allergy for certain plant life. Built-in workstation with electric typewriter. Overhead storage areas require use of stepstool to access.

Exhibit 3-6 (continued)
Sample Job Description B

SUMMARY

The job description is an important part of the job evaluation process, but it can accomplish much more if the organization demonstrates its commitment to the project and the entire process.

To consider job descriptions something all organizations should have may be a major act of folly: without senior management's commitment, the project will merely be given "lip service." To undertake a half-hearted or incomplete effort will hamper the effective operation of the organization in several ways, one of which is an impaired wage and salary administration function. The poor commitment to job descriptions may be part of a larger problem.

With the arrival of the Americans With Disabilities Act (ADA), job descriptions will play an even more important role in the growth and development of any organization. Jobs will have to be studied more carefully to include an analysis of essential and nonessential functions and also to consider what may be done to deal with reasonable accommodation. See Appendix II for a sample *Essential Functions Analysis Form* that may be used together with the job description forms mentioned earlier in this chapter, whenever a position becomes vacant.

Without job descriptions, organizations may miss opportunities to be truly effective in meeting the needs of people with disabilities. This fact, though, only masks the real issue: whether organizations can function effectively without job descriptions even without the impetus provided by the ADA.

chapter four ————

DESIGNING A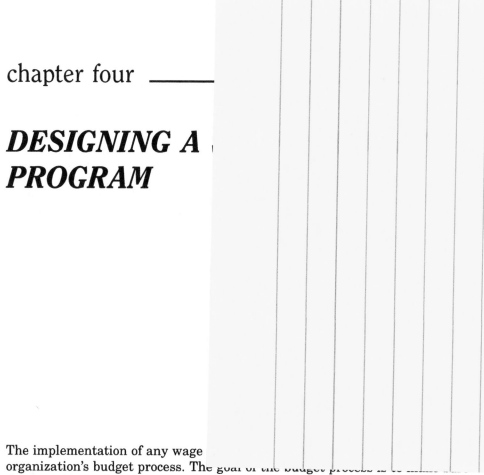
PROGRAM

The implementation of any wage
organization's budget process. The goal of the budget process is to insure that
the organization has the appropriate-sized staff at the most cost-effective salary
level to accomplish its goals and objectives. The budget process will encourage
an organizational departure from the belief that the larger the staff the greater
the power. This belief has hampered many United States organizations in their
efforts to compete in the global marketplace of the 1990s.

There are five major reasons for a wage and salary budget:

To make policy decisions in advance

One major reason for a staff budget is to get all salary decisions made
up front. For anyone who has ever been responsible for an organization's wage
and salary program, the most difficult situation that one must face is the need
to get approval for each recommended salary increase. This is the "mom and
pop" way of handling this effort. It is usually a sign that the organization is
still in the grip of one individual or a small, tight-knit group that continues
to maintain control over all the important aspects of the organization.

To encourage organizational planning

Another reason for a budget is to encourage planning for business reasons and to link organizational objectives to staff planning. Too frequently, strategy sessions that are held to discuss the direction of the organization for the next three to five years are held without the participation of the senior member of the personnel/human resources staff. The reason for this oversight is apparently the same as that given in the U.S. subsidiary of a major Japanese bank. When the senior (Japanese) member of management was asked why there was no senior ranking American member in attendance at the all-important sessions of the *konbukai* or senior management sessions, the American query was answered with what seemed to the Japanese management an obvious answer: "The meetings are in Japanese."

American management is often accused of myopia. The budget process will help to eliminate the waste and embarrassment (as well as the potential legal risk) when planning for staff changes. Through staff budgets, an entire overview is achieved so that one division of an organization is not planning to reduce staff while another attempts to increase its ranks. Not giving each other opportunities to do as much as possible with current staff before either dismissals begin or executive search firms are retained is a waste of time, energy, and financial resources. It leaves an organization open to the charge that "the right hand doesn't know what the left hand is doing."

To foster a "bottom-line" approach

A third reason for a budget is to show human resources expertise for a "hardball" approach and concern for the bottom line in a language that other members of management understand.

The fact remains that in order for personnel/human resources to obtain invitations to the important meetings, it is crucial for them to demonstrate they know how to speak "the language"; and the language in this case is numbers. The design and implementation of a staff budget, complete with both salaries and staffing requirements, is a big step in that direction.

To share human resources expertise throughout the organization

The fourth reason is to foster training and disseminate personnel/human resources expertise throughout the organization. The best training is that which is not perceived as such. The staff budget process is a fine opportunity to demonstrate, on a regular basis, that the wage and salary administration function is in fact a unit that has all its oars in the water and is working with line managers throughout the organization to help them to plan staff allocation effectively.

Additionally, by calling on all members of the organization to consider the budget from the human resources standpoint, the organization is saying that there is a need to pay attention to staff matters and to plan this part of the operation in the same organized, cost-effective manner as each manager is expected to do for other aspects of the operation.

There is no doubt that line managers will also appreciate having to go through the approval process just once, because the personnel/human resources unit will also be able to convince senior management that after this budget process is completed, only variations and changes will need one-on-one approval.

To provide training opportunities for line managers

The training/educational element of developing a staff budget should not be overlooked. The budget process will be an opportunity for managers to sharpen their skills on a human resource issue. By designing this process, the managers will have to take time out of their other activities to deliberate over their own staff, reviewing both its size and performance. Additionally, this exercise will provide managers with the opportunity to understand the difference between people and positions. Other personnel/human resources concepts are raised that can sharpen their skills as they learn to more effectively determine the human resources required to accomplish their own mission.

DEFINING BASIC TERMS

Before developing a wage and salary budget, a working knowledge of certain terms and their specific relationship to the budget and to the wage and salary program is needed.

An organization's expense ledger contains four items related to wage and salary, as follows:

- payroll expense
- payroll-related expenses
- benefit expenses
- pension and retirement expenses

It is important to understand the difference between *payroll expense* and *salary;* the staff budget is one way to reinforce this important concept.

Payroll expense is that amount actually paid out for services provided by employees. This figure includes all actual wages, including shift differential, any other premiums such as hardship duty, allowances for meals and transportation, and any other allocations directly related to wages received that may be granted (for example, uniform cleaning). All mandatory payments that are directly tied to wages paid will also be included and are known as *payroll related expenses.* Other *payroll-related expenses* are those voluntary benefits impacted by any pay increase—life insurance, pension and time off are three examples. Benefit expenses (including pension and retirement) are all the direct and indirect expenses the organization incurs when it decides to offer any benefit. These include mandatory benefits, such as workers compensation, social security (FICA), unemployment tax (FUTA), and disability (if in a state with mandatory short-term disability).

Salary expense, on the other hand, addresses anticipated payroll expenses that may or may not occur and affords opportunities for alterations in budget planning that will not affect the total budgeted figure at all but may alter the payroll expense significantly.

Following are examples of payroll expense and salary expense.

- Employee A is hired at an annual *salary* of $25,000. A special project is begun in the unit requiring the employee to work several weekends. Additionally, after the project's completion Employee A will be required to go overseas to train staff members in the project's new procedures.

After considering overtime, transportation, and overseas-pay differential, Employee A's *payroll expense* totalled $48,750.

- At Company B, all employees are given an annual salary increase that is effective on January 1. In this situation, it is easy to assume that the total *salary* and the total *payroll expense* appear the same, but they may not be equal. Consider what must occur for *salary* to equal *payroll expense:*

  —Everyone must stay the entire year;

  —no one will be docked for time not worked; and

  —there must be no new hires unless the person joining the organization is going to receive the identical rate of pay as the exiting employee and will start the instant the current staff member leaves.

Even in this hypothetical circumstance, it is virtually impossible for *budgeted salary* to be identical to *actual payroll expense.*

IMPLEMENTING A WAGE AND SALARY BUDGET

In strategy sessions with senior management, you will make decisions regarding the parameters for the next cycle's salary increases. You must provide senior management with results of the most recent research as a foundation for the pay increase recommendations presented. (See Chapter 9 for methods of assessing marketplace salary issues.)

After the strategy has been decided with senior management, set the process in motion. Begin with disseminating information first, through written budget forms and second, through training sessions. Exhibit 4-1 shows the progression of steps in the budget process.

Distributing Budget Worksheets and Instructions

Before the training meetings, you should distribute the budget forms you will be using to supervisors and managers so that they can become familiar with them prior to the meeting. Consider the sheets a puzzle, with the various parts to be completed in logical order. Seemingly unrelated bits of information are collected and, like a puzzle, the bits do fit together to form a complete budget picture. The more the worksheets are used, the greater the buy-in from the managers (or their subordinates) responsible for actually completing the task. When the budget worksheets are distributed to the participants in advance of the training sessions, the group dynamics at the meeting are positively affected. Advance distribution leads to greater familiarity with the forms, more interaction in the meeting, and more teamwork during the actual budget process. If the forms are sprung on the participants at the meeting, resistance to the process may ensue.

THE ANNUAL STAFF PLAN

The Wage and Salary Administration Unit can plan for staffing and salary needs by using the Annual Staff Plan—the basic form used in the budget process. Regardless of employee position, this form helps to determine current payroll expenses as well as to project salary costs.

This Annual Staff Plan includes three separate Schedules:

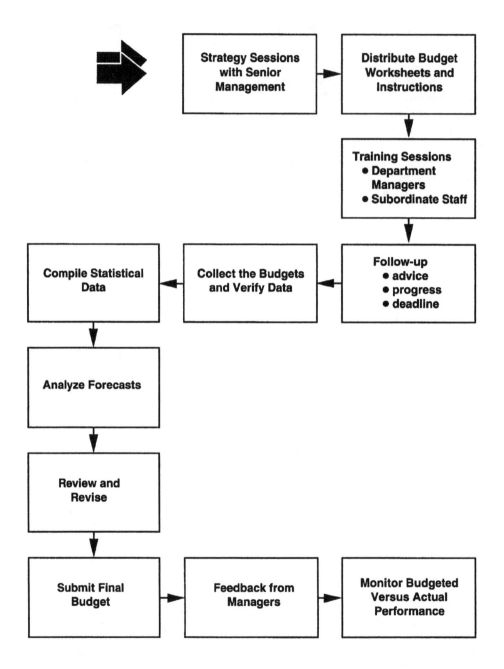

Exhibit 4-1
The Budget Process

- Departmental listing, by employee
- Departmental summary, by month
- Alternative departmental summary, by month

Depending on the form and the degree of detail desired, the following information is required:

- raw data regarding annual salaries
- ratings
- review dates
- planned retirements and separations
- departmental increases or decreases in staff size
- types of increases planned
- details regarding job codes, titles, and classes

Departmental Listing, by Employee (Schedule A)

Section 1, columns 1 through 7 on this form (Exhibit 4-2) requires a listing of the employee name, job code, salary classification, next review date, rating, compa-ratio, and current salary of all current full-time staff as of the established cutoff date. Expected salary levels are to be posted even for those positions that are not yet in place.

This same type of data is required in Section 2 in the lower portion of the form for all part-time employees. Calculations for these part-time employees must be based on hourly rates.

For both Sections 1 and 2, columns 8 and 9 request any increases that have occurred between the cutoff date and the end of the calendar year. These figures include raises in pay as well as the salaries of new staff members hired since the cutoff date.

An important figure, each employee's year-end salary is asked for in column 10. This figure (year-end salary) then becomes the beginning salary for the plan year, on which further increases are based.

Columns 10 through 22 in Section 1 are intended to report proposed salary increases, month by month, through the end of the plan year.

Column 23 totals the new salary level for each month in the plan year but still does not reflect the actual expense. (The actual expenses are reflected

STAFF PLANNING SCHEDULE A

Cut Off Date: _____
For Budget Year: _____   Dept No. _____   Dept. Name _____   Location _____   Division/Group _____

FULL TIME STAFF PLANNING---SECTION 1

(1) Employee Name	(2) Job Code	(3) Salary Class	(4) Next Review	(5) Rating	(6) Compa Ratio	(7) Current Salary	(8) Increases Current	>12/31 New	(9) >12/31 New	(10) Year end 12/31 Salary
(A) TOTALS For Full Time Staff:						$			$	$

Exhibit 4-2

Staff Planning Schedule A

PART TIME STAFF PLANNING---SECTION 2

Employee Name	Job Code	Salary Class	Next Review	Rating	Compa Ratio	Current Rate/Hour	Increases Current	>12/31 New	Year end 12/31 Rate/Hour
(B)			TOTALS Part Time Staff:			$	$	$	$

Instructions: 1. This schedule should include only the names and salary data of individuals already in your employment. All other additions or deletions should be listed on Schedule B.
2. Eliminate the names and salaries of employees who have left the department since the cut-off date.
3. Add names, salaries, and proposed salary increases for staff hired since cut-off date.
4. Part-time names and rates appear as a memo item only; this information will be used in completing Schedule B.

Prepared By: _____ Title: _____ Date: _____

Exhibit 4-2 (continued)
Staff Planning Schedule A

STAFF PLANNING SCHEDULE A

Cut Off Date: _____ Dept. No. _____ Location: _____ Div/Group _____
For Budget Year: _____ Dept. Name _____

FULL TIME STAFF PLANNING---SECTION 1

PROPOSED—SALARY—INCREASES

(11) JAN	(12) FEB	(13) MAR	(14) APR	(15) MAY	(16) JUN	(17) JUL	(18) AUG	(19) SEP	(20) OCT	(21) NOV	(22) DEC	(23) Total Salary (10 + 11>22)	(24) Total Incr (23 -10)	(25) % Rate (24 /10)

(A) TOTAL

PART TIME STAFF PLANNING---SECTION 2

PROPOSED—SALARY—INCREASES

JAN	FEB	MAR	APR	MAY	JUN	JUL	AUG	SEP	OCT	NOV	DEC	Total Salary (10 + 11>22)	Total Incr (23 - 10)	% Rate (24 / 10)

(B) TOTAL

Exhibit 4-2 (continued)
Staff Planning Schedule A

Reprinted here with permission of Panel Publishers from the 1993 edition of *Personnel Recordkeeper* by Matthew J. DeLuca, © 1993.

in Schedule C, which follows; a weighted factor is used to assess the different impact of a "January" increase and a "December" increase.)

Column 24 reflects the amount of the increase/decrease (column 23 minus column 10) as a dollar figure. Column 25 shows the percentage rate of increase/decrease (column 24 divided by column 10).

Totals for the full-time staff are located on the bottom of Section 1 on Line A. All figures contained in columns 7 through 24 are totalled vertically. The percentage increase is calculated in column 25 (total in column 24 is divided by the total in column 10).

In Chapter 5, the figures contained in Schedule A (Sections 1 and 2) will be used in the human resources information system (HRIS) to compare actual payroll expense to the budgeted salaries.

Section 2 of Schedule A is reserved for part-time staff. Use the same calculations as for full-time employees in Section 1, but on an hourly basis. The figures are totalled both horizontally, on a per employee basis, as well as vertically, for each category with the key totals reported in columns 23, 24, and 25.

Annual Staff Plan Summary (Schedule B)

This form (Exhibit 4-3) is an aggregate of the information gathered in Schedule A. This form, however, summarizes all activity by month, so that the actual payroll expense can be measured against the new annual rate.

Full-time employees

Using the information contained in Schedule A, columns 6 through 22, complete columns 1, 2, and 3 of Section 1 on Schedule B. Note that further details regarding the specific number of employees as well as the break-down on hires and separations are required.

Line A at the top of column 4 requires the total salary as of the cutoff date, a figure calculated on line A of column 7 on Schedule A. Below this figure, on line B vertically in columns 1 through 4, are the staff increases/decreases from the cutoff date through year end. Line C then becomes the total salary figure to begin the plan year.

Adding up all the monthly figures (columns 1 through 3) carried over and totalled into column A, the figure arrived at is written on line D. Line E then is the total for salary and for staff for the plan year.

FULL TIME STAFF---SECTION 1

TOTAL Full Time Staff as of Cut Off Date: (from Schedule A, Total Line 7A) $ ___ (A)

MONTH	(1) Total Salary Increases From Schedule A		(2) Staff Increases		(3) Staff Decreases		(4) Entire Plan Year (1 + 2 - 3)	
	Annual Salaries	# Emp	Annual Salaries	# Emp	Annual Salaries	# Emp	Annual Salaries	# Emp
>12/31	$						$	(B)
Total Full Time Staff & Salaries Start of Plan Year (A+B): (1)			(2)		(3)		$ (4)	(C)
JAN								
FEB								
MAR								
APR								
MAY								
JUN								
JUL								
AUG								
SEP								
OCT								
NOV								
DEC								
TOTAL MONTHS							$	(D)
TOTAL FULL TIME STAFF & SALARIES @ END OF PLAN YEAR (C+D)							$	(E)

Exhibit 4-3
Annual Staff Plan Summary, Schedule B

PART TIME STAFF---SECTION 2

	PART TIME (more than 20 hrs)			PART TIME (less than 20 hrs)			
	─(5)─ Total Hours	─(6)─ Avg Hrly Rate	─(7)─ Salary Expense (5 x 6)	─(8)─ Total Hours	─(9)─ Avg Hrly Rate	─(10)─ Salary Expense (8 x 9)	
TOTALS: as of cut off date							(A)
	XXXXX XXXXX	XXXX XXXX	XXXXXXXX XXXXXXXX	XXXXX XXXXX	XXXX XXXX	XXXXXXXX XXXXXXXX	
TOTALS: Start Plan Year							(B)
JAN							
FEB							
MAR							
APR							
MAY							
JUN							
JUL							
AUG							
SEP							
OCT							
NOV							
DEC							
TOTALS:		$		TOTALS:	$		(C)

Exhibit 4-3 (continued)
Annual Staff Plan Summary, Schedule B

STAFF SUMMARY---SECTION 3

| | Number of Employees on Staff (one decimal point only) | | | | |
	(11) Fac tor	(12) Staff Equivalent PT+20 (5/11)	(13) PT-20 (8/11)	(14) FT Staff Col.4	(15) Total Staff 12+13+14
TOTALS: as of cut off date	154					(A)
	XXXX XXXX	XXXXXXX XXXXXXX	XXXXXXXX XXXXXXXX	XXXXXXX XXXXXXX	XXXXXXXXX XXXXXXXXX
TOTALS: Start Plan Year	155					(B)
JAN	154				
FEB	140				
MAR	154				
APR	150				
MAY	155				
JUN	150				
JUL	154				
AUG	154				
SEP	150				
OCT	154				
NOV	150				
DEC	155				
			TOTAL STAFF:			(C)
TOTAL NET STAFF CHANGE (B - C) INCREASE(DECREASE)						(D)

Exhibit 4-3 (continued)
Annual Staff Plan Summary, Schedule B

SUMMARY DETAILS---SECTION 4

Section 4: Enter information for all staff changes since cutoff date (Section 1, Col 2 & 5)

Line No.	Job Title	Job Code	Plan Mo.	Annual Salary	Explanation

Exhibit 4-3 (continued)
Annual Staff Plan Summary, Schedule B

Reprinted here with permission of Panel Publishers from the 1993 edition of *Personnel Recordkeeper* by Matthew J. DeLuca, © 1993.

Part-time employees

In Section 2 on Schedule B, part-time employees are broken down into those working 20 hours or more, and those working fewer than 20 hours per week. This differentiation will permit coordination with the benefit program; part-timers' benefits could add a significant expense to the payroll and must be considered. This form assumes that the 20-hour work-week (when allowed) is the determining factor for benefits eligibility.

As in Section 1 for full-time staff, figures as of the cutoff date and totals for the beginning of the plan year are carried over from Schedule A, Section 2. Lines 7 and 10 are entered into columns 5 through 10 on line A and line B.

Monthly figures are entered for both part-time categories, with totals entered on the bottom of columns 7 and 10 on line C.

Section 3 of Schedule B totals the number of employees on staff each month. All part-time staff members are "translated" into full-time equivalents by multiplying the total hours worked by a "factor." These "equivalents" are then added monthly, vertically and horizontally, to calculate the total number of staff members at the end of the plan year and the net increase (decrease) in staff on lines C and D, respectively.

Details

One last section, Section 4 on Schedule B, provides an area to note the detailed information in support of the increases/decreases for the period between the cutoff date through the end of the year. These details specifically relate to the totals listed in Section 1, line B of Schedule B.

Any salary changes listed on either Schedule A or B must be consistent with the organization's policies regarding salary reviews, increases, and promotions. (During the year, monthly audits are performed to monitor recommended changes against these policies; refer to Chapter 5.)

Salary and Staff Recap, (Schedule C)

This format takes into consideration the time factor in budgeting increases. (See Exhibit 4-4.) It further discriminates between "promotional" and "merit" increases for those organizations whose policy requires tracking types of increases.

Starting with line A, the beginning plan year base salary and staff is listed in the top of columns 7 and 8. Columns 1 through 4 are then completed

(A)

YEAR END 12/31 BASE SALARY TOTAL: $ #

MONTH	(1) STAFF INCREASES SALARY	#EMP	(2) STAFF DECREASES SALARY	#EMP	(3) PROMOTION INCREASE	(4) MERIT INCR.	(5) TOTAL SALARY	(6) X FACTOR	(7) SALARY IMPACT	(8) TOTAL # EMP
JAN								1.000		
FEB								.9167		
MAR								.8333		
APR								.7500		
MAY								.6667		
JUN								.5833		
JUL								.5000		
AUG								.4167		
SEP								.3333		
OCT								.2500		
NOV								.1667		
DEC								.0833		

TOTAL SALARIES: $ XXXXXX   (B)

TOTAL # EMPLOYEES: (C)

Exhibit 4-4

Salary and Staff Recap, Schedule C

Reprinted here with permission of Panel Publishers from the 1993 edition of *Personnel Recordkeeper* by Matthew J. DeLuca, © 1993.

for each month of the plan year and each month is totalled for total salary in column 5. Using the appropriate X-factor for each month, the totals in column 5 are multiplied by the factors in column 6 and the product written in column 7 to determine the salary impact. The number of employees on staff each month is calculated for column 8.

Columns 7 and 8 are totalled vertically and the respective sums are written on lines B and C.

Other Forms

Depending upon the detail required and the method used in HRIS (computer or manual records), elements of both Schedules B and C could be combined with the resultant form being tailored to the particular needs of the organization.

CONDUCTING TRAINING SESSIONS

Introduce the process to managers within the organization by means of brief (two-hour) training sessions. The key to garnering support among the management levels is the presence of senior management, either with a senior management kickoff at invitation-only sessions or with a special announcement stating that the decision has already been made to go ahead with the budget process. Either in the training sessions or in the announcement, discuss salary ranges and market data.

These training sessions may in fact be in two stages if the size of the organization warrants:

- Stage 1: Unit or department managers
- Stage 2: Lower-level or subordinate personnel

In these group sessions of department heads or their designated subordinates (who may be the individuals completing the forms), go over the basics of the forms, how they are to be completed, how the forms are related, and when the budget is due to be submitted. In addition, discuss the approval process after budget submission. Last, provide a question-and-answer period so that all persons involved in the budget process have the information needed to complete the task.

Unless the budget process is tied into the organization's goals or mission, the process may be perceived as another "paper blizzard" with more forms to be filled out and filed away. A budget program in a vacuum, with no feedback or relationship to the particular organization, will not be as effective as a budget program tied to specific goals and objectives, with incentives tied to achievement of the goals. Meeting budget objectives should be a consideration when reviewing both departmental/unit performance and individual performance. If the entire performance appraisal program in place in an organization does not compare actual performance with budgeted goals, then despite your efforts the management is sending a contrary signal to the organization. The staff must have a clear understanding of the importance of the budget, as it effects the entire organization as well as them individually. (For a discussion of methods to encourage staff participation, refer to Chapters 6 and 7.)

FOLLOWING UP WITH ASSISTANCE AND ADVICE TO STAFF

Offers of assistance and advice are an essential part of the budget process. One of the problems with wage and salary professionals and other compensation professionals is that they are often perceived to be aloof, "ivory tower" types. Taking the initiative with offers of assistance will be well received by those who need help in completing the budget. When offered, the goodwill generated will enhance existing relationships over the long run and the budget process immediately. Keep lines of communication open to determine each department's progress and ability to meet the deadline for budget submission.

COMPLETING THE BUDGET

Regardless of the method of human resource information system (HRIS), computerized or manual, it is essential that the individuals actually preparing the budgets have access to accurate and up-to-date information regarding all the members of their staff. Additionally, as the budget may be done in pieces, with various portions assigned to different individuals, all employees involved in the budget process—from department heads to typists—should observe the confidentiality of the information being collected.

Follow these seven steps to complete the budget process:

Step 1. Collect and verify data

It is extremely important that if the organization commits to a staff budget process the requisite resources are committed to verifying the accuracy of the data collected. If errors are allowed to go undetected, they will surface later at the expense of credibility to the wage and salary administration function. Comparing the initial payroll expenses to actual payroll records year-to-date, headcounts for departments to number of pay statements monthly, other organizational plans for the department (e.g. automation of the function, relocation, or reallocation of resources) should be reflected accurately in the budget.

Step 2. Compile statistical data

Once the data has been verified, the data must be compiled so that analysis can begin. The data must be presented in such a way that is consistent with the method of HRIS currently in place.

For example, on a manual HRIS system preprinted forms with categories presented in comparable form will permit easy transfer of figures. Similarly, automated HRIS systems will plan for formatted budget forms that can provide easy-to-read data entry capabilities as well as categories/captions consistent with the existing program.

Step 3. Analyze forecasts

Analyze the compiled forecasts to determine whether the guidelines determined by senior management have been complied with and to identify those areas that require additional work and alteration.

Step 4. Review and revise

After reviewing the data, determine which budgets require additional work or revision. Then meet with those managers to work out a solution within the guidelines of the program established by senior management.

Step 5. Submit final budget

After the numbers have received final adjustments and revisions, report the final budget to senior management for its approval.

Step 6. Report to managers

The next step is to report back to unit managers the final results as approved by senior management. Unit managers should retain a copy of the finalized budget for audit and review purposes.

Step 7. Monitor budgeted vs. actual figures

Throughout the year, you are responsible for monitoring the budget process by reviewing every salary action request. This monitoring will ensure that each recommendation has the proper authorization. You must also report the impact of each action on the staff budget. (This entire monitoring process is covered in Chapter 5.)

OTHER BUDGET ISSUES

To fully appreciate the interrelationships between various budget factors and the policy decisions regarding increases and staff changes, you should be familiar with all the budget "puzzle" pieces.

Impact of Anniversary Date Increases on Salary Expenses

What happens when increases are granted on each person's anniversary date of employment? The real impact of the increase (a full year with the increase at the new rate of pay) will not be felt by the organization—nor impact the organization as an expense for the full year—until the following calendar year.

Example

When company policies dictate that salary (wage) increases are effective on each individual's annual "date of hire" anniversary, the following formula is used to calculate the anticipated salary:

X = Current rate of pay

M = Number of months from anniversary date to end of budget year

INC = Monthly amount of increase (Annual salary × Annual increase/12)

CALCULATE THE SALARY EXPENSE:

$$X + M(INC) = \text{Budgeted Salary Expense}$$

Employee A currently has annual salary of $30,000. Anniversary date is April and Employee A is given an 8% increase.

$$\$30,000 + \frac{9(\$30,000 \times .08)}{12} = \$30,000 + 9(200) = \$31,800$$

Impact of Staff Changes on Salary Expenses

Any changes in staff will have an impact on salary expenses that will be different in the current year than in subsequent years. This will always be true unless the situation occurs on January 1 and there are no lingering payments to be made for all other increases or decreases to staff. In all other situations that occur or have an impact beyond January 1, then the current year's impact will always differ from all subsequent years.

Example A: Staff decrease

Staff decreases, whether voluntary or involuntary, have a direct impact on actual pay expense but not necessarily on the salary budget. If the decrease is involuntary but temporary, the effect will be negligible on the salary budget because the staff level will stay the same and so will the rate of pay for the same job. The actual payroll expense will be different and will depend on the following:

- The length of the severance payment. The amount of the severance payment will result in additional payroll expense after the person has ceased working for the organization. It is possible and sometimes does occur that the severance payments will continue to be made even after the temporary layoff has ended and a new person is hired. In this instance the payroll expense will temporarily reflect two payments for the same position; the salary budget will not.

- The length of time between the date the incumbent leaves (and payments cease) and the start date of the newly hired person. New staff member is obtained either on a transfer or from outside the organization; for this specific position it will not matter where the person was obtained, unless of course a "sign-on bonus" is made.

If the staff decreases are involuntary and permanent, the salary budget will show a decrease in staff level and an accompanying reduction in salary levels at the date the change is to be effective. On the other hand as far as the payroll expense is concerned, payroll costs will continue to accrue for as long as the person continues to draw pay either because of the actual termination date or the severance pay that is agreed to.

Example B: Staff increase

The actual expense of the wages of any staff increase and the projected salary impact of that staff addition will be quite different and will be increasingly so as the year goes on before that addition becomes a member of the staff.

An employee with a base annual salary of $120,000 per year will only earn $10,000 the first year if he/she is only employed for the last month of the year. However, the impact of his/her salary will be the full $120,000 the first full year he/she is with the organization. This salary, of course, should also include an estimate of the related benefit expense.

SUMMARY

A well-designed wage and salary administration program is cyclical in nature: budgets lead to audit and review; audit and review are linked to incentives and performance appraisals; current performance leads to new budgets or revisions; establishing pay levels and strategic total pay plans allows the organization to attract, retain, and motivate according to its needs, financial resources, and market.

The key provisions in a budget enable the organization to evaluate itself in terms of progress made to achieve its stated goals and objectives. Because staff is a prime resource for the organization, establishing and measuring goals in relationship to salary and staff size are prudent objectives of the wage and salary administration program. If the organization is able to maintain the proper sized staff and offer an affordable yet competitive total pay package to each employee it attempts to attract, retain, and motivate, the organization may win in several ways: It will have the best staff to help it to accomplish its goals, and its pay package should be affordable due to the effort and concern demonstrated throughout the organization to the development of a sound budget planning program for its staff.

chapter five _____

AUDITING AND REVIEWING THE WAGE AND SALARY PROGRAM FOR OVERALL EFFECTIVENESS

The audit and review process of the wage and salary program is an essential part of the overall program. The purpose of an audit and review system is:

- to review the policies and practices within the organization relative to wage and salary issues;
- to interface with the financial planning areas of the organization through budgetary review; and
- to recognize issues that may be potential problems, either financial or legal.

The program should be designed to include various control and monitoring procedures to ensure that it accomplishes what has been intended. Controlling costs and guaranteeing the lowest exposure to decisions that are illegally discriminatory are two critical goals. Auditing, or monitoring, should be an integral part of the program and therefore included in the design phase.

Use of the personal computer is one of the most effective aids in supporting any monitoring efforts. The personal computer allows for the sorting and resorting of data in innumerable ways, limited only by the imagination and

105

skill of the user. This sifting and sorting will allow you to identify potential problems by bringing to the surface any items that require additional investigation.

PERFORMING THE WAGE AND SALARY AUDIT

There are two prime issues to consider during the performance of a wage and salary program audit:

- financial/budgetary aspects of wage and salary decisions
- external and internal equity factors of the program itself (including legal discrimination based on performance)

Determining if Budget Guidelines Are Being Met

Assuming there is a budget, the first consideration from an audit standpoint is to determine whether budget guidelines are being adhered to. A staff budget (as covered in Chapter 4) is a comprehensive way to establish an orderly approach to the wage and salary program.

Any auditing of actual payroll expenses, either comparing month-to-month or actual-to-budget will require you to obtain information from the payroll unit. Payroll should have a report, prepared either manually or through an automated HRIS, that will list all the employees by annual salary and by individual pay periods. A report of this nature will enable you to compare totals for payroll expenses and staff size for monitoring purposes.

As discussed in Chapter 10, the interdependencies between payroll and wage and salary administration are such that both functions must have a good working knowledge of each other. To achieve an effective program of audit and review, an open environment of shared objectives between payroll and wage and salary administration is needed. This includes awareness of the type, frequency, and basis of reports generated as well as an understanding of the practices and procedures of both units.

Comparing Budgeted and Actual Individual Salary Increases

This is the simplest form of review, whereby the budgeted increase for each individual (as shown in Schedule A in the Staff Budget, Chapter 4, Exhibit

4-2) is compared to the actual increase to determine whether there has been any alteration to the budgeted amount.

Changes from the initial recommendation should be allowed, because circumstances do change from the time the budget was submitted to the time the actual increase became due. The longer the period between the completion of the budget and the actual salary increase, the greater the possibility that intervening circumstances will create variances. Establish an ongoing monitoring system to review all variances from the budget, on a person-by-person basis, to determine whether the new recommendation is warranted, justified, and within the authority of the person making the change.

In order to establish an ongoing monitoring system, you must be able to verify all changes to individual salary bases. If you are on an automated HRIS, a Daily Change Log, listing all changes (increases, terminations, status changes) to employee salaries can be generated and provided to you. These data entries can be compared to the authorized documentation both for accuracy of information and to verify adherence to the organization's policies and practices. On a manual basis, you would need to compare the physical items, for example, salary cards (see Exhibit 10-2) or salary authorization forms (Exhibit 10-3).

Exhibit 5-1 provides sample questions for an individual audit review, and an aggregate audit review.

Comparing Budgeted and Actual Aggregate Expenses

By reviewing budgeted figures to actual expenses on an aggregate basis (as shown in Schedule B of the Staff Budget, Chapter 4, Exhibit 4-3) as well as in individual comparisons, you will be performing a thorough analysis of the entire program. Again, this exercise requires the support of the payroll unit in providing actual payroll expenses by unit categories.

Even if all individuals are receiving increases that are within guidelines for the budgeted year, it is still possible that the total increase for the unit may exceed guidelines. By tracking monthly actual and budgeted figures, the situation should be reviewed if and when a variance occurs to immediately determine its cause. Failure to do so will not only reinforce undesirable behavior on the part of the line managers but will also give notice to those who are sensitive to such matters, regardless of organizational level, that there is no effective auditing procedure in place. This, in turn, will send a clear but undesirable message to staff members throughout the organization that budgets are merely make-work exercises and disregard for policy and guidelines is condoned if you can "get away with it."

INDIVIDUAL AUDIT REVIEW

1. Is the increase processed on time?   yes   no

2. Does it have the authorized approval?   yes   no

3. Is the increase within guidelines?   yes   no

4. Is it consistent with the budget in terms
   of the amount?   yes   no

   of date of increase?   yes   no

5. Is the supporting documentation consistent
   with the salary action?   yes   no

If the answer of any of the above questions is "no", then investigate to determine the appropriateness of the salary action(s).

AGGREGATE AUDIT REVIEW

1. Is there a variance when comparing
   budget to actual figures for the unit?   yes   no

2. Will the current recommended variance
   have an impact on the budgeted figures
   for rest of the Plan Year?   yes   no

3. Will the impact be included in next
   year's budget?   yes   no

4. When including the next higher level,
   is there a consistent variance to the
   actual when compared to budget?   yes   no

A "yes" response to any of these questions would indicate that you should update budget figures as well as follow-up with appropriate departments to ensure their understanding of the financial impact of their staffing decisions.

Exhibit 5-1
Sample Questions for the Individual Audit Review
and the Aggregate Audit Review

Another important reason to consider an effective monitoring device for aggregate figures is for the savings that may occur because of staff changes that alter salary decisions. For example, if a member of the staff has announced a decision to terminate his/her employment, that specific budgeted salary increase will not be awarded. According to organizational policies, the amount budgeted could be:

- Allocated to the position (increasing the base salary) when it is filled;
- retained by the unit as part of the pool of funds to be used by others within the unit; or,
- lost to the unit and not reused or reallocated under any circumstances.

An ongoing, monthly auditing process would be the effective way to determine that the appropriate policy is being followed.

As the year progresses, the line manager typically anticipates a cushion in the budget that is there for the asking. He/she then begins to realize that rewards to staff (or salary increase decisions) may be more generous due to circumstances not anticipated when the year began. This may have occurred due to staff turnover, forced staff decreases, or the failure to fill a budgeted position at the time anticipated. You must determine if company policies have been applied consistently. If policies have been disregarded or if so many exceptions have been granted as to nullify the stated policy, it is incumbent upon you to discuss with management the need for different policies or guidelines. Any changes should then be circulated, in writing, to all relevant line managers.

Recognizing Legal Discrimination

Many aspects of most wage and salary administration programs are discriminatory; in fact, the law allows them to be so. The three goals of the wage and salary administration program is to attract, retain, and motivate employees. If the program is meeting those goals in an effective manner, then it is also terminating those who are not appropriate to the organization. The entire process is by its very nature discriminatory; it is discriminating in favor of those who are conforming to the needs of the organization and discriminating against those who aren't.

If, as discussed in Chapter 11, the discrimination is based on solid business reasons (as stipulated in Title VII of the Civil Rights Act of 1964 and the Civil Rights Act of 1991) such as a bona fide seniority system or a merit system, then the employer may discriminate in its wage and salary program.

Additionally, certain classes of employees may get increases and or bonuses at a higher rate than others—if the class is a legal class. Executives, revenue producers (for example, traders, account representatives, and sales people), or those with specific technical expertise in high demand, may end up receiving increases on a higher scale than others in the organization. The frequency of the increases may be another way to handle this situation.

Recognizing Illegal Discrimination

Illegal discrimination may appear in several guises.

First, the audit program should consider whether increases to any classes seem to be higher than to others. Here the audit should compare male Caucasian wage or salary increases with those given to women and people of color, on a percentage and dollar basis. Other comparisons should be older to younger workers, then within departments by these categories.

Second, consideration should be given to male/female comparisons. Here not only should the numbers be reviewed but titles, job descriptions, and performance appraisals should also be considered to identify any potential illegal discrimination before the situation explodes.

Third, exempt/nonexempt status should be reviewed. Hours should be recorded for both exempt and nonexempt employees to monitor practices and determine whether the organization or some persons in it are trying to bury overtime expenses.

Monitoring External Markets to Ensure Fair Pay Practices

A proactive audit function in the wage and salary administration unit will be concerned about problems before they occur. One way to accomplish that objective is to do more than address the legal and other issues mentioned above. One more subject that calls for ongoing attention is the matter of external equity.

External equity is a fairness determination that attempts to peg an organization's wages and salaries to other organizations with whom it feels it must compete for staff. On a regular basis, external markets should be observed to notice any shift in pay practice that signals an increased demand for talented staff to fill one or more positions at a higher rate. The sooner this shift is noticed, the earlier you will be able to alert management to the potential problem and to suggest alternative solutions—one of which may be to do nothing at all, and that may be an appropriate decision in certain circumstances. The point is, however, that the wage and salary unit ought to be aware of the external marketplace at all times to identify changing conditions as they occur.

Methods to audit for external equity include:

- using surveys
- frequently scanning the newspapers for advertised job openings
- monitoring exit interviews
- developing a network of contacts to share accurate market information

REVIEWING THE ORGANIZATION'S CURRENT WAGE AND SALARY PROGRAM

Develop an awareness of all the steps in the process of making a change in a person's status, salary, or both. This awareness begins with a complete knowledge of the procedures followed by both payroll and wage and salary administration functions. A review of the information gathered in the Wage and Salary Administration Procedures-Draft Document (see Appendix B) would be a logical beginning. If the program has not progressed to the point of having a written manual, information contained in the Wage and Salary Administration Program Review (Appendix A) would also provide you with a review outline of the current program.

Using the Human Resources Information System (HRIS) for Wage and Salary Administration Audits

At this time, reconsider the information requested in the budget forms (Chapter 4) and prioritize a list of those elements that you wish to track. There are many permutations of information that can be tracked, ranging from daily to annually. Exhibit 5-2 provides a sample Audit and Review Data Checklist.

After you have determined what data you will track and the frequency of audits, consider what resources are currently available to perform the audit and review. Although computers certainly make the job faster, a computer is not necessary to complete the task. In fact, if information "overload" results

	Monthly	Quarterly	Annually
CORPORATE			
DIVISION			
DEPARTMENTAL			
SHIFTS			
SALARY CLASS			
JOB CODE			
INDIVIDUAL			

Exhibit 5-2
Audit and Review Data Checklist

from too much data being submitted, an automated system may add to the problem.

On a manual HRIS, ledger sheets or cards can be set up in advance with periodic postings of actual payroll expenses and staff increases/decreases. Variances to the approved budget can be calculated. The policies of the organization will determine the range of variance permitted and what actions, if any, are to be taken when variances exceed expected boundaries. Exhibit 5-3 contains an example of a manual reconciliation of annual base pay rates.

The Expense Detail Report (Exhibit 5-4) is an example of an aggregate review of budget to actual salary expenses prepared on an automated HRIS.

By comparing both current month and year-to-date figures, you are able to examine those areas where budget variances exist. For example, in Exhibit 5-4, you may note the 6.19 percent variance over budget year-to-date for service staff members, and then may obtain the detail budget/actual records for all employees in that category to analyze the cause of the variance. The reason may be timing: staff members who were budgeted to be hired in subsequent months joined the staff earlier than expected; systems problems required unplanned additional temporary staff, which might provide cost savings in later years; or, a marked upswing in volume occurred (revenue is not included in these figures).

A comparison month-by-month of actual annual base pay rate:		
a)	**PRIOR MONTH'S ANNUAL BASE PAY RATE:** $	**BUDGET** $
b)	**ADJUSTMENTS/ CURRENT MONTH**	
	+NEW HIRES $	$
	+PROMOTIONS $	$
	-TERMINATIONS $	$
	-LAYOFFS $	$
	-RETIREMENTS $	$
	+/-CHANGES $	$
c)	**END OF MONTH ADJUSTED ANNUAL BASE PAY RATE** $	$
A comparison of month-by-month staff size:		**BUDGET**
a)	**PRIOR MONTH'S STAFF SIZE** #	#
b)	**ADJUSTMENTS/ CURRENT MONTH**	
	+NEW HIRES #	#
	+PROMOTIONS #	#
	-TERMINATIONS #	#
	-LAYOFFS #	#
	-RETIREMENTS #	#
	+/-CHANGES #	#
c)	**END OF MONTH ADJUSTED STAFF SIZE (number of pays)** #	#

a = Obtain figure from payroll department or from last month's reconciliation.
b = From Daily Change Log, Salary Action Forms, documents.
c = Reconciles to payroll; carryover to next month.

Exhibit 5-3
Annual Base Pay Rate/Staff Size Reconciliation

FORMAT NO. 198

EXPENSE SUMMARY BY ACCOUNT

-HUMAN RESOURCES-DIV

EXP/CC NO	DESCRIPTION	CURRENT MONTH BUDGET	CURRENT MONTH ACTUAL	YEAR TO DATE BUDGET	YEAR TO DATE ACTUAL	VARIANCE CURRENT MONTH ACTUAL VS BUDGET AMOUNT	VARIANCE CURRENT MONTH ACTUAL VS BUDGET PERCENT	VARIANCE YEAR TO DATE ACTUAL VS BUDGET AMOUNT	VARIANCE YEAR TO DATE ACTUAL VS BUDGET PERCENT
	SALARIES								
00004	MEDICAL SUPPORT		2,500		26,311	(2,500)		(26,311)	
00005	REGISTERED NURSES	206,553	202,568	2,685,188	2,685,372	3,985	1.93	(184)	(.01)
00006	MANAGEMENT	60,810	60,756	790,530	753,556	54	.09	36,974	4.68
00007	CLERICAL & SECRETARIAL	126,987	121,073	1,650,832	1,548,698	5,914	4.66	102,134	6.19
00008	SUPPORT SERVICES				18,841			(18,841)	
00011	OTHER PAID ABSENCES	137,665	260,513	1,789,646	2,456,728	(122,848)	(89.24)	(667,082)	(37.27)
00017	TEMP SECRETARIAL SVCS	5,714	6,647	74,280	86,671	(933)	(16.33)	(12,391)	(16.68)
00019	SHIFT DIFFERENTIAL	6,040	6,801	78,526	92,278	(761)	(12.60)	(13,752)	(17.51)
00021	OVERTIME	56,317	73,109	37,563	57,569	(16,792)	(29.82)	(20,006)	(53.26)
00038	ACCRUED SALARIES	18,002-		234,026-		(18,002)	(100.00)	(234,026)	(100.00)
00041	EST SALARY SAVINGS-BUDGET		527		29,050	(527)		(29,050)	
00045	TERM LEAVE PAY-VAC				1,000			(1,000)	
00046	TERM LEAVE PAY-SICK		527-		30,663	527		(30,663)	
00047	TLP OFFSET				59,713-			59,713	
00049	PERSONNEL TEMPS	4,693	14,117	55,475	145,548	(9,424)	(200.81)	(90,073)	(162.37)
00050	PERSONNEL TEMPS RECOVERY	167,788-	292,850-	1,981,000-	2,848,898-	125,062	74.54	867,898	43.81
	TOTAL SALARIES	418,989	455,234	4,947,014	5,023,674	(36,245)	(8.65)	(76,660)	(1.55)

Exhibit 5-4
Expense Detail Report

FRINGE BENEFITS

Code	Description								
00101	FICA	302,637	339,292	4,043,360	4,330,986	(36,655)	(12.11)	(287,626)	(7.11)
00102	COMPENSATED ABSENCES	50,620	121,897-	604,800	432,283	172,517	340.81	172,517	28.52
00106	HEALTH BENEFITS-B.C./B.S.	558,148	558,147	6,668,384	6,668,384	1			
00107	HEALTH BENEFITS-HMO'S	26,632	348,452	318,176	639,996	(321,820)	*******	(321,820)	(101.15)
00109	INSURANCE-UNEMPLOYMENT	14,529	94,883	173,600	350,982	(80,354)	(553.06)	(177,382)	(102.18)
00110	INSURANCE-LONG TERM DISAB	8,944	18,326	106,800	188,792	(9,382)	(104.90)	(81,992)	(76.77)
00111	INSURANCE-NYS DISABILITY	9,144	8,656	109,200	84,624	488	5.34	24,576	22.51
00112	INSURANCE-HOSPITALIZATION				359	359		(359)	
00113	INSURANCE-GROUP LIFE	29,232	65,292	349,200	381,638	(36,060)	(123.36)	(32,438)	(9.29)
00119	INSURANCE-DENTAL	65,316	102,498	780,360	817,542	(37,182)	(56.93)	(37,182)	(4.76)
00120	INSURANCE-PRESCRIPTION DR	40,496	58,559	483,840	435,213	(18,063)	(44.60)	48,627	10.05
00122	RETIREMENT-ANNUITY	74,310	110,840	887,760	983,481	(36,530)	(49.16)	(95,721)	(10.78)
00123	RETIREMENT-VOL PAYMENTS	474	333	5,600	3,994	141	29.75	1,606	28.68
00126	POSTRETIREMENT BENEFITS-C		1,433,000		1,433,000	(1,433,000)		(1,433,000)	
00127	POSTRETIREMENT BENEFITS-P		11,627,000		11,627,000	(11,627,000)		(11,627,000)	
00141	TUITION AID-EMPLOYEES	4,158	3,633	202,400	189,726	525	12.63	12,674	6.26
00143	TUITION AID-DEPENDENTS		11,200	45,000	56,621	(11,200)		(11,621)	(25.82)
00150	FLEX CREDITS PROVIDED		160,076		2,035,396	(160,076)		(2,035,396)	
00151	FLEX BENEFITS ELECTED	39,760-	175,527-	516,880-	2,312,689-	135,767	341.47	1,795,809	347.43
00155	COBRA-DENTAL				84-			84	
00156	COBRA-MEDICAL		5,580-		42,542-	5,580		42,542	
00158	RETIREES-MEDICAL		8,415-		111,855-	8,415		111,855	
00170	OPERATIONAL IMPROVEMENTS	2,494-		29,818-		(2,494)	(100.00)	(29,818)	(100.00)
00198	EMPLOYEE BENEFITS APPLIED	139,003	334,868	1,725,719	1,730,514	(195,865)	(140.91)	(4,795)	(.28)
00199	EMPLOYEE BENEFITS RECDVRU	1,141,912-	3,001,435-	14,226,182-	16,561,854-	1,859,523	162.84	2,335,672	16.42
	TOTAL FRINGE BENEFITS	139,477	11,962,201	1,731,319	13,361,507	(11,822,724)	********	(11,630,188)	(671.75)
	TOTAL SALARIES/BENEFITS	558,466	12,417,435	6,678,333	18,385,181	(11,858,969)	********	(11,706,848)	(175.30)

Exhibit 5-4 (continued)
Expense Detail Report

Once the individual expense detail reports are analyzed, you may be required to either refer to the payroll records or to speak directly to the department head to obtain the needed information/explanation.

You need not wait for monthly or quarterly expense reports to be prepared to review all salary changes. [In the overview of the wage and salary program (Chapter 1), a Staff Planning Schedule (Exhibit 4-3) was used to obtain information about the existing Wage and Salary Program.] The same information regarding reports generated in the unit and elsewhere in the organization may serve as a guide in establishing an audit and review format. For example, request for review a Daily Change Log, listing all additions, deletions, and changes to payroll records.

You will find a sample Audit and Review Worksheet in Appendix D. It may serve as a menu of choices from which to determine appropriate items to audit, given the particular needs of the organization and the flexibility of the HRIS currently in use.

SUMMARY

Each organization has unique systems and procedures in place to carry out its stated policies. If establishing a wage and salary budget is akin to assembling a puzzle, then an audit and review program for the wage and salary function examines how the pieces fit together and assures that the fit is correct.

The prime requirement for a well-established audit and review system is a well thought out, consistent wage and salary administration program. Once the program is in place, audit and review the program regularly to look for inconsistencies, errors, and sources of improvements. It will not be sufficient to merely locate potential problem areas. The real value added is in proposing solutions to prevent recurrence of the problems and in developing improvements in the wage and salary administration program itself.

USING THE PERFORMANCE APPRAISAL PROCESS TO DETERMINE WAGE AND SALARY CHANGES

The performance appraisal process, also called the performance appraisal system (PAS), is the term frequently used for an organization's formal efforts to evaluate individual performance. Developing a performance appraisal system—a most complicated task—frequently falls under the responsibility of the wage and salary administration function. Regardless of all the other purposes that may be expected of the performance appraisal process, the one that it is almost universally used for is determining wages and salaries. The most frequent use of performance appraisal is evaluating performance for merit pay increases, granted or withheld.

DEVELOPING A PERFORMANCE APPRAISAL SYSTEM

Although a customized system is usually designed for each organization, every performance appraisal system has certain characteristics, described in the following paragraphs.

A form or forms

All performance appraisal systems have forms. In fact, frequently the form is mistaken for the system. To be truly effective, the required form should be designed with the organization and its members in mind and should be considered just one element of the system.

An approach and underlying philosophy

An approach and philosophy are needed to address basic questions in the design phase of the program to ensure the system established is meaningful and consistent with the intent and purposes of those who have made the decision to go ahead. See Exhibit 6-1 for questions to consider when discussing the philosophy and approach.

Policies and procedures

Once attention has been given to the approach and the forms, you need to develop policies and procedures to support the performance appraisal system and ensure that all possible scenarios have been considered. Give attention to the tone set by the organization's performance management process. The forms should support the organization's performance management process, while the process should work in harmony with the rest of the performance appraisal system.

These policies and procedures should include adequate discussion of matters such as fairness issues. There will be demands placed on supervisors to evaluate the persons under their responsibility, but care should be given to respect the dignity of each individual and to be fair but consistent in each situation.

With the issue of fairness, the question of a review and grievance process should be included. An open-door policy is one to boast about, but if management is not able to deal with this issue, having one may be worse. A manager who is unable to deal with the employee with a complaint may cause irreparable harm and embarrassment. A major computer manufacturer recently found this out after an employee tried to use the open-door policy that had been established by the current management's predecessors. He went all the way to the chairman and CEO only to be given a form memo as a response—all this came to light when the employee disclosed the situation to the press.

Will the approach be one that considers all persons "excellent" or one that insists on following a "normal curve"?

Will the entire organization use one form? If not, how many different forms will there be? How will the employee groups be divided?

Will there be emphasis on process or results?

Will staff members be evaluated for activities or results? Will effective staff planning budget execution be considered?

Will promotions and transfers, including EEO and Affirmative Action commitments be recognized? Regardless or emphasis, what will be the criteria? Single or multiple criteria?

What will the performance time period be for the evaluation?

Will there be mandatory periodic meetings and review sessions, or one session at the end of the rating cycle?

What will be the purpose(s) of the performance appraisal system? Will it be only for salary review? For other organizational objectives?

Who will perform the evaluation? Will it be done by superiors, peers, self, customers, subordinates, or a combination?

Exhibit 6-1
Questions to Consider When Determining
Performance Appraisal Approach

Guidelines

If guidelines are well written, this is where managers earn their pay. Managers will understand that the policies and procedures are not intended to take their authority from them but to create an environment that provides them with the authority and responsibility to evaluate staff member performance. These guidelines also will provide the framework for managers to want to evaluate employee performance in a fair, equitable, and consistent manner.

Training

There should be consideration given for the comprehensive training of raters to be effective in their roles as evaluators in the performance appraisal process. Only an ongoing and effective training process will ensure the successful implementation of the program.

One other point to consider when discussing the training aspects of the performance appraisal program is that persons affected by the program should be trained also in what they should expect and what is expected of them. For the personnel/human resources staff to include a module on the importance of employee performance during the new employee's orientation will be time well spent.

USING PERFORMANCE APPRAISAL FOR VARIOUS PURPOSES

Measuring performance, to determine pay rates is usually the prime reason for the performance appraisal system. This use encompasses the measurement of past performance and the determination of whether continued employment (or layoff), pay increase (or decrease), transfer, or promotion ought to be considered. If the performance appraisal process were used for this purpose alone it would more easily be able to tie the system's approach to performance standards. By staying focused, the system would be more effective.

The performance appraisal process, however, is also used for the following purposes.

Providing a feedback mechanism

The performance appraisal is intended to provide a formal feedback opportunity so that at least once every appraisal period every employee covered under the program will have the opportunity to learn how well he/she did during the appraisal period.

Professional/management development

The performance appraisal system offers managers the opportunity to determine the future performance of individual employees by considering their potential, as well as current and past performance.

Human resources planning

The performance appraisal system can serve as the auditor of the skill level of current staff members with consideration given to current and anticipated organizational needs for staff planning purposes.

Encouraging legal compliance on issues of discrimination

The performance appraisal system undertakes a process that has federal and other governmental encouragement to provide a framework for legal discrimination based on performance standards as implemented through the performance appraisal program.

Enhancing communication with employees

The very existence of the performance appraisal system itself communicates signals about the organization to its employees. Each employee is thus offered a mechanism for enhancing the communication process by being a participant in the sessions.

Progressive discipline

This is an element that should be part of the performance management process. In this role, the performance appraisal system should work in coordination with the performance management program. Frequently the past performance appraisals complicate the issues regarding current performance of the employee because the forms were not given as much attention as they should have been or the forms were not supported by documentation when the performance of the employee began to change.

Basis for career path determination

If the performance appraisal form measures past performance, does it make sense for the form to also serve to determine the potential of the employee?

There may be an argument for the past as an indicator of future performance, but it is tenuous. To make matters worse, some organizations have a category on the performance appraisal form for indicating the anticipated next promotion for the employee and a time frame for the promotion. It would take a truly astute supervisor to be realistic about each of his/her employees. In a difficult job market, to be conservative or ignore this category entirely would be to make the organization the loser. If the current situation has changed with a recessionary climate so that promotions will be fewer and farther between, then the form should be altered to suit the times.

Determining effectiveness of selection procedures

The performance appraisal program is sometimes used to address the question of the effectiveness of the selection process. By considering the on-the-job performance level of current employees it is quite simple to consider whether there may be better ways to select "ideal" employees for a particular organization.

PLANNING A PERFORMANCE APPRAISAL SYSTEM

The performance appraisal system has four elements to support it: job analysis; the selection of the method to assess job behaviors or outcomes as well as choosing which behaviors or outcomes to include; communication; and establishment of a feedback mechanism to ensure that the process is effective.

Conducting a job analysis

In order to evaluate performance, the output or some other standard for each job needs to be identified and, ideally, the process determined as well. The simplest way to do this is by conducting a job analysis. There needs to be an analysis performed for each job that will be included in the performance appraisal program. The responsibility for the performance appraisal program is usually given to the wage and salary administration unit because responsibility for job analysis frequently rests in that unit. (For further discussion of job analysis see Chapter 2.)

PLANNING THE SYSTEM

- Job Analysis
- Selection of Performance Appraisal Method
- Communication of the Process
- Development and Implementation of Feedback Mechanism

DESIGNING THE FORM

- Performer-Oriented Approach
- Behavior Approach
- Results-Oriented Approach

RATING ERROR RECOGNITION

- Contrast Effects
- First Impressions
- Halo Effect
- "Similar to Me" Effect
- Central Tendency
- Positive/Negative Leniency

RATER TRAINING PROGRAM

- Rating Errors
- Form Completion
- Interview Skills
- Performance Evaluation Techniques
- Documentation
- Feedback and Follow-up
- Legal Issues
- Reasons for PAS

Exhibit 6-2
The Performance Appraisal Process

Selecting a suitable and valid performance appraisal method to evaluate job performance

In addition to performing job analysis to determine what performance is to be evaluated, you must also need to determine the method by which employee performance will be measured. Further discussion of the alternatives available as well as examples of performance appraisal forms using the various options in both a behavioral and an outcome format are found in Appendix E and Appendix G.

Communicating the process

A description of the process and its expectations (including the basis upon which performance will be evaluated) needs to be communicated to supervisors and incumbents before beginning the program.

This step is perhaps the most important because the feedback obtained is so valuable. The more that feedback has been obtained before and during the performance appraisal process, the more likely there will not be any surprises when the process is completed.

Developing and implementing a feedback mechanism

Unless the organization is hoping to play "gotcha," the goal of the program is to tell employees when they are doing something right as often as when they are doing something wrong. This feedback mechanism should include an audit and review of the performance appraisal program to consider its effectiveness in achieving its objectives.

Here is where many organizations drop the ball. The performance appraisal process is considered just that. There is no target to hit, and therefore the only situations that get addressed are those that cause problems. Often, an employee questioning his or her appraisal is the incident that instigates the review.

Including a proactive ongoing performance appraisal review element in the performance appraisal program not only helps to determine the effectiveness of the program on a regular basis but it also serves as a legal monitor. One last service that such an activity provides is a clear, ongoing signal to all of the members of the organization that the performance appraisal program is important and really works.

AVOIDING POTENTIAL PROBLEMS WITH
PERFORMANCE APPRAISALS

The evaluation of anyone's job performance is difficult, even in the best of circumstances. To establish an optimal program and then formalize the process becomes more of a challenge because of the complexities of human beings and the wide variety of expectations that everyone—executives, managers, supervisors, employees—brings to the workplace.

Psychologists agree that we all like to know how we are doing, and the closer the feedback is to the performance, the greater the impact the feedback will have. On the other hand, there is another aspect to consider: Any activity involving the evaluation of another's performance on the job is considered distasteful by most people (on or off the job), and therefore to be avoided whenever possible.

This is just one illustration of the difficulties that must be dealt with when designing a performance appraisal process. Any performance appraisal process is complex and requires a lot of support from many well-placed individuals throughout the organization to succeed. The following issues should be considered before determining whether to proceed with a performance appraisal system.

The recent (and current) legal environment, believe it or not, is part of the problem. In spite of the fears that should be aroused in every organization because of the Civil Rights Acts of 1964 and 1991, as well as recent court decisions regarding the need to only utilize valid and reliable tests (and performance appraisals have consistently been determined to be a form of test), the widespread use of vague and invalidated performance appraisal systems (without even considering the biases and rating errors of those responsible for implementation of the evaluations) may be largely attributed to the lack of careful scrutiny by the courts and civil right enforcement agencies at the federal, state, and local levels throughout the United States. In spite of the laws, it is easy to see the reasons why neither party—management nor employees is ever truly happy with the result.

If there already is a performance appraisal system in place, the items mentioned below should be considered carefully to see how to improve the performance appraisal process.

Inherent Conflicts

The process itself has several inherent conflicts.

The most basic conflict stems from the roles of the supervisor and subordinate. The supervisor is charged with the responsibility of completing a performance appraisal for each of his/her subordinates. He/she brings a judgmental perspective to the table to determine the employee's performance level. He/she is under pressure to avoid being labeled too generous when evaluating staff while holding the employee accountable for as much as he/she is able. The supervisor is constantly thinking about what to do with an employee's evaluation while knowing that he/she will have to confront the employee sooner or later.

On the other hand, there is the subordinate who is reluctant to admit any personal faults and would rather attribute any problems to circumstances within the system.

There is an inherent conflict in goals that comes with the difference in function of the supervisor and the subordinate. The supervisor is responsible for getting things done through others. The subordinate may have many different reasons for his/her behavior. The supervisor alone needs the subordinate to realize that their objectives regarding on-the-job performance must be consistent with the supervisor's view.

In addition to this relationship, there is one more layer to consider: peer pressure among fellow workers. Employees are really not only evaluated by their supervisors formally but they are also appraised on a frequent basis by their peers and colleagues. In fact, because of pressure from the group, this evaluation may be of more importance to the individual employee than the organizationally generated one.

Defensiveness is one other factor for the wage and salary professional to keep in mind when considering the conflict in goals that exists for supervisors and subordinates. The very concept of the process suggests that the party with less control over the parameters determining performance will be more inclined to look elsewhere to explain less-than-perfect performance.

Psychologists claim that, human nature being what it is, each mention of a specific situation that results in negative feedback to a person demands the identification of several instances that allow for positive feedback to restore the sense of worth and well-being to that person. Most supervisors are not aware that it takes more than twenty positive comments to offset one negative comment.

If the most effective behavioral change will come from feedback as close to the desired behavior (or its opposite) as possible, there is little value to be obtained from a performance appraisal system that requires perhaps no more than one meeting and one completed form per year.

Often there is a difference in the perception of the employee regarding his/her performance and that of the person evaluating his/her performance. The more the cultures differ for the two individuals involved, the more likely there will be serious perceptual differences between the person being evaluated and the person performing the evaluation. One example to consider is that of the recently arrived expatriate Japanese manager. Traditionally, the expatriate Japanese (who have a cultural difficulty sharing their negative and positive comments) will harbor a concern that if he/she shares his/her opinion of a person's positive aspects of performance by complimenting him/her, if that subordinate does something poor anywhere in the future it will seem contradictory with previously made comments so the best thing to do is to not say anything.

Avoiding Organizational Problems with Performance Appraisals

A basic difficulty with any performance appraisal system is that organizations frequently exempt highly visible staff members from being a part of the program. Regardless of level of performance for the individuals occupying those positions, the signal sent by management encourages a "we–they" attitude. The persons who are subject to the performance appraisal system are then perceived not only as accountable but also subordinate. If the logic is taken to its conclusion, those who are in the powerful positions are not judged by their performance on the same basis as everyone else.

In addition to the problems an organization may inflict on itself, there are other existing conditions that may inadvertently detract from any performance evaluation standards the organization is trying to establish.

Often in organizations performance evaluation actually leads to performance punishment. Consider, for example, the employee who is invariably given the most work to do—it is always the best employee. And if we consider why, it is always because the work is so important that no one considers giving it to someone with lesser skills.

A second detriment to effective employee performance may be due to the organization inadvertently giving rewards to employees for nonperformance. Consider the malingerer who, year after year, continues to get paid for all the nonscheduled time he/she takes when giving the excuse that he/she is "ill". Every year this person just takes the number of sick days he/she is allowed, but no more—and guess what? If the organization's policy is to pay for sick days not worked to a certain time then the organization is rewarding nonperformance.

A third behavior that is encouraged is one that comes from questions asking whether performance really matters anyway. This is true in those functions where nothing can be better than "zero defects": if there is no crisis, there is no problem. Auditing is one function where this is true: can there be a better audit of an area than one in which no exceptions are found? Other examples are readily found in many areas (especially operations related) where it is difficult to show that individual and team performance does matter because only when there is a problem do people stand up and take notice. Phone systems, heating, security, and safety all easily fit that profile.

One more example is payroll: payroll is most definitely a function that only receives attention when there is a problem. In fact, the only problem that gets noticed is a missing paycheck or an incorrect (most likely smaller) amount. No one though, including the manager of the payroll unit, would consider congratulating the payroll department for an error-free payday. The result? Sending the signal that performance really doesn't matter.

The fourth behavior that is frequently displayed in organizations that detracts from effective individual performance is the willingness of the organization to allow the existence of obstacles that affect individual performance. These obstacles may be the little things like drafty work areas or poor lighting or more serious circumstances such as broken furniture and equipment.

DESIGNING FORMS FOR THE PERFORMANCE APPRAISAL SYSTEM

The design of the form is such an important aspect of the process because it addresses the issue of determining performance requirements. Once that is done, you can select an appropriate appraisal method that will allow the organization to measure the level of performance on the established criteria.

You must also decide whether one form or more than one form is appropriate for the organization. Regardless of setting, there are usually at least two forms that are used for determining employee performance. The breakdown is typically between nonexempt and exempt staff. Industrial psychologists frequently argue that to be truly meaningful, each position should have its own performance appraisal form.

If the organization has the resources to do it, position-specific forms would be ideal. That would allow for the performance of each position to be evaluated strictly on specific questions that are relevant and appropriate to the job occupied by the incumbent.

In addition to the issues mentioned above, the forms should be easy to complete and simple to understand, both for the rater and the ratee. With the arrival and nearly universal acceptance of the personal computer in the workplace, the cost for altering the form will be hardly as great as when the only alternative was the commercial printer. Today even the smallest companies should consider the economies that frequently come with desktop publishing; the performance appraisal form can be designed and duplicated internally.

Designing the Form Using a Performer-Oriented Approach

Performance appraisal forms using a performer-oriented method compare employees to each other in certain categories (for example, "Who is the best member of the group?" "Who should be let go if we have to reduce our workforce?"). Before going this route, remember that all performer-oriented methods look at overall performance and are highly subjective. The following methods all take a performer-oriented approach:

Ranking (straight or alternative)

This is the process of listing all the employees in a unit and ranking their performance from strongest to weakest. Straight ranking is a simple comparison going alternately from the best to the worst, then second best and second worst, and so on. Alternative ranking compares each employee by ranking them to each individual in the group regardless of the level of performance.

Traits

Even though difficult to validate, traits are used probably because they are so familiar in a traditional environment. Loyalty, leadership, and attitude are frequent terms that organizations using this type of form are trying to determine.

Skills

This is an appraisal method that determines the skills an employee has from established standards. Speed, accuracy, and ability to operate equipment may all be considered and real data regarding the past period of performance obtained. Even here, though, there are skills that are difficult to measure (for example, customer service), and there is always the possibility that some important skills may be ignored by the evaluator and then will subsequently be ignored by the employee—perhaps to the detriment of the organization.

Using Behavioral Approaches for Performance Appraisal

Appropriate behaviors are easier to determine once the evaluator has been trained. These are skill- and performance-based approaches that directly tie behaviors to the job. More commonly used examples are the following:

Graphic rating scales

The graphic rating scale is the most popular form of performance appraisal. The scales are most useful for jobs where it is not required to emphasize direct output. They may vary in terms of performance dimension, format of scale, and forced choice/unbroken line determinations. Appendixes E and F provide examples of performance appraisal forms using the forced choice graphic rating scale format.

Critical incidents

In this approach the supervisor maintains a log for each employee to record instances of importance on the job that demonstrated superior performance or substandard performance. This approach is difficult to apply because there are no quantitative techniques tied to it. Additionally, when being watchful for those extraordinary situations, the rater may fail to notice the performance by an employee who, day in and day out, accomplishes all that he/she is expected to accomplish without occurrence of a critical incident.

Behaviorally anchored rating scales (BARS)

This is a labor-intensive approach that requires a scale of standards derived from job analysis, with emphasis on critical incidents, for each job in the organization. These standards are then weighted for their importance in the job's contribution in meeting the organization's objectives.

Mixed-standard scales

Like BARS, the mixed-standard scales approach is labor intensive and uses critical incidents. The difference is that it uses a three-level answer request (performs better than, exactly like, or worse than the statement).

Using Results-Oriented Approaches for Performance Appraisal

Management by objectives (MBO) was very popular for several years, and it continues to enjoy great popularity to evaluate managers. When used effectively, MBO will enhance consistency in meeting goals throughout the organization. Usually the person being evaluated meets with his/her supervisor at the beginning of the appraisal period to negotiate objectives for the coming period. Periodic meetings should occur subsequently to discuss the employee's progress by considering the attainment of midperiod targets. The employee will then be rewarded at the end of the appraisal period by the results attained in meeting the goals that had been agreed to.

Appendix G provides an example of an outcome-based performance appraisal form.

Selecting the "Right" Form

There is no "right" form for every organization. Each organization is unique and so are its staff composition (both raters and ratees), values, priorities, objectives, and traditions. When selecting the form, consider whether the form is:

- useful both in assessing employee performance and serving as a feedback mechanism;
- cost effective both in terms of design and ease of use;
- valid as a job-related tool and free from rater bias; and,
- credible both to raters and ratees alike.

RATING ERRORS IN THE SYSTEM

When designing a performance appraisal system, give careful consideration to the rating errors that may occur unless proper precautions are taken. Rating errors are errors in judgment that a rater makes when evaluating the performance of another. They may be defined as the difference between the judgment of the rater and an accurate assessment of performance. They are particularly difficult for the rater to accept because he/she is unaware of making them. Such a rating may lead to incorrectly retaining, promoting, transferring, or terminating an employee. There are several forms of rating errors.

Error caused by comparison with others

When this error occurs, the rater evaluates the employee in comparison to others rather than to standards for the job itself. We all have met the employee who not only accomplished all the tasks of his/her particular job, but who also managed to perform other tasks of a voluntary nature and always seemed to anticipate problems before they occurred. Frequently this is the person who volunteers for years to run the holiday party, picnic, or some other time-consuming, thankless task that makes everyone else green with envy—not that this person is doing it but that they seem to do it so effortlessly. What an act to follow! How can any other employee compare favorably with this performer, no matter what performance appraisal form is used?

Errors caused by first impressions

Sometimes an evaluator puts such emphasis on the employee's actions during his/her first days on the job that whatever the person does afterwards is always shaded (or glows) with those first remembered actions. Pity the person who arrives late on his/her first day, or on time but dressed inappropriately. Then there are the new employees who are "tested" in all sorts of ways. There is also the story of the executive who was not shown the executive restroom by his peers, but was only told about it weeks after he had started work. It seems his supervisors had pegged him as a weakling from his first actions and he was never able to correct that impression right until the time he was hounded into termination three years later.

Errors caused by the halo effect

The halo effect takes place when a rater overlooks major areas of the ratee's performance and magnifies one or a few aspects. One example that comes readily to mind is the person who is in early every day (and has never missed a day in years), but whose on-the-job performance is less than adequate and has been so for quite a long time. In another example is the person who has excellent skills, but you readily identify a problem when his/her supervisor adds, "when he/she is here, that is." Usually, to exacerbate the problem, the employee is transferred and the halo effect has taken its toll.

Errors caused by the "similar to me" effect

This is the "clone" theory in action. Here the rater thinks highly of the employee because, whatever the reality is, the perception by the rater is that the employee represents something of positive worth to the rater.

Errors of central tendency

If the rater has a difficult time envisioning an excellent or a terrible performer, chances are the rater is committing the error of central tendency. This error may be the most damaging to an organization, because if great employees cannot be determined and recognized as outstanding, they will tend to leave in frustration. If, at the other end, poor performers are allowed to stay, then the best employees will be discouraged for two reasons: The best employees will readily see that they aren't highly regarded and the worst performers aren't poorly regarded. The result will lead to the departure of the best employees and will continue a downward spiral until something is done to stop the flow and change the mindset of the supervisor—or to change supervisors.

Errors caused by positive or negative leniency

The opposite error to central tendency is the error of positive or negative leniency. This error occurs when the rater is perplexed by the thought of making a judgment (either positive or negative) regarding the employee and as a result selects the path and the rating of least resistance. There may be reasons, as in the U.S. military, to rate the employee on a high level: if you don't, your career is over. So as a result, everyone rates everyone they are responsible for on the highest level. On the other hand, if the organization insists that each department, regardless of size, must rate at least one employee in the lowest category, the rater (feeling the pressure) will place the mandated quota in the lowest category.

DESIGNING A RATER TRAINING PROGRAM

The way to reduce the tendency of raters to commit errors is to offer them ongoing training. Simulation exercises and videotapes in a group setting are an effective way to combat these errors and reduce the likelihood of their occurrence. The process must be ongoing; in fact, the performance appraisal process must be constantly monitored in an attempt to provide a broad and consistent standard of evaluation.

Training may either take place in groups, to increase raters' ability to implement the process, or one-on-one. These approaches should include a pre- and post-test element and should include the following key topics.

Identifying rating errors as part of the training process

Rating errors should be identified as part of the performance appraisal process. By recognizing them in a training setting, it is hoped that the participants will be more sensitive to their own biases in the workplace.

Completing forms as part of the training process

Leaving nothing to chance, program participants ought to be given ample opportunity to practice completing the forms that they will use. Raters sometimes lack the training or desire to evaluate others. This dislike of holding other people's fates in their hands can result in biased evaluations, which are damaging to the system, the organization, and the evaluated employees (not to mention the harm this unchecked behavior does to the supervisor). Familiarity with the forms, the various ratings possible, and the terminology will help to break the ice for novice raters.

Developing Interview Skills

The most obvious opportunity for feedback both for supervisor and subordinate comes during the performance appraisal interview. The fact that it takes place at all is not without problems for both parties.

The supervisor may try to avoid the interview, especially for the more difficult employee. The reason is simple: no one relishes the thought of having to confront any person with weaknesses in his/her performance. It becomes more difficult if there are other related reasons for the meeting, such as salary increase considerations.

The subordinate, too, is concerned about the meeting because he/she has a lot at stake. He/she knows that the supervisor has an obligation to be open and frank, but if the supervisor detects any "defects" in the subordinate at this meeting it could damage his/her career. So if performance improvement is the key, the employee won't seek open comments because there may be (and usually are) other reasons for the meeting and any frank discussion may negatively affect those other considerations.

Practicing performance evaluation techniques

An essential element of any performance appraisal training program—and one that is absent from many—is attention to the evaluation of on-the-job performance. Practice is a basic requirement of any training activity and it is particularly important in a complicated process such as this.

In an effort to mirror on-the-job performance evaluation as closely as possible, it is essential that each program participant receive several hands-on opportunities during the training program. If possible, practice rating sessions should include videotapes of on-the-job performance wherever possible. In this way, each of the trainees will start the process by evaluating the same actual performance, and then comparing their evaluations with the evaluations of the other members of the class.

Developing documentation skills

Documentation is the backbone of any performance appraisal system. The organization cannot assume that persons responsible for getting their work done by supervising, managing, and leading others in the performance of their duties understand what that responsibility entails. Again, through practice, program participants will realize the importance of well-written documentation to support their conclusions.

Building a system for feedback and follow-up

Do not assume that program participants understand the nature and importance of feedback and follow-up. One of the training modules should specifically address the issue of building a feedback and follow-up loop into evaluation of the process.

Understanding legal issues

From a legal standpoint it is important for each program supervisor to know his/her limits in employee evaluation. Supervisors must be taught how to reduce their risk, so that difficult performance evaluations will not come back to haunt you.

Understanding the benefits of the performance appraisal process

Given the confusion that frequently surrounds performance appraisals, it would be time well spent to devote at least one module to explaining why the organization has decided to introduce this particular performance appraisal program. Include in the module a brief discussion of the benefits both employer and employee will obtain from the performance appraisal program.

Using the performance appraisal form in training

The last variation that training may take is through the form itself. A well-conceived form should contain understandable directions and should be logical and effective to its user. Time spent on the design of the form is time well spent and may eliminate the need for some of the training topics mentioned previously. There should, however, always be training for the improvement of interviewing techniques. The performance appraisal process must be constantly monitored in an attempt to provide a broad and consistent standard for evaluating the performance of others.

AVOIDING LEGAL PROBLEMS IN THE PERFORMANCE APPRAISAL PROCESS

The first requirement of any performance appraisal system, if it is to avoid legal problems, is to determine the reliability of the appraisal instrument and the validity of the job criteria that have been identified as critical to satisfactory job performance. This is a difficult process that requires the organization to tie the appraisal and its criteria to the jobs occupied by persons whose performance is being appraised. If there is no commitment to this process there should be concern for the legal viability of the program.

The Civil Service Reform Act of 1978 provides great assistance in ensuring legal compliance in the performance appraisal process and contains details that will help organizations develop sound performance appraisal programs. The Act is only applicable to federal agencies but contains useful advice for any organization. It includes the following steps that federal agencies must perform when establishing a new performance appraisal system:

- Encourage employee participation in the development of performance standards.
- Set performance standards that lead to accurate job performance evaluations.
- Advise employees of these standards before the appraisal period commences.
- Provide written periodic appraisals of job performance at least once a year.
- Use appraisal results as a basis for developing, rewarding, assigning, promoting, demoting, retaining, or "removing" employees.

SUMMARY

There seems to be growing discontent with the performance appraisal process as it has been traditionally implemented. The growing diversity of the workforce, the increasingly litigious nature of U.S. society, the legal climate, and the current wide disparity of standards in the area of performance appraisal will continue to put pressure on the people responsible for performance appraisal in any organization.

Innovations—total quality management, high performance work teams, participative management—will have an impact on the performance appraisal process. Performance management is one attempt to address the matter of appraising employee performance in a comprehensive manner.

MAKING INCENTIVES PART OF THE WAGE AND SALARY PROGRAM

Since the end of World War II until recently, there have been only insignificant changes in the ways that wage and salary programs were implemented in most organizations. The five elements (base pay, short-term incentives, long-term incentives, benefits, and perquisites) were there, but the primary emphasis was on the base-pay component for all but the executive level staff. Jobs were evaluated on a functional basis and a "scientific approach" toward compensation was taken by most practitioners in the field. Job descriptions were written for the function or position rather than the employee, with the thinking that no one is indispensable in the workplace. (It seemed to go without saying that if a machine were cheaper, then that would be the preferable choice).

If an incumbent got "hit by a truck" there would be another employee quickly available to do the job and, with proper planning, not a minute of production time would be lost. There were "slots" and people got slotted into positions. There was a rigid hierarchy and people moved up according to set patterns. The clearly defined organizational structure gave the appearance of stability, impermeability, and wisdom.

Benefits were offered to complement base pay and were a small part of the total package. A ten-year vesting plan for pension benefits helped to keep the cost of benefits down. Without a close eye on the potential future costs of the commitments being made, the focus was the pay element.

Base pay frequently has been considered an entitlement that was expected to grow each year. A person is entitled to payment in exchange for his/her labor and that right is protected in the United States by the Fair Labor Standards Act of 1938 (FSLA). From a legal perspective, it is not a reward but something a person has earned and was promised by agreement in advance.

Base pay increases were tied to inflation, with workers customarily receiving regularly scheduled increases. Because of the formula for calculating benefit entitlements, any increase in base pay directly affected benefits. Organizations were not overly concerned, however, because it seemed that benefit costs were minimal. Bonus payouts were also usually tied to base pay, on a percentage basis, so that was all the more reason to fight for larger increases.

The manager of the wage and salary unit called the shots, understood the complex processes, and made the decisions.

In this environment, the wage and salary professional operated primarily in a maintenance mode. He/she maintained the salary structure with periodic adjustments, more frequent "adjustments" in periods of high inflation and fewer when the economic situation was less volatile.

The situation in the United States is changing. The economics of the workplace have evolved, and a dominant theme is now competitiveness. With increasing local and global competition, an organization must be responsive to survive. That organization must send an important message to its employees: "We are in this together, so tell us what is important to you to enable you to work as effectively as possible. You, in turn, must realize what is necessary for the organization to succeed. If we are to succeed, we need you to succeed also. We will either succeed together or we will all fail together."

Offering incentives to motivate employees to perform in a desired manner—to meet or exceed expectations—is an important part of this process. Cash payments, stock ownership, noncash awards, or combinations of the three are considered incentive payments.

Motivation is a complex behavior but one that must be dealt with if there is a serious commitment to functioning effectively.

Pay is a complicated and important piece of the puzzle used to attract, motivate, and retain employees. When not used effectively, it serves as a dissatisfier. With the emphasis on the diversity of today's workforce, pay becomes an even more complex issue because it means different things to different people. Current research confirms that in our culture people in the workplace are motivated by the promise of reward—as opposed to receipt of the reward itself. If, therefore, the wage and salary program is structured to make certain that employees are promised a reward for performance on an individual and team basis, then the employee should be motivated to perform effectively. If this message is conveyed clearly throughout the organization, then the entire organization will know this philosophy is not to be taken lightly and will respond appropriately.

Whatever incentive program is developed, it should be done with the uniqueness of the organization in mind.

IDENTIFYING THE KEY COMPONENTS OF A SUCCESSFUL INCENTIVE PROGRAM

The biggest challenge today is linking incentives to performance. Both large and small organizations have made a variety of efforts to do so, with mixed results. The problems have ranged from a lack of communication to a change in the business environment. Chapter 6 discusses dysfunctional signals that are often communicated to employees, for example, rewarding nonperformance, punishing the best performers, showing indifference to good performance, and providing obstacles.

The current emphasis is on making the most of limited resources. The need, therefore, is to get the "most bang for the buck."

Ten key components are needed for a successful incentive program:

- Tie plan to organization business strategies.
- Relate pay increases to organizational performance, both bottom-line and quality driven.
- Consider (and encourage employees to consider) part of pay to be variable, related to organizational performance.
- Involve employees as partners.
- Switch from the concepts of pay as reward, and of reward as entitlement.
- Transfer more risk to the employee.
- Separate variable pay from benefits, especially pensions.
- Eliminate the word *bonus;* use the term *incentives* instead.
- Award incentives on both individual and team bases.
- Use the compensation professional as an internal consultant.

In the programs discussed in this chapter, the key concepts are employee participation and the opportunity to win. Another essential element for success is organizational trust.

IMPLEMENTING SPECIFIC TYPES
OF INCENTIVE PROGRAMS

A variety of incentive programs are relevant today. Regardless of the program considered, each one assumes a certain underlying philosophy.

Offering Long-Term Incentives to Motivate Employees

Long-term incentives are those that have a payout longer than a year in duration. Terms between three and five years are the most common, and they are most frequently provided to those at the highest end of the pay spectrum. There are two reasons for this: first, the higher the position in the hierarchy, the longer the time span for the position; and, second, the hope is that these long-term payouts will provide incentives for the long-term growth of the organization, linking the length of time needed to earn the incentive with the time it takes to obtain the desired results.

It is hoped that this long-term vision will offset any reduction in motivation due to the date of payment relative to the targeted behavior being reinforced. Because of the long time frame, psychologists are skeptical of the impact of the reward on the person's behavior. In addition, because of the complexities of both the position and the marketplace, there may be some question as to what impact is attributable to the efforts of one person and what is attributable to the circumstances surrounding that person's tenure in the position.

Frequently, stock options are offered as long-term incentives to those whom the organization perceives as being particularly desirable to retain over the long run. Typically, senior executives are participants in this arrangement, with a payout longer than one year and with a deferred vesting schedule as well. The more the "layers" of payout dates that are created, the more difficult it will be for this person to leave the organization without leaving a piece of something behind.

Profit-sharing plans frequently also have a deferred vesting schedule that may be payable over three years. This too is an effective way to retain employees of any level, because any time the person decides to depart, there are pieces of profit sharing that will be sacrificed if the person has already stayed one or more years.

Offering Short-Term Incentives to Motivate Employees

Short-term incentives are those with a payout of a year or less. The time element is believed to be more motivating because the time between the performance and the payment are closer together, allowing the employee to see the link between the two. The following short-term incentive programs have varying time frames and may be used together.

Gainsharing. In a gainsharing plan, any financial gains in organizational performance are shared with all employees in a single plant or company location on a formula basis. Such a plan is effective in situations where quantitative measures may be applied to production and organization effectiveness. When standards that have been agreed to by management and employees are reached or surpassed, the payment is made. Awards are frequently granted on a quarterly or annual basis.

An example is a manufacturing company whose shipping department, due to a concerted effort to become more efficient and meet delivery deadlines, had set a target of decreasing overtime expenses by 25 percent in the first six months of the calendar year. An incentive to do so was offered by management, with the agreement that if the 25 percent reduction was met, then the equivalent dollar amount would be paid out as an incentive payment to the eighteen employees in the department.

To achieve the goal and to enable all members in the department to benefit from the gainsharing, the entire department had to agree to work as a team and develop efficient methods of operation in order to reduce the overtime. This was the goal of the organization: "To promote a team approach and award directly the efforts to improve the organization's overall performance."

Working towards the goal also created an awareness that "we are all in this together," which promoted a spillover of efficiency past the initial six-month period.

Profit sharing. In this arrangement, the employer promises employees a cash payment based on the organization's performance, usually as that performance is tied to earnings. Guidelines are established to trigger payment, but usually there is no strict formula that requires an automatic release of funds. All or a portion of the payment may be converted to unit shares and a deferred vesting schedule to encourage using the payment for retirement savings and staff retention.

Profit sharing was a popular benefit in the late 1960s and early 1970s among many major companies in several industries. It has fallen into disfavor mainly for two reasons. First, heightened economic uncertainty has forced employers to consider the wisdom of a payout to employees that may not be as substantial as in prior periods, if a payout is declared at all. Employers had inadvertently created another "entitlement" rather than a motivator that created a sense of team spirit.

Second, despite the hoopla and popularity of the plan among consultants (along with the encouragement of the program through its tax benefits), both organizational experience and research studies showed that the profit-sharing plan in most organizations—especially the largest—was not an effective motivator. Everyone received it regardless of level of performance, and the language of the discretionary formula governing the plan was so complex and dry that most employees felt they did not understand it. In fact one major banking institution, no longer in existence, had a tradition of declaring a 15 percent profit sharing year in and year out, regardless of results.

Variable pay. Variable pay is a one time payment that an employee receives in exchange for meeting a predetermined result that may be dependent strictly on the employee's individual performance, linked to the business unit's performance, linked to another level's performance, or linked to organization-wide performance or results.

Variable pay is that portion of an employee's pay that is "at risk." Historically, the total amount of an employee's pay was a given. Assuming continued employment, the employee would continue to receive the pay that had been promised on a regular basis. Each payday, that concept continued to be reinforced when the payment was made.

In this traditional pay-plan arrangement there are wage or salary increase considerations on a regularly scheduled basis—most commonly, the annual review. The annual review usually results in a merit increase, a discretionary percentage that is used to award wage or salary increases as a reward for the past year's performance.

Awarding annual merit increases rather than one-time payments presents a twofold problem. First, the increase sends a confusing signal due to the fact that in this country cost-of-living (COL) increases are all too often considered part of the merit increase. So, if the actual merit portion is considered after the COL (keeping up with inflation means only staying even), the reward for merit is minuscule. If paid on a weekly basis, that annual increase divided by fifty-two weeks (after taxes) really reduces the size of the payout. Particularly at the lower end of the pay scale, these increases are "reduced" to such an extent that a rise in pay is barely noticed. At the highest pay levels, it may appear to be negative if the effective date of the increase coincides with the first payment of the new calendar year; employees in this group will have hit their FICA maximum before the end of the year and, with the current level of employee's portion of social security tax over 7 percent, will have enjoyed a period of paychecks larger than usual without the FICA deduction. Come the annual increase in the beginning of the year and the reinstitution of the FICA deduction, the pay increase must exceed 7 percent for any increase to be recognized as having taken place at all.

Even if the one-time payment award is 1 percent of base pay, because it is a one-time hit, the payment is larger than a merit increase spread over fifty-two or twenty-six payments in the course of a year.

The one-time payment is nonrecurring. If the plan continues and the participants hit the targets, the payment is triggered again. Each of these payments has no relationship to the other. The formula for the award may be triggered by one series of events one year but not another. Because this payment is nonrecurring, there is no escalation, either in terms of direct or indirect payments. That is, any payment made is linked to the reward alone, and therefore no tie is made to pension formulas or insurance policies.

AWARDING DISCRETIONARY INCENTIVES BASED ON "SUGGESTION SYSTEMS"

Incentives may be discretionary, that is, given at the will of the person authorized to make the payments. Such incentives frequently lose whatever motivating effect they have, because the award is given without identifying a clear connection between the recipient's behavior or performance and the award. There is little reason to call the payment an incentive, because the reason for the award is not clearly understood by the recipient.

Suggestion Systems enable employers to give discretionary awards for specific ideas and suggestions that contribute to the growth of the organization. Around for years and remembered for the ubiquitous boxes, suggestion systems have become more popular since discussed in books on Japanese management practices where case studies have shown the annual generation of thousands of ideas but minimal rewards. In at least one instance, a piece of cake was distributed during working time to all the program's participants. An organization of professionals in the United States working in this area recommends that the first thing to do is destroy the box, and second, to take all suggestions seriously.

The key to determining whether such a program is desirable for any particular organization is the level of trust present. There must be a high enough level of trust that the staff will be willing to participate and share their ideas. Without this trust the organization's employees will consider the program another opportunity by the management to either exploit the employees or to demonstrate dysfunctional behavior for one reason or another.

The initial requirements for a suggestion program are:

• management commitment

- review and award procedures
- form to submit suggestions
- internal resources to maintain program

In order for a suggestion system to work, the organization must be committed to:

- generating new ideas from employees
- building an organizational team
- creating a partnership environment
- steamlining the organization
- recognizing employee participation

If the commitment to execute such a program is there, the suggestion system is a valuable tool, particularly because success of the program doesn't depend as much on the amount of the reward as the climate in which the program is introduced. If finances are particularly tight, a suggestion system can be helpful for quality improvement because it conveys to the staff their importance in identifying opportunities for improvement and that they will be recognized for their efforts.

There are organizations that have elaborate procedures, elaborate ceremonies, and six-figure awards for individuals and teams that have come up with winning ideas. Cash payouts are not the only form that the reward may take. Letters from the CEO, tickets to dinner, a play, or a sporting event, a trophy, or a desk item (particularly worthwhile because the people who win them will have them prominently displayed) have all been successfully used as awards. Employees obtain intrinsic satisfaction from the recognition and the rewards.

Suggestion systems are not a panacea, however. Organizations ought to consider their introduction carefully. There must be an internal commitment to follow through with the program once introduced. That commitment includes a review procedure that answers and reviews all suggestions on a timely basis.

As with all other wage and salary administration issues, any new program will not change the organization overnight. Rather, each of the plans introduced will help to create the climate management is trying to develop. Wage and salary programs are a highly visible way for management to get attention.

CHOOSING DIFFERENT TYPES
OF INCENTIVE PAYMENTS

There are three basic forms of incentive payments: cash, stock/options, and prizes.

Awarding Cash Payments as an Incentive

Cash payouts may be considered incentives if the cash paid is linked by the recipient to the behavior or results the organization wants to reinforce. Here there are real opportunities to tie behavior or results to the award. Company-retained "shoppers" may make a payout to employees who give them superlative service—right after the transaction. Retail store managers have been known to give their superior buyers and other staff members cash payments on a departmental walk-around. Other executives and managers give out cash awards at biweekly or monthly meetings in front of the unit's staff.

Sign-on bonuses. The sign-on bonus is an instrument that is frequently used to encourage the applicant being offered a position with the organization to actually accept the offer. It is currently used frequently for certain positions in banks and other financial services institutions and for nursing and other technical positions in the health care industry.

If there are difficulties offering higher pay as an incentive because of organizational issues, the sign-on bonus may be an innovative approach to close the deal. The advantage is that it is a one-time cash payment, although step payments may be considered to protect the organization's investment in the new employee. The purpose of the payment is to entice the candidate to accept the offer. For maximum impact and to control cost, the more there is an understanding of what is on the candidate's mind, the greater the amount arrived at will be appropriate and effective in the particular situation. Examples include: relocation expenses (or a portion thereof in those instances where the organization does not want to make it a matter of policy); an amount to cover security deposit for newly rented living quarters; or a "bump" of $5,000 to make a lateral move more enticing.

Some oppose such an enticement because they perceive it as a bribe. They may take a high-handed approach to the effect that "anyone who doesn't see the advantages of working here is making a mistake, so we shouldn't encourage him/her with any cash payment up front." Conversely, the sign-on bonus may been seen as a method to arrive closer to a candidate's "ballpark" salary figure without causing long-term ripple effects to base pay and/or benefits.

One other way available to the employer to entice a prospective employee to join the organization is through a stock grant. This could be effective and extremely attractive to the start-up organization and will be effective in communicating the "partnership" vision that the organization may wish to offer. One advantage to the employer offering stock (or options) in this situation is that it may be offered on a deferred vesting basis so that continued employment will be required to obtain the full value of the reward. Performance should not be an issue in a sign-on award. If performance is an issue, the award should be treated as a short-term or long-term incentive.

Awarding Stock/Options as an Incentive

A stock or option award may be given on a formula or discretionary basis. Unless there is some link to performance, such an award should be considered a "bonus" or a benefit rather than an incentive. For an incentive to have impact, the recipient must see a link with performance: the stronger the link, the greater the impact. A drawback of awarding stock is the negative impact that occurs when the organization's stock price falls.

Awarding Prizes as an Incentive

Prizes are an alternative to cash and stocks/options and provide another perspective on the incentive arrangement. Depending on the approach, the prize may be shared by a nonemployee and may range from a dinner for two to a trip. This is a great opportunity to try to elicit from the employee population what is particularly attractive to the group that is targeted for incentives. The other great aspect of prizes is that they can be quite economical; the organization award might even be its own products or services.

The organization must be careful to select prizes that are particularly appropriate to its circumstances, values, and financial condition. Start small and build up in prizes and ceremonies; each time awards are given expectations are raised. If the organization decides to cut back, a message will be conveyed to the employees—intended or not.

A WORD ABOUT INTRINSIC REWARDS

The incentives discussed to this point have been extrinsic—that is those received from outside oneself, from the organization and the environment surrounding the work.

There is another opportunity for the organization, and that is the opportunity for employees to perform because of incentives that are intrinsic in nature. External rewards might be highly visible and very costly, but if they have little or no value to their recipient, their positive, motivating effect will be weak.

Intrinsic rewards include recognition, participation in the decision making process, increased responsibility, perceived opportunities for personal growth, interesting work, and diversity of activities.

The concept of incentives is complex because of the complicated nature of people and the diverse nature of our population. When considering external incentives, the organization will be wise to consider the makeup of the employees they are trying to motivate and reward. The intrinsic and the extrinsic aspects of the incentives being proposed should be considered as a whole. If adequate time is given to both facets of this matter the incentives finally decided upon will be more successful and probably less costly.

NEGATIVE INCENTIVES

[In Chapter 6, four common forms of organizational behaviors tied to performance that are negative in nature were discussed.] Below is a brief discussion of two negative incentives that are tied to cash payments.

The key to using any form of incentive is to ensure that there is sufficient consideration given not only to the desired result of an action, decision, or program but also to any underlying effects that may result.

Using a Two-Tier Pay Program

An economic alternative to consider if resources are limited and the current workforce is being paid a premium because of historical circumstances is the two-tier pay system.

This program attempts to hire new people at a level below those already on board in an effort to build a more effective wage and salary administration program. The premise is that those already on the job will have no problem seeing persons hired after them paid at a lower level, because the senior staff members will be told that they will be working alongside persons earning less than them for the same jobs. Whether they will be unfazed by this revelation is open to question. It is difficult to imagine that anyone would not be concerned about his/her job, particularly in this economic climate, when informed that the organization had found others to work in the same capacity for substantially less money.

Experience bears out that there have been two major problems with two-tier programs. First, the senior employees are concerned about their jobs, especially when management shows the people in personnel/human resources that they have been able to find candidates willing to work for less money. Second, the people who accept the jobs quickly become irritated that they are being paid less than their fellow employees for essentially the same work.

How Severance Pay Can Be Used as an Incentive

Severance pay may be defined as that payment given to a departing employee to help his/her uncertain personal financial situation due to an unexpected job loss.

If not mandated by statute or required by formal company policy—in a union or non-union environment—the choice is the decision of the employer. If anything, severance pay will be perceived by the employees—both those who are members of the current staff as well as those recently departed—as an incentive to take the time and effort to pursue other employment opportunities and not spend the time to consider legal action. In fact, if the employee is asked to sign a release in connection with leaving employment, the incentive for the employee to do so would be the underlying assumption of obtaining the severance payout. No employer would like the publicity of being taken to court by a terminated employee who is telling the world that he was coerced into signing a release because the employer threatened to withhold any severance payment until he did.

For it to be considered a true incentive, however, it should be given on an individual basis. If severance pay is provided to some employees and not others who are leaving the organization under similar circumstances, the employer may be thinking it is preserving its right to give severances to only those to whom it wishes. Nonetheless, the organization is at legal risk because of the perception of discrimination on the part of the employees regarding the organization's basis for the granting or withholding of the severance payment. For this reason, severance pay, if granted, is usually considered a benefit.

HOW TO BUILD AN INCENTIVE PLAN

Too often incentive plans arise from an idea or a need that is seized upon before in-depth consideration can be given. The result is a plan that does not meet expectations. This lack of detailed planning raises the question whether an incentive plan will ever work, and those who remember past failures will adopt an "oh no, not another incentive plan" attitude that will infect the minds and attitudes of peers and colleagues and help to scuttle the next plan.

Another reason to be careful when considering an incentive program is that it may cause more problems than it solves. By rewarding certain desirable behaviors to the exclusion of others, the organization may inadvertently discourage these other equally desirable behaviors. Incentives—whether team or individual—to a certain extent will divide the workforce between those who get the incentives and those who do not. Incentives require time and attention if they are going to be effective. At the same time, they could be damaging to the organization because their introduction may excite some employees while annoying others. This is not to say that incentives should not be used; rather, caution should be taken. Carefully choose your incentive program and be mindful of its potential consequences. Exhibit 7-1 shows the steps required to develop any incentive program.

Ten Steps to Implementing an Incentive Program

1. **Determine the targeted result/behavior.** Since the incentive must tie into the desired result, in meeting with senior management identify those areas within the organization that require improvement. The type of results may indicate the type of incentive to offer. For example, if employee turnover is the prime problem facing the organization, then instituting "service awards" for 1-year, 5-year, and 10-year terms of employment might be considered. If additional sales volume is the target, tying in the number of new customers brought in over a certain "sales promotion" period to "prizes" would directly tie performance and rewards. The first priorities are to determine exactly what the goals of the incentives are and when the goals are to be achieved.

2. **Look for opportunities for incentive programs.** The better known the organization—its leadership, employees, values, culture, traditions, and business—the more recognizable will be opportunities to consider as foundations for an incentive program. By wandering around and perhaps conducting a survey, running a focus group, or by sitting in on the staff meetings of one or more units, situations will arise that may be considered for incentive programs. Also initiate a legal discussion with counsel representing the organization (internally or externally) regarding the possibility of an incentive plan.

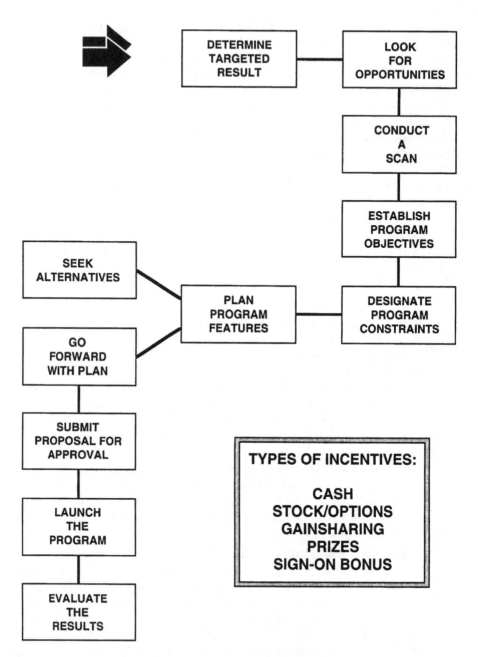

Exhibit 7-1
Steps in Developing an Incentive Program

3. **Conduct a scan of organizational needs.** Look at the organization from inside and outside to gain additional insight into its markets and those of its competitors. If the desired improvement is in the customer service area, see what turns customers on. Consider incentive arrangements in other companies in the same industry or in other organizations in the same geographical area; see what has worked and what hasn't. For methods to gain this type of information through surveys, refer to Chapter 9.

4. **Establish program objectives.** When the decision has been made to propose an incentive program, the next step is to establish program objectives. These objectives should be pegged to some quantitative improvement wherever possible, and the objectives should also be reachable. If the incentive program is not perceived to be attainable, it is doomed to failure even before it is introduced.

5. **Consider design constraints.** Perform an analysis of the supportive and restraining elements that will confront the introduction of such a program. Include finances, current market conditions, staff, management, plan elements, and any other circumstances that should be considered before the final decision to go ahead is made. It will be better to identify constraints before any plan introduction to see if they could be dealt with or worked around if necessary. The better the incentive plan is able to meet the organization's particular needs, the greater the likelihood of success.

6. **Determine plan features.** After an in-depth consideration of design constraints, define the features of the plan. Keep it simple and brief, but keep in mind the constraints mentioned in step 5.

   When designing an incentive program for lower-echelon employees, consider the following factors:

   • They have less control over larger issues/projects.

   • They have shorter-term task orientation, and therefore less need for long-term incentives.

   • They have less desire and understanding for stock options and "future value" from capital gains.

When designing an incentive program for higher-echelon employees, consider these factors:

   • They have more responsibility and control over issues/projects.

   • They have longer-term task orientation, and therefore greater need for long-term incentives.

- They have greater control over and impact on organization's objectives.

- They have greater interest in stock options.

7. **Determine whether to go ahead.** With all the necessary information in hand, it is time to determine whether to proceed. Going back to the initial step, perform a Gap Analysis (see Chapter 12). This analysis compares the current state of affairs at the organization to the outcome desired after the incentive plan is instituted. Determine what results are measurable and what role, if any, the incentive program will play in filling the "gap."

   The program may be designed for a single unit, for the entire organization, or for something in between. Unless there is a clear set of expectations at the outset, it will be impossible to establish a track record and to determine whether the program was a success.

8. **Make the proposal to management.** With all the details of the proposed incentive program in writing, you are now in a position to present the program to senior management for approval. In order for the proposal to be considered seriously, the meeting should be formal, with the organization's key players in attendance. In order to have an informed discussion, distribute an outline of the proposal in advance of the meeting; elicit comments, suggestions, and opinions.

   The proposal itself should clearly define

   - the objectives of the incentive plan (the "gap")
   - how the incentives will bring about the desired behavior
   - direct and indirect costs
   - constraining and supporting forces within the organization
   - the time frame for the program
   - any additional information regarding similar programs within the industry/competition
   - methods and parameters for measuring effectiveness of the program

9. **Discuss the program with managers and staff to gain their support.** Once the proposal has been approved, then the next selling phase begins. Meet with managers and staff to enlist their support for the plan. The perception should be that this is their plan and it needs their support if it is to be effective. Listen to their comments and suggestions. It may not be too late to make adjustments. Once the program is running, continue to use the communication channels

that were opened when this program was under consideration. (The initiation of an incentive program constitutes a change in the organization; refer to Chapter 12 for a discussion of managing change.)

10. **Evaluate.** Initiate the evaluation process, the most important part of the program. Refer to the original proposal submitted to management for those factors which will determine the effectiveness of the program. Submit a written evaluation specifying which elements of the program worked and which elements didn't work. Use this critique for future reference when considering other programs. Solicit the opinions of colleagues, peers, plan participants and recipients, coworkers, and any others who have a professional relationship with the eligible work group.

HOW TO EFFECTIVELY COMMUNICATE THE PROGRAM

Regardless of the program chosen or the nature of the organization, it is crucial to the success of the program that communication be an unceasing effort. Even the greatest of programs, if communicated poorly throughout the organization, will suffer.

The key is to take advantage of every opportunity to mention the program, whenever possible. In the United States today it is estimated that each person is barraged with at least three thousand messages daily, from the time he/she awakens until he/she returns to sleep. To penetrate that onslaught is difficult because of the number, quality, and attractiveness of the messages coming from so many different directions. For you to gain the attention of the targeted employees it is not enough to have an attractive message; it is also necessary to convey it often enough to ensure that it is received and "recorded" for impact.

In communicating an incentive program there is never the danger of being repetitive. In fact, the more frequent the communication; the more likely the message will be heard.

The variety of podiums from which the message is sent should range from the President/CEO all the way down to the line supervisor motivating his/her work unit. Make sure that it is given in orientation to the newest employees, at the twentieth anniversary awards ceremony, and at every other opportunity in between.

Frequently organizations change priorities and programs without sufficient communication. If nothing else, the constant, repetitive retelling of the incentive program will reassure the employee population that the rules have not changed and the program continues to be important to the organization.

The start of the program is a perfect opportunity to make announcements in in-house publications, at staff meetings, on bulletin boards, and even in payroll stuffers. Each audience is unique as are the circumstances surrounding the announcement unique. Telling and retelling will present the program in a different light each time, but the message will always be clearly the same.

When the program is up and running, convey messages regarding the program through progress reports, newsletter articles with comments from a "roving photographer," and at other opportunities. As soon as the first winners are announced, articles and announcements should appear all over; perhaps an award ceremony can be held. Even a visit from the President/CEO to the recipient's unit can be a real photo opportunity.

BENEFITS AND PERQUISITES AS INCENTIVES

The last two elements comprising the compensation package are benefits and perquisites. These are included in this chapter on incentives to consider what they are and what they aren't.

Benefits

Benefits may be defined as those noncash payments that encompass health, welfare, time off, and services. They include mandatory benefits (Social Security, Workers Compensation, and unemployment protection) as well as those voluntarily offered. They are provided to all employees of a specific level regardless of performance. Typical voluntary benefits commonly provided include medical protection, a retirement plan, and time off (vacations and holidays) with pay. Employers also provide other services that are frequently tied to the business they are in. Airlines, for instance, might offer employees free flights. Computer companies might offer discounted hardware. Retailers often offer discounts on whatever goods or services they provide.

Historically organizations were encouraged to offer benefits as a low-cost alternative to increases in pay. Tax advantages were offered by the federal government if an organization offered benefits to its employees, provided they did not favor the highly compensated. (If they do, they are considered as any other payment and taxes must be paid accordingly—which makes them less attractive to the employee receiving them and to the employer offering them.)

Because benefits are offered to all employees of a specific level regardless of performance, they may be considered totally as nonincentives. With rising concern for adequate medical and retirement coverage in this country, however, employers and employees each from their own perspectives are paying more attention to their cost and provision: that there may be an incentive in keeping them to the employee who understands and appreciates their value.

Exhibit 7-2, published annually by the United States Chamber of Commerce, depicts by industry the percentage of pay that employers contribute to meet the various costs of the benefits provided. It is a valuable source and reference point to be used when considering the cost of the total compensation package in an organization's attempts to ensure that it is paying at the right level for the work force it wishes to attract and retain.

Perquisites

Perquisites are the last element of the compensation package. They may be defined as benefits provided on a selective basis that are directly or indirectly tied to the person's on-the-job performance. Usually available only to a select few at the top, the more that attention is paid to them, the more these "throwaways" are realized as being sometimes quite costly. Perks may, in fact, become the source of a performance problem.

For example, there was a rising star in a major financial services institution who was promoted to president and CEO. As soon as the promotion became effective he had access to the company plane. Before long, he was flying all over on any excuse. Not long after, he left the company. By providing the perk, the organization spent a lot of money for something that eventually led to the loss of a valued employee.

Perks are complicated in terms of evaluation. They do bring value to the table and should be looked at from the perspective of employee interest and employer cost.

DEVELOPING AN INCENTIVES PROGRAM: CASE STUDY

The incentive plan described in the following case study was geared to the specific requirements of the organization at a particular point in time. The unique qualities of each organization must be recognized in order to develop an effective incentive plan.

Type of Benefit	Total, all industries	Total, all manufacturing	Food, beverage and tobacco	Textile products and apparel	Pulp, paper, lumber and furniture	Printing and publishing	Chemicals and allied products	Petroleum industry	Rubber, leather, and plastic products	Stone, clay and glass products	Primary metal industries	Fabricated metal products (excl. machinery and transportation equip.)	Machinery (excluding electrical)	Electrical machinery, equipment and supplies	Transportation equipment	Instruments and misc. manufacturing industries	Total, all nonmanufacturing	Public utilities (elec., gas, water, telephone, etc.)	Department stores	Trade (wholesale and other retail)	Banks, finance companies and trust companies	Insurance companies	Hospitals	Miscellaneous nonmanufacturing industries*
Total employee benefits as percent of payroll																								
1. Legally required payments (employer's share only)																								
a. Old-age, Survivor, Disability and Health Insurance (employer FICA taxes) and Railroad Retirement Tax	6.9	7.1	7.2	7.3	7.4	7.2	7.1	6.7	7.2	7.0	7.7	7.4	7.7	7.0	7.3	6.7	6.7	6.9	7.3	7.2	6.2	7.1	7.1	6.2
b. Unemployment compensation	0.6	0.6	1.0	1.9	1.1	0.8	0.6	0.6	0.8	0.7	1.4	0.7	0.8	0.5	0.5	0.6	0.6	0.5	1.0	1.1	0.6	0.6	0.2	0.5
c. Worker's compensation (including estimated cost of self-insured)	1.2	1.1	1.4	1.3	4.1	1.7	1.5	2.0	2.0	2.5	3.6	5.2	1.2	0.4	1.4	0.8	1.2	0.8	2.0	3.2	0.2	0.4	1.3	1.7
d. State sickness benefits insurance and other	0.6	0.3	0.0	0.1	0.7	0.2	0.1	1.8	2.9	0.2	0.3	0.3	0.1	0.0	0.0	0.1	0.7	0.2	0.0	0.1	0.1	0.0	0.7	1.6
2. Retirement and savings plan payments (employers' share only)																								
a. Defined benefit pension plan contributions	3.6	2.9	2.4	1.5	2.1	4.3	2.7	0.2	4.7	4.9	1.6	3.4	3.6	1.9	3.3	4.0	4.7		0.0	0.7	2.3	4.6	2.5	4.4
b. Defined contribution plan payments (401K type)	2.0	1.9	1.2	1.1	0.5	1.6	1.7	2.0	1.0	2.5	1.0	1.2	2.0	2.3	1.7	1.5	2.0	2.2	0.6	1.7	2.2	2.0	1.6	1.7
c. Profit sharing	4.4	8.6	11.8	0.1	2.0	4.8	1.9	7.8	1.6	2.2	3.0	3.1	7.0	10.7	0.8	5.4	1.8	3.3	3.3	1.5	2.0	2.8	3.2	1.1
d. Stock bonus and employee stock ownership plans (ESOP)	1.7	1.9	0.8	0.3	1.1	7.3	2.4	3.5	6.7	0.0	0.0	7.6	5.4	2.3	0.9	0.4	1.5	1.4	1.3	1.2	1.2	3.6	2.4	1.2
e. Pension plan premiums (net) under insurance and annuity contracts (insured and trusted)	1.8	0.6	3.2	0.2	0.0	0.1	0.0	0.3	6.1	0.0	0.0	3.0	0.8	0.8	0.1	0.2	2.1	5.2	0.0	2.1	0.2	0.5	0.2	1.3
f. Administrative and other cost	0.8	0.6	0.5	0.4	0.8	0.4	0.2	1.0	0.3	1.0	0.5	1.6	0.4	0.2	1.0	0.5	1.0	1.0	0.0	0.6	0.4	1.3	0.6	1.1
3. Life insurance and death benefit payments (employers share only)	0.5	0.5	0.5	0.2	0.6	0.7	0.5	0.7	0.5	0.8	1.5	0.7	0.6	0.3	0.6	0.8	0.5	0.8	0.2	0.2	0.4	0.5	0.2	0.5
4. Medical and medically related benefit payments (employers' share only)																								
a. Hospital, surgical, medical and major medical insurance premiums (net)	7.4	3.4	7.5	7.3	9.0	7.1	7.5	5.9	7.7	9.3	8.8	9.3	8.5	8.8	9.0	6.9	6.7	8.6	3.4	7.6	4.9	6.3	6.9	5.7
b. Retiree (payments for retired employees) hospital, surgical, medical and major medical insurance premiums (net)	1.4	1.8	0.9	0.5	1.1	0.8	3.8	1.1	2.1	2.9	1.5	0.8	0.7	2.0	1.1	1.1	1.1	1.6	0.5	0.6	0.4	0.9	0.7	1.1
c. Short-term disability sickness or accident insurance (company plan or insured plan)	0.6	0.6	0.6	0.3	0.3	0.9	0.1	1.0	0.7	0.3	0.3	0.6	0.5	0.7	0.3	0.2	0.6	1.1	0.5	0.3	0.5	0.4	0.5	0.3
d. Long-term disability or wage continuation (insured, self-administered, or trusts)	0.3	0.3	0.5	0.2	0.3	0.2	0.3	0.1	0.8	0.3	0.1	0.2	0.5	0.2	0.4	0.2	0.4	0.3	0.0	0.3	0.2	0.6	0.3	0.4
e. Dental insurance program	0.8	0.9	0.8	0.4	0.8	0.7	0.7	0.8	1.0	1.0	0.6	1.0	0.8	1.0	1.0	0.8	0.7	0.9	0.3	0.6	0.5	0.7	0.6	0.6
f. Other (vision care, physical and mental fitness, benefits for former employees)	0.6	0.5	0.3	0.4	0.5	0.1	0.2	0.2	3.1	0.6	0.3	0.4	0.9	0.3	0.5	0.3	0.6	1.0	0.6	0.9	0.2	0.4	0.3	0.3
5. Paid rest periods, coffee breaks, lunch periods, wash-up time, travel time, clothes change time, get ready time, etc.	3.8	3.3	4.7	5.5	5.1	4.3	3.4	3.1	4.4	3.9	2.8	2.7	3.7	3.8	2.0	3.2	4.2	3.1	5.3	5.4	4.4	5.2	4.6	4.7
6. Payments for time not worked																								
a. Payments for or in lieu of vacations	5.6	5.7	5.4	4.6	6.4	4.8	5.6	6.0	5.6	5.2	5.0	4.9	5.3	6.2	5.6	3.4	5.5	6.2	3.3	4.5	4.0	5.2	6.2	5.6
b. Payments for or in lieu of holidays	3.4	3.4	3.8	2.9	3.6	2.4	2.9	3.1	3.7	3.1	3.5	3.7	2.7	3.3	4.3	3.5	3.4	3.7	2.6	2.5	3.2	3.5	2.6	3.6
c. Sick leave pay	1.5	1.3	0.6	0.2	0.7	1.4	0.5	1.3	1.0	0.5	1.0	1.7	1.3	1.1	2.0	1.6	1.6	1.6	1.3	0.8	1.1	1.7	1.9	1.8
d. Parental leave (maternity and paternity leave payments)	0.1	0.1	0.2	0.0	0.0	0.1	0.1	0.0	0.2	0.0	0.0	0.0	0.0	0.0	0.0	0.1	0.1	0.1	0.0	0.1	0.2	0.1	0.6	0.3
e. Other	0.6	0.7	0.4	0.3	1.5	0.3	2.4	0.2	1.6	0.9	0.6	0.6	0.7	0.3	0.7	2.5	0.6	0.7	0.2	0.5	0.6	0.5	0.7	0.6
7. Miscellaneous benefit payments																								
a. Discounts on goods and services purchased from company by employees	0.8	0.4	0.4	0.4	0.0	0.2	0.6	0.0	0.2	0.7	0.1	0.5	0.0	0.6	0.1	0.2	1.0	0.4	2.8	2.1	0.1	0.2	0.5	0.2
b. Employee meals furnished by company	0.4	0.5	0.3	0.0	0.2	0.0	0.7	0.5	1.1	0.0	0.1	0.8	0.2	0.5	0.0	0.2	0.4	0.3	0.2	0.7	0.2	0.7	0.4	0.3
c. Employee education expenditures	0.3	0.3	0.1	0.1	0.1	0.4	0.1	0.2	0.2	0.2	0.2	0.2	0.3	0.4	0.2	0.3	0.3	0.2	1.1	0.1	0.3	0.4	0.3	0.4
d. Child care	0.1	0.0	0.0	0.0	0.0	0.0	0.0	0.0	0.0	0.0	0.0	0.0	0.0	0.0	0.0	0.0	0.1	0.0	0.0	0.0	0.1	0.0	0.2	0.0
e. Other	0.4	0.4	0.3	0.5	0.4	11.2	0.1	0.3	0.2	2.6	0.2	0.5	0.5	0.7	0.2	0.4	0.5	0.4	0.1	0.1	0.4	0.7	0.5	0.5

*Includes research, engineering, government agencies, construction, etc.

1991 Employee Benefits Report

Exhibit 7-2
Average Benefit Cost as Percent of Payroll for
Companies Paying Employee Benefits, 1990

Reprinted with the permission of the Chamber of Commerce of the United States from the 1991 edition of *Employee Benefits* © 1991. *Employee Benefits* may be ordered by calling 1-800-638-6582.

Scenario

A biotech firm located on the east coast was beginning its fourth year of operation. At a weekly meeting with the wage and salary professional, the president stated that to be economically viable, the company had to increase its volume and profits during the coming year. As a publicly held company, the investors recognized it as a long-term growth situation, but inroads had to be made to attract new customers and to develop and market profitable products on a more timely basis.

The staff consisted of fifty employees, all highly-educated. A performance appraisal system had been put into place last year. It had been difficult to combat a "think tank" environment and promote a "bottom-line" approach across staff lines.

The wage and salary professional suggested an incentive program to help the staff focus on increasing sales and profits while also developing a "team" aware of the company's goals and committed to the company's future.

The wage and salary professional conducted informal discussions with company managers regarding the scope and basics of a possible incentive plan, with various suggestions and comments being offered.

Gap Analysis

A review of the company's operations over its first three years of operation highlighted several areas open to improvement:

- too few profitable and marketable products
- lack of controls and runaway expenses for materials and supplies
- profit margins on new products too low
- period between design and introduction of new products too long
- sales team ineffective in finding new markets.

Organizational Constraints

As a start-up, the company needed to conserve cash. It also needed to maintain its competitive edge within the biotechnical industry, necessitating continued research. While the company needed short-term results over the next year, it recognized that long-term relationships with its staff and customers were of prime importance for sustained growth. Any incentive plan would have to minimize negative impact on the financial statements, while maximizing positive effect.

Program Features

A combination cash/stock option program was designed to reward employee performance on both short- and long-term bases. Basic terms of the incentive program were as follows:

- Corporate goals for year 1 of the plan were total sales of $5 million and net income before taxes of $575,000. Annual review of the plan would provide for new goals yearly.
- Threshold range of 80 percent of goals to 120 percent of goals was established for year 1 of plan to determine levels and eligibility for awards. Only if minimum goals were achieved would awards be granted.
- Award agreements were to be written at the beginning of the year as part of the performance appraisal process, with the promise of grants to be awarded at year-end.
- Process was to be an "iterative" up/down plan with management setting appropriate goals for various departments. Supervisors and staff would incorporate these goals into their individual objectives tied to the existing performance appraisal system. There were to be two written reviews annually.
- All employees were to be included in the plan. New employees become eligible after 6 months on a pro rata basis. Opportunities for rewards were linked to positions in the organization's hierarchy:
  —Lower positions eligible for 5 percent to 20 percent reward
  —Higher positions eligible for 35 percent to 75 percent
  —Awards tied to base salary figures for current year
- Stock option awards were linked to achievement of corporate goals, with a staggered vesting schedule:
  —After 6 months: 33 percent
  —After 15 months: 66 percent
  —After 24 months: 100 percent
- Stock option award to be adjusted at year-end to reflect any appreciation of stock price.
- Cash portion to be fully vested at year-end.

Program Approval and Introduction to Staff

An outline of the proposed plan was presented informally by the wage and salary professional to company managers for feedback on the specific terms of the incentive program. A formal proposal outlining the terms of the program, anticipated direct and indirect costs, and pro forma figures estimating award payouts at various threshold levels was presented to senior management and the board of directors for approval. The written proposal was reviewed by legal counsel.

A full staff meeting for all employees was held by the president to introduce the program. A thorough discussion of the company's long-term financial goals and the importance of each unit's role to the achievement of their objectives brought about several suggestions for improvement. A brochure detailing the program features was given to each employee, and follow-up meetings within each department were scheduled for the next week, with the wage and salary professional available to attend. Several posters were designed and placed in strategic areas to remind staff of corporate goals and the importance of this team approach.

- During the course of the year, quarterly financial statements were issued to all employees, with positive and negative impacts of various units highlighted.
- Semiannual performance reviews pointed out progress made towards unit and individual objectives.
- Departmental meetings focused on ways to increase sales volume and decrease expenses.

Results

Upon receipt of audited financial statements, thresholds for both sales volume and net income before taxes were calculated. The wage and salary professional then translated figures to determine each individual's award percentage. Individual percentages were then converted to dollar amounts, tied to the base salary effective at the beginning of the plan year. The dollar figures were converted into cash and stock option award values. Stock option award values were converted to options, as adjusted for stock price gains since the program inception.

An official awards ceremony was scheduled at a luncheon attended by the entire staff and conducted by the president. In addition to announcing the results, thanks were given for everyone's contribution to the effort.

Evaluation

At a follow-up meeting of senior management and all department heads the past year's performance was discussed in detail. Suggestions for improvement and for year 2 company goals were tendered. It was agreed that the incentive program fostered a "we are all in this together" approach and focused attention on the long-term business goals of the company. It was decided to continue the incentive plan for another year.

SUMMARY

A panel discussion by consultants and senior compensation staff members from major corporations at a recent gathering of compensation professionals all agreed that the compensation profession is undergoing an "exploration" of current and past practices to determine what is and isn't working. It is becoming difficult for compensation professionals who are trying to do the same old things by continuing to convince everyone that their "expertise" is out of the reach of others in the organization, therefore, all in the organization must rely on the compensation professional for guidance, support, and direction—and the formula to make it all work.

In the current environment, the successful compensation professional will be the one who considers his/her role as that of an internal consultant and change agent. The professional will determine the stakeholders that are essential to any program's success and will work towards the program's success by "wandering around" the organization with open eyes and mind, depending on focus groups, and facilitating employee buy-in.

A recent study of quality improvement initiatives through the management of human resources conducted by KPMG Peat Marwick found that compensation is coming of age as a separately defined discipline. New programs emphasize involvement and buy-in. The traditional top-down approach has been replaced in a vast majority of instances with broad-based task forces designing new pay programs. By establishing a pay strategy that provides a base pay that is competitive and around the median of its group, more organizations are emphasizing other elements of the pay package. A broad-based task force and employee involvement through focus groups arrive at more meaningful programs that do not increase cost but rather use the same dollars in more effective ways. Variable pay, gainsharing, and a slight reduction in the merit pay allow organizations to change the mindset of the employees. Instead of the unintended message of the past that encouraged employees to think in term of entitlements, the shift has been made to a shared arrangement. The "we're all in this together" approach is a win-win situation because the employer is dependent upon the employees for effective organizational performance and the employee is dependent on the organization as a source of livelihood. With this perspective, opportunities for employer and employee should continue to grow.

_____

chapter eight

STAFFING AND MANAGING THE WAGE AND SALARY ADMINISTRATION UNIT

Doing more with less is the cry from business leaders everywhere. How to heed the call is the real question that the wage and salary professional must address. This chapter explores the role of the wage and salary administration unit within the personnel/human resources function, and the composition of the wage and salary administration unit. Staff breakdown will be considered for both large and small organizations in both centralized and decentralized environments.

DETERMINING THE ROLE AND SIZE OF COMPENSATION WITHIN THE HUMAN RESOURCES FUNCTION

More often than not, the wage and salary administration unit is located under the umbrella of personnel/human resources. A recent Society for Human Resource Management/Bureau of National Affairs (SHRM/BNA) survey of current personnel/human resources practices found that, out of 506 organizations reporting, 79 percent had the wage and salary administration located totally within the personnel/human resources department. Another 19 percent reported that the responsibility is shared with another department. Only 2 percent have the responsibility located in another department entirely.

The personnel/human resources function may be responsible for as many as fifteen separate major areas. They include the following:

- Recruitment
- Employment
- HRIS Administration
- Staff/Labor Relations
- Performance Management
- Research
- Staff Planning
- Management Development/Succession Planning
- Compensation
- Benefits
- Wage and Salary
- Employee Assistance
- EEO/Affirmative Action
- Training
- Safety

The size of the wage and salary administration unit within the personnel/human resource function is dependent upon the scope of activity and the other requirements of the function.

There is an argument for strategic planning when building the personnel/human resource team. By going through the process in a strategic, long-term manner, the structure of the unit may be considered both in terms of meeting today's needs as well as those anticipated three to five years into the future. By focusing on the mission of the organization and the desired output (the results needed from the personnel/human resources function), determinations may be made about the projected composition of personnel/human resource staff, including that of the wage and salary administration unit.

It is fairly common for personnel/human resource professionals to take a more generalist position in smaller (fewer than 2,500 employees) organizations, after having spent time in a larger organization in a more specialized role.

Staffing, wage and salary administration, and benefits are the three specialties from which candidates are frequently selected. A primary reason for hiring persons with that kind of background is the perception by senior management of the needs of the organization doing the hiring at the time.

In organizations with fewer than 2,500 people the wage and salary administration unit often has only one full-time professional providing leadership for all the tasks and responsibilities involved. For organizations with more than 2,500 employees, the specific size of the wage and salary administration unit is totally dependent on the nature and mission of the personnel/human resource function and of the wage and salary administration unit within the function. The extent of automation, the political environment, perceived needs of key decision makers, and the extent to which the organization is a centralized personnel/human resource environment all play a part in determining the size of the wage and salary administration unit.

Another way to determine the size of the wage and salary administration unit as part of the personnel/human resource staff is to consider the annual personnel/human resource department expense and compare it to the organization's operating expenses. The SHRM/BNA survey periodically provides information on this topic, by both organizational size and industry. Here the range in the latest survey is quite wide and stretches from a low of .1 of 1 percent (manufacturing companies with more than 2,500 employees) to a high of 12.1 percent (nonmanufacturing companies with 500 to 900 employees).

If the organization is at the low end or below it for its size and industry, a review of personnel/human resource expenses may point to the conclusion that there are activities being ignored by the personnel/human resource mission and only the bare minimum requirements for the function are being met. Additional salary expense for an increase in wage and salary administration staff may be considered an option.

On the other hand, if an analysis of operational expense in comparison to personnel/human resources expenses indicates a high percentage, the function should be explored in more detail in an effort to determine the reasons for the additional cost. A possible option here, with respect to the wage and salary unit, is to decrease staff size.

Determining Staff Size Within Larger Organizations (2,500 or more employees)

In the largest organizations, several different functions may report directly to the head of personnel/human resources. Wage and salary administration is considered to be a subfunction of the compensation and benefits function(s). The wage and salary administration unit frequently has a counterpart on the benefits side that reports either directly to, or one step removed from, the senior person responsible for compensation and benefits. The structure is hierarchical, and the hands-on activities of wage and salary administration are delegated to the lower-level professional staff. [Exhibit 8-1 shows a typical personnel/human resources structure organized by function.]

In this type of organization, the functional units of human resources are typically considered as a division, and the scope of activities is such that the persons in each personnel/human resource sub-area, including wage and salary administration, are functional specialists. Economies of scale allow for breadth and depth that would not be possible in smaller organizations. Research, automation, outside consultant support, and major sophisticated communication efforts are all a part of the system and the way things get accomplished. In this type of organization, the compensation function is the policy and research arm that takes a big-picture, long-term approach to the subject. The wage and salary administration function is charged with the primary responsibility for program implementation.

Because of the organization's size, the wage and salary administration function is primarily a volume activity and production is an ongoing process. Typical responsibilities include:

- Professional support for updating and revising job descriptions.
- Processing monthly salary actions.
- Follow-up on outstanding reviews.
- Distribution of the next month's reviews.
- Generation, analysis, and distribution of "budget plan to actual" salary expense reports.
- Audit of salary actions to ensure conformance to organizational policies and procedures, as well as legal compliance.
- Job evaluation for new jobs and those radically changed.
- Maintenance of salary survey information to guarantee up-to-date information.
- Consideration of range and grade changes to reflect internal needs and external conditions.
- Ongoing training efforts to ensure that line managers and supervisors understand and are effective in implementing all of the program's elements.
- Compensation committee preparation and follow-up.

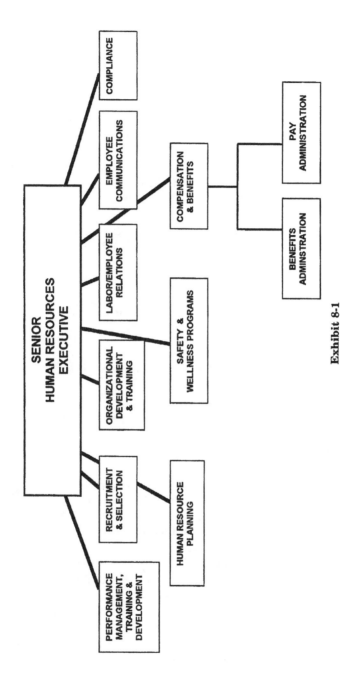

Exhibit 8-1

- Incentive program administration.
- Special projects.

The larger organization is one that by nature has the infrastructure to support the wage and salary administration programs that have become intertwined with the other practices that have, over time, become hallmarks of the organization. The advantage of this arrangement is that the support mechanisms are there to carry out current wage and salary programs effectively. The disadvantage is that great effort is required to introduce or inject anything new into the system. One reason for this is the complex infrastructure in a large organization and the various internal constituencies within this infrastructure. The decision makers and middle management in each constituency have their own set of values and purposes. The time and effort to install the change effectively becomes a difficult and trying endeavor. It requires enormous persistence and focus on your part, as well as a keen sense of organizational dynamics to make sure the change is introduced effectively.

Determining Staff Size Within Smaller Organizations (fewer than 2,500 employees)

In this environment the structure is much flatter, as a rule. The reason for the cut at 2,500 employees is because generally up to and including that level, the senior HR professionals must perform in a hands-on manner when the situation requires. Above that staff level, the senior personnel/human resource professional tends to take on the role of functional leader/manager who is dependant upon others to provide the technical subject matter details.

The manager's role is to select the right persons to enable him/her to respond to the organization's needs appropriately. If the effort is inadequate, either because the persons selected are not up to the task or because the infrastructure or resources are not sufficient, the senior personnel/human resource professional will have the wherewithal to personally get the task done in the manner he/she expects.

In the smaller organization, the SHRM/BNA survey reported that the median ratio of personnel/human resource staff per hundred employees goes from .5 for the organization with more than 1,000 employees up to 1.0 for the organization that has 250 or fewer employees. In these organizations, the personnel/human resource staff is required to wear several, if not all the specialist "hats." Obviously, if the position is a single incumbent function, the personnel/human resource professional must be able to deal with any of the fifteen major functions as they arise.

The wage and salary administration function in this environment is a particularly difficult one, because the design of the system may allow for resources such as consultants outside the organization in the attempt to develop the wage and salary program. There may be support from a task force created with senior management's blessing to help develop the program, yet to sustain the effort internally and externally after the program has entered its implementation phase is difficult to accomplish. In the smaller organization the advantages of an infrastructure don't exist, and the senior management team will not have the advantage of the same big-company perspective and values to allow the system to get the support and attention it needs—especially after the program has been introduced.

With this scenario in mind, the senior (or only) personnel/human resource professional must be particularly careful to consider the design of a wage and salary administration program that is simple to use and easy for line managers to implement with little effort or attention.

The last item to consider in the personnel/human resource function in the smaller organization is the need for the personnel/human resource professional to build an appropriate dependence on others, especially those in the personnel/human resource unit, so that they will grow as professionals and, in this case, as wage and salary administration specialists.

The personnel/human resource professional in the smaller organization must be sensitive to the consultative and project aspects of the position. If the incumbent develops systems in any of the fifteen areas without sufficient line buy-in, each of those additional activities will be added on to the activities already being performed. The key to avoiding this no-win situation is to identify internal and external persons and organizations that will see win-win opportunities.

One example demonstrates the point: In a major city there was a group of forty smaller companies (with staff sizes ranging from approximately 48 to 1,500) that needed salary survey information. Year after year they pooled their resources and they did it all themselves. After several years, automation played an increasingly important role, but was a time-consuming activity for all the people who worked on this project. After a while they realized they also wanted to conduct a benefits survey, but that took away more time from other activities for almost half of every year.

One day, one of their number suggested going to a major consulting firm and giving them a win-win proposition. He suggested that the consulting firm consider conducting the salary survey as a marketing effort that, if properly priced, would be at least a breakeven venture, if not actually profitable. In return, the group would serve on the steering committee for the survey and provide input into each year's survey before the actual survey was conducted. The only other piece of the proposal was to give the survey for free to this group of participants, if they participated in the survey themselves.

The consulting firm bought the idea and considered the project so success-ful that they subsequently agreed, under the same conditions, to conduct a biannual benefits survey as well.

The personnel/human resource professional with wage and salary admin-istration responsibilities in the smaller organization must find the time for creative thinking to identify and address critical issues.

Outsourcing for Assistance and Support

Outsourcing, looking outside the organization for assistance and support for the personnel/human resource function and the wage and salary administra-tion unit within the function, is another staffing option to consider.

Dependent on size, the personnel/human resource function needs a level of expertise that the smaller organization may not be able to support in as complete a manner as it wishes. There are three options available:

1. Select a junior-level staff member, or someone with the potential from another discipline or skill area to go through an on-the-job apprentice-ship, and depend on that person to use their own abilities to create their own training program.

2. Hire a seasoned professional with specific expertise and experience. In the smallest organizations, the person will be either performing below level most of the time (and may even in fact be eligible for overtime wages) or will not be sufficiently able to address issues in which he/she has had no experience.

3. Outsource the function: Hire an organization to provide personnel/ human resource expertise on a full range of activities. Instead of requir-ing one or two additional staff persons and spreading them over all the activities that must be serviced, the organization retained will be required to provide the expertise on the full range of required activities. This external organization will be able to do so by drawing on its staff of full-range personnel/human resource professionals who have expertise in a variety of subfunctions, including wage and salary administration. These organizations will be able to accomplish the task because they will have the economies of scale. They will be effective because they will treat the personnel/human resource unit as cus-tomers.

HOW TO STAFF THE WAGE AND SALARY ADMINISTRATION UNIT

The wage and salary administration unit, in both the smaller and the larger organization, should be considered a separate function within personnel/human resources. This applies even to smaller organizations, where the function might be performed by a part-time person, perhaps on an irregular basis.

Use the following levels of positions, usually found in the wage and salary function in larger organizations, as a guideline for meeting staffing needs.

Manager, Wage and Salary Administration Unit

This position represents the most senior person in the function, reporting usually to the vice-president–level manager of compensation or the vice-president–level manager of both compensation and benefits. This position is charged with the responsibility for policy and program revisions as well as for providing leadership for the function and professional development for all the members of the unit. This person sits on the compensation committee and is the subject matter expert in the organization on all wage and salary administration issues.

Wage and Salary/Compensation Specialist

The person in this position is a senior specialist responsible for high-level issues and problem solving in the wage and salary administration unit. He/she may be designated the acting manager of the unit and assume day-to-day operational responsibility even when the manager of the unit is present. If the wage and salary program is automated to any extent, this is the person who takes responsibility for coordination of the project with the vendor and the internal members of the support team. This person is responsible for audit and control of the actions taken by each member of the wage and salary unit. This person takes responsibility for determining the scope and nature of the salary survey program.

Wage and Salary Administrator

The wage and salary administrator is the middle-level expert responsible for maintaining the program and bringing problems beyond his/her experience level to the attention of the compensation specialist. This person considers complicated tasks such as insufficient documentation or over-budget increases and determines whether he/she is able to resolve the matter or must bring it to the attention of his/her supervisors. This position is more responsible for report analysis than the staff at junior levels. This person is responsible for the initiation of salary surveys and their swift and effective completion.

Compensation Analyst

This person is responsible for the generation of reports and range and structure analysis as well as more complicated and senior job analysis.

Job Analyst

The person in this position performs job analysis and basic job evaluation. It is an entry-level position.

Database Administrator

This person is responsible for maintaining the records and systems required to generate the reports needed in a personal-computer–based environment. Those units in organizations with a heavy commitment of human resources to automation may also have a staff of programmers (to write software or applications code) and programmer analysts (to make systems adjustments and install bulletins or software/applications updates) to support the mainframe/midrange system. This group may be part of the wage and salary administration unit, be a separate and distinct HRIS unit, or may report to another area of personnel/human resources.

Administrative Assistant, Wage and Salary Administration

The administrative assistant performs most of the clerical tasks and is responsible for processing data—input as well as output. He/she is an essential link in the wage and salary administration function. This position is truly administrative and provides the support that ensures the unit's mission is accomplished day in and day out.

HOW TO MANAGE THE WAGE AND SALARY ADMINISTRATION UNIT

There are two organizational approaches to the management and administration of the wage and salary administration function. They can be either centralized or decentralized.

Keep in mind when considering each structure that neither is "correct" and each has its advantages and disadvantages. For all the parts of the organization to be "in sync," regardless of structure, the organization must carefully consider which approach is most suitable. For a decentralized wage and salary function to expect a steady flow of directives from the larger personnel/human resources unit is as contrary to the nature of its approach as it would be for the centralized personnel/human resource function to allow line units, to go their own way in essential human resource services—such as wage and salary administration support—without any guidance, direction, or feedback for months (or even weeks) at a time.

How to Centralize the Wage and Salary Administration Function

In a larger organization with a centralized functional structure [as portrayed in Exhibit 8-1,] the major personnel/human resource functions are all located in close proximity at a headquarters location, and policies and procedures are developed and interpreted centrally. Personnel/human resources representatives are appointed to serve as liaisons with specific line support functions and work with line managers to implement the organization's wage and salary program. The amount of delegation is kept to a minimum and decisions such as those affecting starting pay, increases, adjustments, range changes, restructuring of grades, and job evaluation are performed primarily with the sanction of the centralized wage and salary administration unit.

Because of the responsibility of the centralized wage and salary administration staff, the size of staff is such as to support the centralized approach of operation. Although the reporting relationship of the line representative may be considered a matrix, it is more likely that the liaison is quite dependent upon the centralized personnel/human resources unit, with due consideration always to the manager of the unit for which the representative is responsible.

Persons serving in the line representative role are generalists who confer with the centralized personnel/human resources staff when the situation warrants. All the responsibility for wage and salary administration, and for the other personnel/human resources functions, lies in the effective implementation of the organization's centrally created personnel/human resources policies and programs.

This may work to the representative's advantage, however, because the line representative should, as an internal customer, be expected to turn to the centralized wage and salary administration function. The service expected from the headquarters staff should be sufficient to provide any needed support.

Regardless of level of automation, the communication is primarily one-way: from the "corporate" level to the line.

In a centralized environment, the wage and salary administration staff must take it upon itself to mingle and mix with their internal customers on a constant and frequent basis, not only to gain credibility but also to maintain relationships outside the organization to ensure a working understanding of the marketplace at all times.

How to Decentralize the Wage and Salary Administration Function

The decentralized structure is more inclined to interaction and dialogue between the "corporate" personnel/human resource function, with its wage and salary administration unit, and the line organization. In this structure, two-way communication and feedback are important, but—depending on the amount of decentralization—the key is the ability and need of the decentralized units to take the initiative within guidelines and be accountable for their activities and actions.

In this type of structure the representative is more dependent on the manager of the unit in which he/she is serving. Although ostensibly a generalist, the representative builds a decentralized unit to support and address the particular needs of the manager responsible for the line unit. The representative is more likely to go to the corporate headquarters staff on a proactive basis of his/her own determination.

In the most radical forms of decentralized organization, there may be an elaborate system of charges for corporate services in which the line units are encouraged to seek outside vendors in competition with the organization's own services. In fact, if the political situation warrants, the line representative may be encouraged to openly avoid contact with the headquarters group in personnel/human resources in general, and wage and salary administration in particular.

The representative in this type of organization often functions like the personnel manager of the local subsidiary of a major multinational organization and relies on the same specific hands-on skills as the senior incumbent in the smaller organization. If the division in which he/she is located warrants, it is quite possible that the position may take on additional staff to support the efforts and perform the activities that are not offered by the headquarters staff.

Here the options available to the representative are as varied as the negotiation skills he/she brings to the job. To be effective, he/she must determine the responsibilities to be developed and maintained. The representative must build staff or otherwise obtain support for those activities beyond the scope and abilities (or time) of the incumbent. The person may be required to maintain a wage and salary program that has been provided to the line unit by the headquarters staff only to find that it is impossible to maintain with the limited resources, including trained staff, provided to support the effort.

If that is the case, and if the centrally created wage and salary administration program is not appropriate for the line organization, the representative will need to work with his/her direct report—either the manager of the decentralized function or his/her subordinate—and work to find a practical solution at the local level.

Managing the Wage and Salary Function in the Smaller Organization

The smaller organization creates an environment for the wage and salary administration function that has some of the characteristics of the decentralized organization, yet it is different in the following ways:

- There is no centralized function in another location to go to for direction, suggestions, and advice.
- Because of the size of the organization and the proximity of the senior members of management, there will be more interaction regarding wage and salary administration issues—which might be both a curse and a blessing.
- There is less likely to be any infrastructure or value system that supports a full-service wage and salary administration program. Its usefulness may be considered very important only in times of crisis (for example, when the accounts payable department threatens to walk out altogether unless their pay complaints are addressed immediately).
- Because of the size of the organization, it is less likely that the line managers are aware of their role in the wage and salary administration process. They will have to be trained to become effective parts of the system, or the wage and salary professional will be required to take on more responsibility personally.

SUMMARY

An understanding of staffing and organizational structure is important to determine the approach that you will take to the position and the opportunities there will be for professional growth. Whether you are a member of a large or small organization, the two key elements to determine are the level of responsibility and service required and where to go for help.

No structure is ideal for all individuals. Each person, because of his/her own unique skills, aptitudes, and experiences, must consider what is the most effective way to work within an organization to maximize personal and professional effectiveness. Regardless of whether there is a staff of twenty or a single incumbent, the ability to realistically determine what is doable within the organizational structure is crucial to effective performance of the job.

chapter nine _____

HOW TO DEVELOP WAGE AND SALARY SURVEYS TO DETERMINE PAY POLICIES

One of the most exciting areas of wage and salary administration is salary surveys. This is a critical area of major interest, and it provides you with an opportunity to be truly creative and innovative. Compensation professionals frequently suggest that the salary survey has a greater impact on salary decisions than any other policy-making tool.

There are a number of reasons for initiating a salary survey:

Management requests

Management may be concerned about the status of the salary levels for particular positions or units. A review of the compensation program will reveal whether these salary levels attract, retain, and motivate employees in a legal and affordable manner. A newspaper article, an employee's complaint, or a discussion with peers from other organizations may all raise this issue.

Internal concerns

There may be a growing concern about current salaries either in comparison with salaries being paid for other positions within the organization or in comparison with salaries being paid by other organizations. To put these rumors to rest, a survey will reveal the facts and then the information can be disseminated. The wage and salary survey will determine whether an organization's pay rates are effective and competitive before there is a sudden mass defection.

Periodic exercise

From time to time, salary surveys should be done as a way to sharpen your professional skills and keep current with changing market conditions for the positions in your organization. These surveys are also a way to develop and sustain relationships with wage and salary administration peers in other organizations. If they're willing to share information about their own compensation programs, your peers can offer valuable suggestions for making your program as effective as possible.

DEVELOPING THE WAGE/SALARY SURVEY

A successful, informative survey that meets the established objectives in a timely manner requires planning. There are three phases to the survey process: preparation, survey, and results. Exhibit 9-1 shows the steps involved in each of these three phases.

Preparing for the Survey

Identify the need

Before deciding to undertake a salary survey, you must always identify the objective, and put it clearly in writing. Conducting a survey is a laborious task, even with the help of a personal computer and the luxury of support staff. It is crucial to focus on the goal of the survey, that is, the specific information you wish to obtain.

Determine the approach

After deciding to do the Wage/Salary survey, it is necessary to determine the approach. Will you do the survey personally or retain a consultant? It can

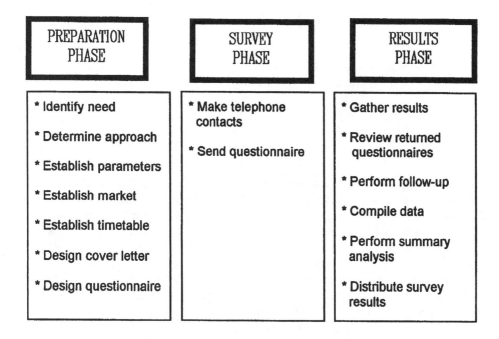

Exhibit 9-1
Steps in the Wage and Salary Survey Process

be easier to select a consultant to do the survey, but you will still be required to:

- interview and select the appropriate consultant;
- communicate the objective of the survey; and
- jointly select the market.

There is an obvious trade-off in time: You will invest up-front time in searching for, interviewing, and selecting a consultant, and you will devote supervisory time to ensure the quality of the end product. If the consultant has not been used before, he/she may not be sensitive to the quirks or peculiar demands of the specific industry involved. An initial time investment is required so that there are no surprises during the survey, or afterwards when the data is compiled.

When initiating a survey, in addition to the choice between hiring a consultant to conduct the survey or doing the survey yourself, there are also the following alternatives to consider:

- Do a "quick and dirty" survey by telephone.
- Use "third-party" surveys.
- Find an existing industry survey.
- Go to various governmental resources.
- Go to a vendor, such as a recruiter.

Set parameters

At this point you must determine the number and type of positions to include in the survey. Again, it is imperative to remember the objective of the survey. Although difficult, it is essential to select the "right" number and type of jobs to survey. In the process, keep in mind that picking the positions and the participants is the primary benefit in conducting the survey personally. It's "your" survey, so you will get the specific information you need.

On the other hand, consider the need to attract participants. Make the survey sufficiently sophisticated and comprehensive so that others will want to participate, but be careful to not ask for too much or others will either be unable or unwilling to participate. There is a fine line between "too much" and "too little" information.

There really is no rule of thumb for determining an appropriate number of jobs to survey. It depends on the complexity of the data being requested and the level of sophistication of the participants. If a starting point for consideration is requested, ten for both exempt and nonexempt positions is a ballpark figure to consider. If information for both nonexempt and exempt levels is needed, then as many as twenty positions may be included in the survey; there should be a fine level of participation. If the group is sufficiently sophisticated and is used to providing data for lengthier surveys, then there should be little difficulty offering a longer survey.

The reason for at least ten positions is that the work involved for ten positions is not much more than for any lower number of positions. If information is needed for only three or four of the ten positions, then the additional data obtained for the other positions will be helpful in determining the relevance and accuracy of the required data provided. Depending on the number of participants, it may come to light that all positions are not a "match," and then the survey will suffer because the sample is too small and the amount of data too scanty. The result: a lot of work and little to show for it.

Another reason for seeking data on at least ten positions is that it helps to get others to buy into participation. Even though information for three or four positions is the prime objective for the survey, the other participants may be more interested in other positions. By including their interests as well, there is more likelihood for participation, enthusiasm, and support for the survey. This is another reason to telephone ahead to get commitments before conducting the survey; if any of the would-be participants makes a request, including their positions in the survey will certainly help to get them to buy in.

Try to anticipate future organizational needs. If the need is for just a position or two at present, consider other positions that may require updated information in the foreseeable future and include those as well. After "going to the well," it is difficult to go again each subsequent time without allowing some downtime to creep in.

The positions included in the survey should be truly "benchmark" positions. These are positions that are fairly standard by definition; are common to other organizations; represent different salary levels; and, are technologically "stable." For all these reasons, these are the very positions that are frequently included in large-scale surveys.

Establish the market

The "market," those to whom the survey questionnaire is directed, may be geographically defined—national, regional, or local. Or, the market may be defined by perceived competition for talent and/or product. It may vary from survey to survey, depending on positions to be included and changing environmental circumstances.

There is never just one market. The market is composed of a variety of markets that overlap to varying degrees and that together form the current marketplace. The problem is that the concept is truly dynamic and constantly changing. The aim of the survey is, therefore, to pinpoint the most relevant organizations by location or other distinguishing characteristics for the specific positions for which you are seeking information. In even the smallest of surveys, always consider at least five relevant organizations and at least ten benchmark positions.

One reason for surveying at least five organizations is that there will be a greater probability that at least two organizations will report data for each position. For ideas on which organizations to select, start with senior management and ask, "Who are your major competitors for talent? Which organizations really develop their people?" Then consider the line managers, current employees, and exit interviews for their opinions on which organizations they perceive to be the competition for talent. Don't neglect your own opinions and those of your peers. Human resource/compensation/wage and salary administration professionals not only offer great suggestions but may also be prime sources for information (either directly or indirectly).

Establish a timetable

Essential to the success of the survey is the establishment of a timetable. Start backwards from the date you need the data and establish deadlines for each of the steps. Include some leeway, and keep in mind upcoming holidays and vacations. Determine whether the participants being depended upon for the data will be able to meet the agreed-upon dates, even with their other commitments. People are sometimes more optimistic than realistic about unexpected demands that crop up at inopportune times.

Choose appropriate participants

Making an initial telephone call is very important in determining the eligibility and availability of a potential participant as well as his/her interest in participating in the survey. To not make an initial telephone contact is to take a gamble on the survey not being returned by the participant as had been requested. "Cold" surveys may be met with a similar reception. To act in such a manner would place you in a poor position: no survey data when compilation was to begin. The solution—to backtrack and make an after-the-fact telephone call to chase questionnaires—bespeaks poor planning and lack of courtesy to the participant whose support is being requested.

It is never too early to make the telephone contacts and get the survey commitments. Watch for those who say, "Send me the questionnaire and then we will consider participation." This is all the more reason to provide a beautiful questionnaire as the selling tool. At the same time, this response may just be a delaying tactic, so do not depend on their response. If a response is received from these "uncommitted" participants, add the data to the list of those who have already participated but, since their participation was not counted on, their failure to participate will not damage the survey. Keep a log of the calls made as a record for future reference; see Exhibit 9-2 for an example.

When choosing survey participants, establish the following:

The level of responsibility and experience of the person at the other end of the phone

Quickly determine whether the person on the other end of the phone is the most appropriate one to deal with for this survey. It is not of great importance whether the person on the phone will do the survey himself or herself or assign it to someone else. The key is whether the person on the other end of the phone has the authority and ability to deliver the data as promised.

TELEPHONE CONTACTS					QUESTIONNAIRE					FOLLOW-UP			SURVEY RESPONSE		
ORG. NAME	CONTACT	PHONE #	DATE	RESPONSE	MAILED	ATTENTION:	ADDRESS:	CODE	ANON	DATE	STATUS	REC'D	DATE	COMMENT	

Exhibit 9-2
Survey Action Log

An appreciation for the effort going into the survey

Ideally, the person agreeing to participate will have an understanding of the effort of such an undertaking and an appreciation for the effort involved. Furthermore, the participant should understand the importance of the program; that the situation is truly a win-win arrangement and that the contact made now will help both you and the participant to work together effectively whenever appropriate in the future.

An understanding of the salary survey process

The prospective participant should be experienced enough to understand the importance, sensitivity, and accuracy of the survey data. If the prospect is a novice, providing a brief summary of what the survey will entail is a good investment of time.

A willingness and ability to provide the data in an accurate and timely manner

Along with experience, the participant should recognize the need for timeliness in his/her commitment to furnish data. All the survey participants should be fully cognizant of the fact that the commitment is not just to obtain the survey result data but to furnish their data as well. Participant should understand that if the data provided are inaccurate or misleading, the results of the survey will be useless.

A sense of urgency

For the survey to be effective, all the participants must individually agree that the time commitment is vital. Even one tardy participant will lead to delays for everyone and is thereby reneging on his/her commitment.

Designing the cover letter

The quality of the cover letter is important because it will convey an image to those persons who have already committed verbally to participate in the survey. The cover letter should exude professionalism. It should make the participants feel pleased with themselves for agreeing to be part of the survey. Additionally, it is helpful to have the cover letter at hand when making initial telephone contacts requesting participation in the survey. The letter may serve as a script to assure that all participants are given the same basic information both over the telephone and in the actual written request.

If you feel that any of the participating organizations will be impressive to any other of the potential survey participants, mention that fact in the individual participant's letter. The cover letter is a sales tool; if the name of any organization will help to encourage any fence-sitters to participate, it would be folly not to mention it—with permission, of course. The letter must be proofread carefully so that you don't inadvertently send a letter to one of the participants that mentions them in their own letter as one of the participants; also do not mention any participants that have indicated their willingness to participate in the survey only on the condition that they remain anonymous.

A sample survey cover letter is provided in Exhibit 9-3. Regardless of contents, details in the letter should include:

1. An expression of gratitude for agreeing to participate in the survey when called. As discussed, regardless of circumstances, it is imperative that the initial contact for the survey be done by telephone.

2. Always be sure to provide the due date for completed questionnaires. Timeliness for surveys is essential to their success. The qualifier for identifying appropriate persons for future surveys rests with prior experience. As survey relationships are built, past experiences are prime indicators as to who can be depended upon.

3. Promise the confidentiality of the data and the results. Include a postage paid envelope for returning the questionnaire so that those who respond are noted, but not their specific identity. If any of the participants does not even want to be identified as a participant in the summary page of the completed document, there is no reason to not agree to their request.

4. Close with a statement of appreciation for participating in the survey. You are developing a relationship, and it is assumed that there will be a need for additional requests in the future.

Designing the questionnaire

The design of the questionnaire is even more important than the cover letter. Think of this document as another selling tool. You are selling your survey to the participants and you need them to agree that this winning idea is worth their time, effort, and, most important, their information. Show that the form is worth their investment because it is as good as (if not better than) any survey questionnaire they have ever seen. This is the document that will

Dear ___ :

Thank you so much for agreeing in our telephone conversation to participate in our current wage/salary survey. We are so glad that you are willing to take time out from your other activities to complete the enclosed questionnaire.

The data you are being asked to provide will be held in strictest confidence. The compiled results will be provided to all participants. To protect your identity you have been assigned a code number; this number is located on the cover of the enclosed response envelope.

As stated in the questionnaire, actual data shall be as of (date). We have tried to make the form self-explanatory, but if you have any questions or comments, please contact me.

Please return your completed questionnaire in the pre-addressed, stamped envelope, also enclosed. You will note that a return date of ___ is stated on the questionnaire. We realize this may appear to be an early response date, but we request your cooperation in returning the survey promptly. This due date allows us to provide the completed results to you by ___ .

Your cooperation in this important project is greatly appreciated. A meeting to discuss the results of the survey is planned; we will telephone your office in approximately one week to schedule a mutually convenient date and time.

Once again, thank you for your interest and participation in this important project.

Sincerely,

Exhibit 9-3
Sample Survey Cover Letter

contain the data required to accomplish your stated objective.

In Appendix H, you will find a sample questionnaire. When designing the survey include the following sections in your format:

- **Contact data:** who is completing the survey and how to contact them if necessary after the survey is completed.
- **Organizational data:** demographics by exempt and nonexempt categories, salary administration data, benefits details, working hours and leave information, and, overtime policy.
- **Job description summaries:** brief but thorough summaries providing the essential elements of each position to be surveyed. Include a written statement of condition that there should be at least an 80 percent match (or some other percentage that feels comfortable). Include space for a comment for each position, stating whether it is a complete match or is greater or less than the position described (but not more or less than the percentage mentioned as the outer limit).

Design the questions carefully and review the document closely to ensure that all items have been asked and the format is logical. It is crucial that the form contain sections that allow room to provide all the data that you seek—in a manner that is easy to understand and unambiguous.

Since much depends on the format and content of the survey questionnaire, it is essential that it be tested before dissemination. Give it to associates or junior members in the wage and salary administration unit to see how they perceive the form; ask for comments and suggestions for improvement.

Conducting the Survey

Send the survey questionnaires out fast and keep a record of the mailing date and the place and person to whom it was directed in case any are lost. Exhibit 9-2 includes space for recording this information. If there is concern about receipt of the questionnaires, telephone each of the participants three business days after the surveys were mailed. If the cost is worth it, consider using overnight mail for its swiftness and guarantee of delivery.

Compiling, Analyzing, and Distributing the Results

The last phase in the survey process involves six steps:

1. **Contact the participants.** One or two days before the stated deadline for returning the completed questionnaire, call the participants to

check on their progress. It is better to head off any problems at this stage than to be "surprised" by a problem later, when you will have less time to deal with it.

2. **Review the returned questionnaires.** Before commencing tabulation, review each of the questionnaires to evaluate the quality and completeness of the results. If any problems are detected, they could be addressed at that time instead of waiting for the other data.

3. **Follow up.** If there are problems regarding missing data, incomplete/incomprehensible responses, or missing questionnaires, follow up immediately to convey the seriousness of the project and the survey's status relative to completion of the project.

   For those surveys that have unanswered questions, take a moment to get the answers over the telephone from the participants. The information gained will help to provide insight into the quality of the work provided.

4. **Compile the data.** Accuracy during this phase of the project is essential to the success of the project. One opportunity to increase the likelihood of accuracy is to provide the line item results as well as the summaries. Then, if any of the participants wonder where they stand in the survey, they can look at the tabulated results, line by line, to consider any discrepancies. This detail work can be performed by a special assistant with a proven proficiency for details, figures, and accuracy. Or you might attend to the project personally, taking responsibility for the accuracy of the report generated. The individuals responsible for the report must have a good understanding of statistical terms, such as *mean, median,* and *mode.* (See Glossary for definitions.)

5. **Perform the summary analysis.** Some participants prefer receiving the data in a raw (untampered) format, but most prefer summaries. Unless you know the participants' preferences in advance, provide both and give an overview as well.

6. **Distribute the survey results.** Since you have stressed promptness in obtaining the survey responses, it is imperative that the results be provided to the participants in a timely manner, as specified in the cover letter.

You must ensure confidentiality at all costs. All of the personnel involved in this step of the survey response must be supervised to be absolutely certain that the material being sent out is the correct material going to the appropriate person in the organization according to the designation specified on the questionnaire submitted by the participant. Any mistake here will compromise your personal reputation, so be extremely careful to have the most diligent staff members coordinate and take responsibility for this aspect of the process.

How to handle late responses

Frequently, for whatever reason, one completed survey arrives just when the compiled results are about to be delivered. Your choices are:

- refuse the data and return it;
- accept the data, retabulate the numbers, provide all new results, and throw out the old reports; or
- accept the data; let all the other participants receive their data without the new numbers, and reformulate the data for the late participant, sending an updated copy to all at a later date.

The ultimate choice is yours. It is a balance between "relationship maintenance" and the difficulty of doing the work over to the work out for everyone on time. If the resources to start retabulating the data are not available, this question is moot. The reminder telephone calls and follow-up on late submissions of surveys will keep these surprise returns to a minimum.

How to handle minimalist responses

The second problem is ethical: What do you do with the organization that submits the barest of data just to get everyone else's results? Do they receive the same results as the others, who did all the work, or is their data returned with the mention that they provided too little data to be considered a participant?

This author's opinion is on the side of liberalism. Share the data, because that particular organization may not have the positions or the match may not be close enough in many instances to provide the information requested within the parameters specified. Keep the person and the organization in mind for future surveys. Follow up and try to get more information both during the survey and after it has been completed to determine whether the organization should be approached again for future surveys.

Distributing the survey's results

The physical distribution of the results requires the following:

- **Cover letter.** The cover letter should express gratitude to the organizations for their participation in the survey, citing return of the results by the agreed on date (if the deadline was met), the code letter of the participant, and, if already in place, confirming the date and time for a meeting to discuss the results, if the decision has been made to have one. See Exhibit 9-4 for a sample survey results cover letter.

- **List of participants.** This should be an all-inclusive list of the organizations that participated in the survey. The listing should always be alphabetical, unless there is a strong reason for an alternative way of listing the participants. Respect the request of any of the participants for anonymity, and make sure their names are omitted from the list before the packets are distributed.

- **Summary analysis of results.** This should be a brief, one-page analysis of results to highlight major findings from the survey. Comments may also be included here about methodology or peripheral items that may not be known by all participants (for example, a flat payment of $5.00 per day for meals that is included automatically in each employee's pay, or taxi vouchers available to all employees who incur overtime).

- **Actual Results of the Survey Data.** The array of the format of the data is dependent upon the sophistication of the group. In many instances, a summary breakdown may be sufficient, and anything more may be perceived as a nuisance to the participants. Other groups may prefer a complete breakdown and want the opportunity to view the raw data (with organizations listed always by code letter only). Needless to say, this responsibility rests with you. In an effort to satisfy everyone at least partially, consider providing both a summary and the data reported by each participant, line by line.

Providing the data on a disk

As an alternative to the "hard copy" result format, consider providing the data on disk for those who prefer it. The data could be provided in a spreadsheet format and be readily accessible for analysis or distribution that the participants may be hoping to offer their internal staff members. It certainly is an option worth considering and may be an effective alternative that would help to convey a state-of-the-art and sophisticated image to your peers.

Avoiding the data through telecommunications

You might also consider providing the survey results through a modem. To make the results available electronically would certainly speed up delivery of the results for those participants having the means and ability to make use of the technology.

Dear ___:

As promised, enclosed is the final report for the wage/salary survey in which you participated. Your code letter is ___.

We hope you are pleased with the results. Let me personally thank you for your support of this time-consuming endeavor. Without your participation and interest, this project could not have been completed so quickly or effectively. Your cooperation in meeting the deadline is particularly appreciated; with your prompt response we are able to deliver the final results as promised.

Please let me know your comments or suggestions on the survey -- in any aspect -- so that we can identify opportunities for improving future surveys.

In an effort to derive additional benefit from the survey, you will have the opportunity to meet the other survey participants at our facilities (location) on (date) at (time). The primary topic of the meeting will be the survey results. I do hope you will be able to attend. Please confirm with me at (telephone number) by (date).

In any event, let me thank you once again for all your assistance. I look forward to working with you again.

Sincerely,

Exhibit 9-4
Sample Survey Results Cover Letter

When using telecommunications or a disk, be even more careful that the data transmitted does not in any way compromise the confidentiality of the results or the identity of the participating organizations.

USING CONSULTANTS TO CONDUCT SALARY SURVEYS

Consultants can be useful in gathering information through salary surveys. Consultants can be expected to go through the laborious process of finding survey participants. They then will proceed to design the questionnaire (if they already have one available for use, that will reduce their fee). The consultant then will also be responsible for obtaining the data and presenting it in a meaningful format.

One major benefit of retaining a consultant to conduct the survey is the prestige that goes with the engagement of an "expert." From a selling standpoint, it is easier to sell a survey to participants through a consultant because the consultant will keep the name of the client confidential (unless the client explicitly requests otherwise). Second, the consultant will convey the fact that, as a disinterested third party, all data will be retained solely with his/her organization and never reach a competitor's premises. Third, the participants are able to obtain desirable data at no cost because the consultant is being paid by your organization to provide that data to them.

Retaining a consultant to perform a salary survey is one method that is frequently mentioned as an opportunity to avoid the legal risk incurred when conducting a salary survey directly. Be careful, though, to retain a hands-on position with the consultant; do not just provide instructions to the consultant when the project begins and never see him/her again until it is completed. The consultant should work with you to establish the specific parameters of the survey and obtain from you the sources to utilize when the survey plan is drafted.

Drafting the Consultant's Contract

Determine the objectives and the parameters of the survey prior to any discussions with a consultant. This will establish a frame of reference that can be subject to revision after discussion with a consultant, who may provide additional ideas for the nature and scope of the survey under consideration.

When working with a consultant, request a written proposal that is concise, but covers all of the points you consider critical to the project. Upon receipt of the proposal, compare it to the stated objectives for the survey, determine that the objectives remain valid, and verify that the consultant's approach will meet those objectives. If necessary, revisions will result in the secondary objective: no surprises.

When there is clear agreement with the consultant as to objectives, approach, price, and timetable, then give the signal to the consultant to proceed with speed; if not, terminate the discussions. By the time this step is reached, it may be difficult to remember that there is still reason to consider the alternative of not using a consultant. Here, instincts as well as your own intellectual skills should be used to determine whether to work with the consultant.

HOW TO USE OTHER SURVEY METHODS

There are other opportunities to consider for survey data. These include consultants (used in a way different from that already described), industry groups, and the much maligned but quite important telephone survey.

Conducting Telephone Surveys

Although less reliable than the written survey these "quick and dirty" telephone surveys are truly helpful in obtaining information in a pinch.

The results of such a survey are frequently and to a great extent dependent upon the relationship between the participant and the person conducting the survey. For example, industry associations frequently provide salary data for positions unique to their membership and often will provide data over the phone for specific positions and follow-up with printed material whenever available. The value of the data is to a great extent dependent on the emphasis the association places on this information. Usually these staff members are very service-oriented, so consider the source a good one.

Even though the survey is conducted over the telephone, preparing for the survey follows much the same process as a formal, written survey. The steps are as follows:

1. **Design a written survey questionnaire.** The prepared list of questions will provide a script for the telephone interview and will ensure a standard format for each interview.

2. **Distribute written results.** Regardless of the length of the survey, promise the participants a written copy of the final results. The relationship-building aspect is not to be forgotten in the telephone survey, and the best way to develop that is by providing written results.

Using Industry-Specific Compensation Surveys

There are compensation consultants who provide surveys on a regular basis. The banking industry has the Cole survey. ECS does broad industry surveys that include human resources and data processing professionals. McGlagen does a survey for trading professionals. There is a cost for these surveys, and there is usually a two tier system—one price for participants and another for nonparticipants. See Exhibit 9-5 for an example of a survey conducted annually by Towers Perrin, also known as TPF&C, a major global human resources consulting firm.

Local Chambers of Commerce are also frequent providers of such surveys. Making contact with a local chapter is an obvious first step to consider in identifying this and other local resources. See Exhibit 9-6 for an example of a survey conducted annually by the New York Chamber of Commerce and Industry.

Using Government Surveys

The United States Department of Labor conducts surveys on a variety of positions and different locations. The results are printed a long time after the data have been accumulated so the information is often of limited value. The reason for the delay in access to the data is to a great extent due to the number of participating organizations, which is usually quite vast so that the sample is at least meaningful.

Obtaining Information from Vendors

If there has been an ongoing relationship with one or more vendors, including suppliers, they may be available to provide current information on an immediate basis. Most vendors love the opportunity to be of service (as should you), because it is the relationship that they are hoping for and they appreciate how these opportunities forge those relationships. Two obvious ven-

TPF&C COMPENSATION DATA BANK

1990

POSITION SUMMARY TABLE

COMPANIES WITH SALES RANGING FROM $1 BILLION TO $3 BILLION
(CORPORATE)

POSITION TITLE: TOP PER EXEC   JOBCODE: 301   NUMBER OF CASES: 74

			BASIC SURVEY STATISTICS			
	10TH	25TH	MEAN	MEDIAN	75TH	90TH
BASE SALARY	$110,200	$120,524	$151,182	$150,000	$169,260	$189,050
TARGET BONUS PERCENT	25	30	37	35	44	51
BONUS AS % OF BASE	0	22	38	34	46	63
TOTAL COMPENSATION	$123,031	$154,984	$212,199	$194,739	$244,319	$280,750
MIDPOINT (N = 61)	$108,320	$125,000	$149,538	$151,852	$170,230	$189,322
EXEMPTS SUPERVISED	8	13	32	24	43	64
TOTAL EMPLOYEES	14	23	60	41	74	148
REPORTING LEVEL	3	3	2	2	2	2
UNIT SALES	1019	1282	1918	1700	2610	2905
CORPORATE SALES	1019	1282	1918	1700	2610	2905
ONE YEAR ROE	0	8	17	14	20	29
FIVE YEAR ROE	0	8	12	12	16	20
AGE	45	47	52	50	57	61
COMPANY SERVICE	4	7	16	14	24	28

BOARD OF DIRECTORS MEMBERSHIP
PARENT(%)	EXECOM(%)	SUBSIDIARY(%)	OFFICER ONLY(%)
3	0	0	62

INTERNATIONAL RESPONSIBILITY
FULL(%)	PART(%)	NONE(%)
1	61	38

INCENTIVE PRACTICES
LTIP ELIGIBLE(%)	BONUS ELIGIBLE(%)	BONUS RECEIVED(%)
85	99	88

Exhibit 9-5
Industry-Specific Compensation Survey A

Reprinted here with the permission of Towers Perrin, New York City.

TPF&C COMPENSATION DATA BANK   1990

POSITION SUMMARY TABLE

COMPANIES WITH SALES RANGING FROM $3 BILLION TO $6 BILLION
(CORPORATE)

POSITION TITLE: TOP MIS EXEC   JOBCODE: 701   NUMBER OF CASES: 31

			BASIC SURVEY STATISTICS			
	10TH	25TH	MEAN	MEDIAN	75TH	90TH
BASE SALARY	$91,824	$108,000	$133,075	$129,000	$160,020	$172,600
TARGET BONUS PERCENT	20	23	28	29	33	39
BONUS AS % OF BASE	15	18	31	24	40	66
TOTAL COMPENSATION	$113,627	$130,900	$176,765	$166,000	$225,000	$258,016
MIDPOINT (N = 30)	$94,166	$112,939	$133,161	$132,415	$154,188	$177,400
EXEMPTS SUPERVISED	41	60	136	111	213	249
TOTAL EMPLOYEES	51	77	202	162	291	491
REPORTING LEVEL	4	3	3	3	3	3
UNIT SALES	2590	2761	3901	3392	5163	5672
CORPORATE SALES	2590	2761	3901	3392	5163	5672
ONE YEAR ROE	0	4	17	15	25	39
FIVE YEAR ROE	2	12	15	14	20	30
AGE	43	46	51	51	56	60
COMPANY SERVICE	3	6	18	21	26	33

BOARD OF DIRECTORS MEMBERSHIP

PARENT(%)	EXECOM(%)	SUBSIDIARY(%)	OFFICER ONLY(%)
0	0	0	23

INTERNATIONAL RESPONSIBILITY

FULL(%)	PART(%)	NONE(%)
0	45	55

INCENTIVE PRACTICES

LTIP ELIGIBLE(%)	BONUS ELIGIBLE(%)	BONUS RECEIVED(%)
84	100	100

Exhibit 9-5 (continued)
Industry-Specific Compensation Survey A

Reprinted here with the permission of Towers Perrin, New York City.

42 PROGRAMMER, INTERMEDIATE

COMPANIES WITH 1-500 EMPLOYEES

COMP. NO.	NO. OF INCUMBENTS	AVG. SALARY	YRS. OF SERVICE	ESTAB. RANGES MINIMUM	ESTAB. RANGES MAXIMUM	ACT. SAL. PAID MINIMUM	ACT. SAL. PAID MAXIMUM	CURRENT HIRING RATE
5	7	33317	1.5	28500	42700	30500	35950	37225
8	4	30901	17.0	37225	55810	27144	37448	-----

COMPANIES WITH 501-999 EMPLOYEES

COMP. NO.	NO. OF INCUMBENTS	AVG. SALARY	YRS. OF SERVICE	ESTAB. RANGES MINIMUM	ESTAB. RANGES MAXIMUM	ACT. SAL. PAID MINIMUM	ACT. SAL. PAID MAXIMUM	CURRENT HIRING RATE
17	3	42447	2.5	39035	46304	39035	46304	-----

COMPANIES WITH 1000+ EMPLOYEES

COMP. NO.	NO. OF INCUMBENTS	AVG. SALARY	YRS. OF SERVICE	ESTAB. RANGES MINIMUM	ESTAB. RANGES MAXIMUM	ACT. SAL. PAID MINIMUM	ACT. SAL. PAID MAXIMUM	CURRENT HIRING RATE
4	4	34164	9.0	19656	31460	31252	36584	-----
11	-	----	--	28911	28911	------		43440

COMPANY SIZE	TOTAL INCUMBENTS	NO. COMPANIES REPORTING	AVERAGE SALARY	NO. OF COMPANIES REPORTING POSITION EXEMPT	REPORTING POSITION NON-EXEMPT
1-500 EMPLOYEES	7	3	31936	2	1
501-999 EMPLOYEES	3	1	42447	---	1
1000 & OVER EMPLOYEES	4	2	34164	2	---
ALL COMPANIES	14	6	34825	4	2

Exhibit 9-6

Industry-Specific Compensation Survey B

From the *1991 Chamber Surveys*, "Savings Bank and Savings and Loan Association Salaries" © 1991, New York Chamber of Commerce Educational Foundation, Inc.

TITLE		SALARY RANGE	AVERAGE
III. ACCOUNTING/CONTROL FINANCIAL ADMINISTRATION			
Controller...................... VP........................		$80-130K	$ 98K
Assistant.................... AVP......................		$55- 75K	$ 65K
Accountant................................		$45- 60K	$ 52K
Junior..		$38- 48K	$ 45K
Accounting Clerk.....................		$23- 32K	$ 30K
Auditor........... Chief..............................		$90-125K	$100K
.... VP...........		$55- 75K	$ 62K
Reconciliation Clerk.................................		$20- 30K	$ 25K
IV. OPERATIONS			
Manager - Domestic............................ VP...........		$68- 98K	$ 85K
International...................... VP...........		$77-110K	$ 95K
AVP...........		$62- 75K	$ 70K
Check Processing Manager.................................		$40- 53K	$ 47K
Proof & Transit......................		$18- 26K	$ 25K
D/P Manager...		$50- 85K	$ 72K
Systems Analyst....................		$48- 65K	$ 60K
Systems Controller.................		$45- 65K	$ 58K
Programmer.........................		$38- 62K	$ 50K
Foreign Exchange Operations Manager.................		$48- 65K	$ 55K
Supervisor..........................		$38- 45K	$ 40K
Clerks................................		$24- 32K	$ 30K
Investigations Officer/Supervisor.....................		$35- 42K	$ 38K
Investigators (FS/US$/CIB)............		$25- 35K	$ 30K
L/C Department, Manager/Officer.......................		$40- 60K	$ 55K
Supervisor........................		$30- 38K	$ 35K
Technician.........................		$25- 35K	$ 30K
Issuance/Reimbursement		$22- 28K	$ 25K
Loan Department, Manager...............................		$35- 47K	$ 44K
Supervisor........................		$30- 37K	$ 35K
Staff................................		$22- 28K	$ 26K
Money Market Operations Manager.....................		$42- 55K	$ 50K
Supervisor........................		$35- 42K	$ 38K
Clerks.............................		$22- 30K	$ 28K
P&R Department, Manager/Officer.......................		$45- 60K	$ 55K
Supervisor........................		$35- 45K	$ 40K
Clerks.............................		$25- 30K	$ 28K
Chips Operator...................		$22- 27K	$ 24K
Telecommunications Manager...........................		$40- 54K	$ 48K
Supervisor........................		$25- 30K	$ 28K
Operator.........................		$20- 25K	$ 23K
Swift Operator...................		$20- 25K	$ 24K
Treasury Operations Manager...........................		$62- 75K	$ 70K
Supervisor........................		$32- 45K	$ 39K
Treasury Clerk...................		$25- 35K	$ 28K
Typist (Operations - Any Specialty)........................		$18- 26K	$ 25K

Exhibit 9-7
Sample Salary Levels by Position, Compiled by
Executive Search Firm

TITLE		SALARY RANGE	AVERAGE
VI. ADMINISTRATION			
Human Resources Manager		$70-95K	$78K
	Generalist	$42-55K	$52K
Personnel Recruiter		$30-47K	$42K
	Assistant	$20-30K	$28K
Administrative Assistant		$28-38K	$35K
Secretary	Executive (to General Manager)	$32-38K	$37K
	Bi-lingual (any language)	$28-38K	$36K
	Steno, W/P	$25-32K	$28K
	No Steno	$19-27K	$25K
	Word Processing	$23-28K	$30K
Receptionist	Typing	$19-23K	$21K
	No Typing	$17-21K	$19K
Office Services Manager		$38-50K	$42K
	Assistant	$22-37K	$28K
Mailroom Supervisor		$20-33K	$27K
	Clerk	$17-22K	$20K
	Messenger/Mail Clerk	$16-21K	$18K

Reprinted with the permission of Kling Personnel Associates, New York City.

Exhibit 9-7 (continued)
Sample Salary Levels by Position, Compiled by
Executive Search Firm

dor groups are executive recruiting firms and employment agencies. Exhibits 9-7, and 9-8, provide examples of the kind of information you can get from these two groups. Others sources are systems vendors (especially for technical positions) particularly if you need information from other organizations using the same hardware or software.

Exploring Alternative Sources of Information

Not all information must come from formal printed surveys. Before considering either hiring a consultant or designing one's own questionnaire, explore alternative sources of information that may not be as factual, current (from the standpoint of when the data was actually accumulated), or specific, but may be sufficient for the particular needs of your organization. In fact, Exhibit 9-9 is an example of a periodic survey published in *The Wall Street Journal* that provides economic forecasts which are useful to consider when attempting to determine salary increase budget levels to ensure that increased spending power will not be eroded.

There are newspapers and other public information sources from which you may extract data; this approach is sometimes referred to as going directly

Base Salary as of 4/1/91

Annual Sales (millions $)	<2	2-5	5-10	10-15	15-25	25-40	40-60	60-100+	Total
Average	85	93	119	119	144	153	192	190	138
Median	75	85	110	118	138	150	180	178	130
1st Quartile	47	68	93	100	108	130	146	150	95
3rd Quartile	120	100	135	137	161	168	200	200	163
1990 Average	79	87	112	113	136	142	173	181	130
90-91 % Change	8%	7%	6%	5%	6%	8%	11%	5%	6%

Base Salary as of 4/1/91 Incentive Program

	<2	2-5	5-10	10-15	15-25	25-40	40-60	60-100+	Total
Average	84	91	121	120	139	150	194	186	143
Median	90	85	116	120	130	150	183	180	132
1st Quartile	45	70	95	100	104	130	150	153	100
3rd Quartile	100	98	138	137	160	165	200	200	168
1990 Average	81	86	113	113	133	139	179	171	134
90-91 % Change	4%	6%	7%	6%	5%	8%	8%	9%	7%

Base Salary No Incentive Program

	<2	2-5	5-10	10-15	15-25	25-40	40-60	60-100+	Total
Average	83	94	114	118	149	173	202	207	125
Median	60	85	108	120	137	156	166	170	108
1st Quartile	47	65	89	90	108	125	92	140	85
3rd Quartile	120	100	125	144	175	200	183	300	150
1990 Average	75	90	110	117	138	164	155	226	117
90-91 % Change	11%	4%	4%	1%	8%	5%	30%	-8%	7%

Short Term Incentive

	<2	2-5	5-10	10-15	15-25	25-40	40-60	60-100+	Total
% Eligible	41%	51%	67%	71%	68%	85%	84%	79%	70%
% Paid	27%	78%	68%	79%	73%	83%	76%	70%	74%
Avg. Bonus	38	22	31	40	49	56	60	67	48
1991 Projected Avg.	40	32	29	43	49	64	60	71	53
1991 Projected Median	20	25	20	40	45	50	57	49	40

Total Cash Compensation

	<2	2-5	5-10	10-15	15-25	25-40	40-60	60-100+	Total
Average	98	105	136	146	175	196	229	229	168
Median	90	98	122	145	173	181	218	200	152
1st Quartile	52	79	100	110	136	154	183	175	108
3rd Quartile	120	123	155	170	200	218	260	288	205

Exhibit 9-8
Sample Salaries of Chief Executive Officer/President:
Manufacturing Companies by Company Size

From *Officer Compensation Report*, Phillip L. Farber CCP Consulting editor, Panel Publishers, Inc., New York City, 1992. Reprinted with the permission of Panel Publishers.

(In percent except for the dollar vs. yen)

| | JUNE 1991 SURVEY | | | | | NEW FORECASTS FOR 1992 | | | | | | | | | |
	3-MO. TREASURY BILLS[1] 12/31	30-YR. TREASURY BONDS 12/31	GNP[2] 2nd HALF 1991	CPI[3] 2nd HALF 1991	DLR. vs. YEN 12/31	3-MONTH TREASURY BILLS[1] 6/30	12/31	30-YEAR TREASURY BONDS 6/30	12/31	GDP[2] 1st HALF	2nd HALF	INFLATION RATE[3] 1st HALF	2nd HALF	DOLLAR vs. YEN JUNE	DEC.
Robert Barbera, Lehman Brothers	6.40	8.50	4.2	3.6	140	3.90	5.00	7.10	7.50	3.1	4.3	3.3	3.3	130	135
David Berson, Fannie Mae	6.18	8.65	2.9	3.6	145	3.80	4.70	7.67	7.93	1.6	3.3	3.4	3.7	122	130
Paul Boltz, T. Rowe Price	6.40	8.75	2.6	3.8	145	3.75	4.75	7.50	8.00	1.8	3.0	3.5	4.0	125	135
Philip Braverman, DKB Securities	5.20	7.80	-1.0	3.0	130	2.75	2.50	7.00	6.75	-1.0	1.0	2.5	2.5	125	123
William A. Brown, J.P. Morgan	N.A.	N.A.	N.A.	N.A	N.A.	3.40	3.65	7.15	7.25	-1.5	2.7	2.7	3.0	125	122
Dewey Daane, Vanderbilt Univ.	6.00	8.75	1.6	3.8	133	4.30	4.80	8.00	8.25	0.8	1.4	3.5	4.5	120	125
Robert Dederick, Northern Trust	5.85	8.25	3.5	3.8	140	3.60	4.00	7.20	7.40	1.2	3.1	3.5	3.5	125	125
Kathryn Eickhoff, Eickhoff Econ.	5.50	8.25	1.4	3.9	137	4.00	4.10	7.00	6.80	2.1	2.9	3.5	3.6	125	130
Gail Fosler, Conference Board	5.80	8.30	2.0	4.9	150	4.00	4.00	7.70	8.00	1.3	2.8	3.5	4.0	120	120
Lyle Gramley, Mortg. Bankers Assn.	5.60	8.30	2.3	3.6	140	3.80	4.00	7.30	7.40	1.9	3.0	3.1	2.9	125	128
Maury Harris, PaineWebber Inc.	5.75	8.00	3.3	3.5	140	3.80	4.30	7.30	7.30	2.3	2.8	3.5	3.5	130	135
Richard Hoey, Dreyfus Corp.	5.80	7.90	4.4	3.1	141	3.65	4.25	7.20	7.70	-0.5	4.1	2.5	2.7	125	135
Stuart G. Hoffman, PNC Fin'l Corp.	6.15	8.25	1.5	3.9	144	3.50	4.20	7.40	7.65	1.4	3.2	3.5	3.7	124	130
Edward Hyman, ISI Group Inc.	5.00	7.30	0.0	3.0	145	3.40	3.50	6.80	7.00	0.5	3.0	2.0	2.0	140	140
Saul Hymans, Univ. of Michigan	5.64	8.19	3.0	3.8	136	4.00	4.20	7.20	7.10	2.7	3.5	3.3	3.5	123	123
David Jones, Aubrey G. Lanston	6.00	8.75	3.2	4.4	140	4.00	4.75	7.50	7.75	-0.6	2.0	3.3	3.5	125	130
Jerry Jordan, First Interstate	6.10	8.00	3.4	3.9	155	4.50	5.10	7.70	7.90	3.1	3.2	3.3	3.4	129	135
Samuel Kahan, Fuji Securities	5.75	7.75	2.0	3.3	140	4.00	4.65	7.25	7.75	2.0	3.3	3.0	3.5	130	145
Irwin Kellner, Chemical Banking	6.00	9.00	1.8	2.9	135	4.25	4.75	8.00	8.50	1.6	3.4	2.0	3.0	115	100
Lawrence Kudlow, Bear Stearns	6.30	7.70	2.7	3.5	145	4.15	4.70	7.20	7.70	3.2	3.4	2.6	2.3	135	140
Carol Leisenring, CoreStates Fin'l	5.80	8.00	2.0	3.6	145	4.00	4.90	7.50	7.80	1.2	3.1	2.6	3.0	122	135
Alan Lerner, Bankers Trust Co.	5.55	8.40	3.0	4.5	150	3.75	4.50	7.50	8.10	1.0	4.0	3.5	3.7	130	155
Mickey Levy, CRT Govt. Securities	5.70	8.40	1.3	4.0	144	3.75	4.20	7.25	7.70	0.4	2.0	3.3	3.6	136	146
William Melton, IDS	6.20	8.10	3.2	3.3	132	4.30	5.00	7.80	8.00	2.1	2.8	3.2	3.4	130	133
Lynn Michaelis, Weyerhaeuser Co.	5.50	8.50	1.2	3.1	135	3.50	3.80	7.20	7.00	0.0	3.1	3.0	2.7	125	120
Arnold Moskowitz, Moskowitz Capital	5.25	7.90	2.0	3.3	138	4.10	4.70	7.40	7.60	1.9	3.5	3.1	2.5	136	139
John Mueller, Lehrman Bell	5.60	8.20	4.6	3.5	133	4.02	4.13	7.40	7.31	2.8	2.9	2.4	3.3	124	123
Elliott Platt, Donaldson Lufkin	5.71	8.00	3.0	4.0	138	4.10	4.61	7.80	8.50	1.9	3.0	3.8	4.3	132	140
Donald Ratajczak, Georgia State Univ.	5.95	8.25	3.0	3.7	135	3.88	4.53	7.45	7.70	-0.5	2.8	3.0	4.0	122	128
David Resler, Nomura Securities Int'l	5.80	8.25	1.5	2.8	145	3.50	4.00	7.00	6.80	0.5	2.9	3.2	3.3	123	125
Alan Reynolds, Hudson Institute	6.60	7.80	3.8	3.0	140	4.20	5.00	7.00	7.70	1.4	3.3	2.4	2.8	131	128
Richard Rippe, Prudential Securities	6.00	7.80	2.7	3.8	135	3.85	4.40	7.40	8.00	1.6	3.6	3.6	3.2	120	130
Norman Robertson, Mellon Bank	5.70	8.50	2.8	3.0	143	3.85	4.20	7.50	7.70	1.0	3.2	2.5	3.5	127	132
A. Gary Shilling, Shilling & Co.	5.80	8.70	1.8	2.4	150	3.25	3.00	6.00	5.00	-3.5	1.0	2.0	1.8	160	180
Allen Sinai, Boston Co.	5.92	8.27	2.0	3.6	133	3.75	4.05	6.93	7.10	0.3	2.8	2.6	2.9	117	123
James Smith, Univ. of N.C.	5.48	7.75	2.8	2.8	148	3.55	3.25	6.75	6.25	3.7	3.4	2.6	2.4	143	151
Neal Soss, First Boston Corp.	6.20	8.50	3.0	4.3	145	3.25	3.75	6.99	7.01	-0.3	2.6	3.5	3.0	130	130
Donald Straszheim, Merrill Lynch	5.95	8.65	2.7	3.9	142	3.85	4.35	7.75	7.95	0.7	3.2	3.3	3.6	123	120
Joseph Wahed, Wells Fargo Bank	5.50	8.00	1.5	3.5	140	3.40	3.80	7.20	7.60	1.7	2.8	3.4	4.0	125	123
Raymond Worseck, A.G. Edwards	6.00	8.00	1.3	3.5	140	4.00	4.50	7.25	7.50	1.8	2.8	2.5	3.0	142	138
David Wyss, DRI/McGraw-Hill	6.30	8.70	3.1	3.0	140	3.60	4.60	7.40	7.50	1.5	4.5	3.8	3.6	120	130
Edward Yardeni, C.J. Lawrence	5.50	7.50	2.0	3.5	140	3.50	3.50	7.00	7.00	-0.5	2.0	3.0	2.5	125	135
AVERAGE FORECAST[4]	5.84	8.22	2.4	3.6	141	3.80	4.25	7.30	7.49	1.1	3.0	3.0	3.2	128	132
CLOSING RATES AS OF 12/31/91 [5]	3.93	7.39	N.A.	N.A.	125										

N.A.-Not available. [1]Treasury bill rates are on a bond-equivalent basis. [2]The June 1991 survey included forecasts for inflation-adjusted gross national product, seasonally adjusted annual rate. The 1992 outlook includes forecasts for inflation-adjusted gross domestic product. [3]Consumer price index, annual rate. [4]Averages for the June 1991 survey, published July 5, are for the 40 analysts polled at that time. [5]Government estimates of second-half economic performance and inflation are not yet available.

Exhibit 9-9
A Sampling of Interest-Rate, Economic and Currency Forecasts

to the marketplace. If, for example, you need an immediate answer for what the going rate is for a particular job, refer to any recent source, such as the classified employment advertisements in a local daily newspaper. Granted that some of the ads may include some "puffery," but by looking at the range for the category in question, the results may very well meet your immediate need. Exhibit 9-9 provides another example of information you can obtain from newspapers and other public information sources.

PARTICIPATION OF WAGE AND SALARY PROFESSIONALS IN SURVEYS

As a wage and salary professional, you can participate in two main types of surveys:

- vendor-supported surveys
- organizational surveys

Participating in Vendor-Supported Surveys

In these surveys, the vendor (for example, Hay, KPMG Peat Marwick, New York Chamber of Commerce and Industry), on a periodic basis, solicits participation and offers a free or discounted service in return. There are advantages to these surveys including:

- A price rebate or discount. In exchange for participation in the survey, the vendor may offer fee incentives.
- Resources and experience that are difficult to duplicate internally. These vendors often see this survey as a marketing tool and therefore will put together their best internal resources and do a very professional job.
- A free forum to discuss the results. This gives you the opportunity to meet peers and evaluate the work of the vendor for future reference in the event that he/she ever needs an external resource for wage and salary administration matters.

Participating in Organizational Surveys

The wage and salary professional is the would-be participant instead of the initiator. In these cases, a decision must be made on a case-by-case basis to determine how many surveys can be supported, given the time and interest required for participation. The wage and salary professional should keep in mind, though, that he/she may be approaching these same people at a later date. There is an obvious trade-off to participating in other's surveys: building relationships and obtaining information that may be needed in the process. These are the same selling points used on participants when you are the initiator.

Oftentimes a survey on behalf of an organization is conducted by a third party, usually a consultant. There are real advantages in participating in such a survey, not the least of which is the visibility you receive and the relationship you can begin to cultivate with the consultant.

SUMMARY

Despite changes, technological leaps, and innovations, the salary survey continues to remain an important part of the wage and salary administration program. Mindful of this fact, it is for you to gain experience in participating and conducting surveys. The amount of time involved is well worth the personal and professional satisfaction you will gain from engaging in this activity.

As an added advantage, initiating wage or salary surveys provides the impetus to get your creative juices flowing because. Each survey is original and unique, and the constant change in the marketplace makes the whole exercise all the more worthwhile.

chapter ten _____

HOW PAYROLL AND THE WAGE AND SALARY ADMINISTRATION FUNCTION WORK TOGETHER TO IMPLEMENT PAY DECISIONS

The wage and salary administration function requires the support and assistance of the payroll unit. The two functions are interdependent, because the decisions made by the wage and salary administration unit are implemented by payroll. The best conceived pay plans can be destroyed by an ineffective payroll unit.

The payroll function is frequently the victim of poor communication and often feels like the stepchild of personnel/human resources. In fact, one major discussion occupying increasing attention in human resources circles is whether, when a personnel/human resources function is about to become automated, the system selected should be one that is integrated with payroll. So far, the prevailing argument has been that payroll and human resources should be interdependent and integrated functions, while remaining separate and unique units within the organization. Exhibit 10-1 summarizes the advantages and disadvantages of integrating payroll and personnel/human resources.

WORKING WITH PAYROLL TO MAKE SURE NEW EMPLOYEES ARE PAID ON TIME AND CORRECTLY

Payroll becomes part of the wage and salary administration process when an employee begins work. It is an essential part of the wage and salary function

ADVANTAGES	DISADVANTAGES
Redundancies can be eliminated.	Payroll is a bookkeeping function; personnel/human resources is not.
Only one system needs to be maintained.	Whenever there is integration, personnel/human resources becomes the "stepchild" (or the other way around, depending on your point of view).
Both have similar needs, e.g., database and file management requirements; both heavily utilize calculations.	
	Payroll is transaction oriented; personnel/human resources is relationship driven.
Direct overlaps provide greater controls for headcount and salary expense purposes.	Payroll needs calculation software and personnel/human resources needs database.
Linkage may reduce inefficiencies and promote the concepts of internal customer and consultant.	Separation is better for audit purposes.
Heightened sensitivity may enhance understanding and support on both sides: may be useful for staff development	Needs of each are different; to meet one function's needs is to detract from the other's.

Exhibit 10-1
Integration of Payroll and Personnel/Human
Resources Automated Systems

because of its importance in ensuring that the new hire is paid on time and correctly from the beginning. This simple procedure can be a difficult one for several reasons.

Providing the Information Needed for an Employee to Be Paid

The employee must provide three items that are required by law:

• Social Security number

- I-9 form
- W-4 form

If any of these required items is missing, there can be penalties imposed, and the employer and staff can be held responsible for allowing any payment to be made without the necessary documentation. This can be a touchy issue if the personnel/human resource staff or the line manager wants the employee to start without the necessary paperwork because of the importance of filling the vacancy.

Determining an Employee's Starting Date

In a well-run unit, the personnel/human resource staff will coordinate the needs of the organization with the starting date of the newly hired employee to ensure that the first paycheck is provided as quickly as possible. However, payroll requirements frequently drive the start date. Mondays were often seen as the best day to start because it was best for payroll—that was the start of the pay cycle. It didn't matter that for everyone else including the line manager, Mondays were the worst of all possible times to start. In the best of all circumstances, personnel/human resources and payroll will arrive at a mutually satisfactory starting date. However, your primary concern must be the productivity and efficiency of the organization.

Another factor to consider when determining an employee's start date is motivation. Research studies show that the best days to start work are Thursdays and Fridays because then a certain amount of acclimation has taken place. The new employee has a chance to reflect Saturday and Sunday on his/her new job so that when Monday comes the new employee is ready to start work with the assignments he/she has already been given. The employee won't need a supervisor to show him/her where to sit or what to do. The employee will be paid on time because all the necessary forms will have already been completed. Sometimes employers ask new employees to fill their forms out before they actually start working. This assignment is allowed under the Fair Labor Standards Act (FLSA) without any payment being made, although a few employers have been known to pay the person for this effort.

Benefits professionals and their clerical support are driven by the need to have all the benefits forms completed before employees are released to go to work. Their rationale is realistic: It is hard enough to get the completed forms on the first hours of the first day; they would never get them back if they had to complete the forms at a different time or on their own. Payroll also prefers to have employees fill out the necessary forms before they actually start work. Here the rationale is "if they don't fill out these forms they won't get paid." This may be the ultimate "gotcha"—especially in difficult economic times when the person getting on the payroll is likely to have come on board after a payroll interruption and might be just barely "making it" to his/her first paycheck. Filling out payroll forms on a Monday start date may even be inconvenient for payroll if Monday starts create deadline problems for the payroll function.

Establishing Salary Records

The wage and salary administration unit is responsible for creating a salary record for the new employee. Include in this record address, start date, job title, salary classification, job code, starting salary, and EEO information. Additionally, classify the job as exempt or nonexempt. An example of such a form in a manual HRIS environment is shown in Exhibit 10-2.

Providing all of this data, however, does not actually get the person paid; that responsibility is not included in the wage and salary administration function for dual control and auditing purposes. Provide the following information to the payroll unit so that the salary promised in the offer is converted into real dollars on payday:

- Employee name
- Identification number
- Dapartment
- Wages/salary for pay period frequency (monthly, biweekly, hourly)
- Start date
- Date input was processed onto payroll database.
- Authorization from the wage and salary unit (should not be given until the person actually reports for work on the start date to guard against payments for "no-shows")

Get authorization from payroll to indicate that someone in payroll with authority has approved the transaction. An example of a form used for this purpose is shown in Exhibit 10-3.

Verifying Payroll Records for Accuracy

When the new employee has been added to the payroll roster and the data recorded, the wage and salary administration unit has the responsibility

SALARY CARD

DATE	DEPARTMENT	TITLE	SAL CL	SALARY	IN-CREASE $ %	BI-WEEKLY SALARY	HOURLY RATE	LAST RATING REVIEW	NEXT RATING REVIEW	REMARKS

NAME LAST FIRST M.I. EMPLOYEE NUMBER SOC. SEC. NUMBER HIRE DATE

BIRTH DATE SEX □ M □ F EEO CODE □ H □ B □ A.I. □ AA □ W ADDRESS No. AND STREET CITY STATE ZIP AREA CODE & TEL. No.

Exhibit 10-2
Sample Salary Card, Front

DATE	DEPARTMENT	TITLE	SAL CL	SALARY	IN-CREASE $ %	BI-WEEKLY SALARY	HOURLY RATE	AMOUNT RATING/REVIEW	NEXT RATING/REVIEW	REMARKS

Exhibit 10-2 (continued)
Sample Salary Card, Back

Reprinted with the permission of Panel Publishers from the 1993 edition of *Personnel Recordkeeper* by Matthew J. DeLuca © 1993.

To: Payroll

FROM: HRIS

SUBJECT: New Hires

	NAME	EMPL. NO.	DEPT.	SALARY BIWKLY/MO HRLY	EMPL. DATE	ONLINE EFFECTIVE DATE
Non-Officers: Perm. Full Time: 1.						
2.						
3.						
4.						
5.						
6.						
7.						
Part-Time: 1.						
2.						
Per-Diem: 1.						
2.						
Officers: 1.						
2.						
3.						

Checked & Approved by:

HRIS	Recruiter	Pers. Off.

Exhibit 10-3
Sample Payroll Authorization Form

Reprinted with the permission of Panel Publishers from the 1993 edition of *Personnel Recordkeeper* by Matthew J. DeLuca © 1993.

for monitoring its accuracy. To do so, the information carried on payroll records should be verified to be correct and complete. Even though some information may not seem particularly important, each of the data items are important for the employee they pertain to. In an effort to ensure that no data regarding the new employee is incorrect, always verify the information with the employee and the payroll unit. Refer to Exhibit 10-4 for a schedule of information to be obtained and verified.

WORKING WITH PAYROLL TO PROCESS SALARY ACTIONS

Another impact of the payroll unit may be felt with the processing of salary actions. This is (and should be) a routine procedure but, as with processing the new employee, any change made in a staff member's pay or location must be verified to ensure accuracy and timeliness. Anyone experienced in payroll matters is sensitive to the importance of the function to employees, and you need to be sensitive to it as well. There are three major activities affecting a person's pay while on an organization's payroll: pay increases, transfers, and promotions.

Implementing Pay Increases

Increases are most frequently made available to employees as a result of an annual review process that may occur either on a calendar year or employee anniversary date basis. Many employees live in expectation of this annual event. Informally, rumors circulate and passions and anxiety grow as the moment of the announcement draws close. The first big event is hearing what the increase will be; the second big event is tearing open the first pay statement to see the impact of the increase on take-home pay.

The payroll unit has a major task on its hands whether the organization provides increases on a calendar year basis or whether it follows the employee's anniversary date. Exhibit 10-5 provides a sample salary action form, and Exhibit 10-6 provides a sample form for notification of salary increase.

Calendar date increases

When employees are all given their increases on the same date, payroll has a once-a-year major event to prepare for so that the increases are present

DATA CATEGORY	REASON FOR VERIFICATION
Name	A poorly managed organization may be the problem if a misspelled name appears on the employee's first pay statement. The clock will be ticking to tell if this is an aberration or indicative of system problems; response time to correct the error is a barometer of the system's problems.
Start Date	An undetected error may have repercussions for review and benefit calculation purposes.
Home Address	If this is the only organizational "mailing list," the error may not surface until year-end mailing of W-2 forms.
Social Security Number	Benefit entitlement problems may go undetected until the employee files for benefits.
Annual Salary	May lead to incorrect calculations of individual pay amounts.
Pay Frequency Amount	Will lead to incorrect pay amounts and deductions.
Work Location	Misdirected pay statements will result in missing a payday, particularly if the employee is in another geographical location.
Department	The wrong department will be charged with the pay expense.
Benefit Eligibility Date	The incorrect benefit eligibility date may allocate the employee the wrong benefit or, for the correct benefit, assign an eligibility date that does not correctly reflect the employee's coverage.
Benefit Deduction Date	If the deduction date is incorrect, the employer will either have to ask for the additional sum that is due at a later date or absorb the expense—neither is an attractive alternative.
Overtime Eligibility	Overtime eligibility detemines the basis for making overtime payments based upon the organization's policies and hierarchy.
Exempt/Non-exempt	The exempt/non-exempt determination is determined under FLSA guidelines. If an incorrect status determination is made, the result can be a complaint by the employee to the Bureau of Wages and Standards with a subsequent audit; or an undetected error could surface during a routine audit. Neither is a desirable prospect and raises the question with employees as to the accuracy of their own payments.
EEO Characteristics	EEO characteristics should be verified so that any statistical analysis will be an accurate portrayal of the racial and gender compositions of the workforce. If during a spot audit an error is found in the data, the credibility of the organization will be called into question.
Miscellaneous Information	Data regarding employee (clock) number, emergency information, and business telephone number or extension may also be included.

Exhibit 10-4
Verification of New Employee Data

SALARY ACTION RECOMMENDATION TYPE OF ACTION: ☐ Merit Increases ☐ Promotion Increases ☐ Merit/Prom. Combined	Employee Name					

Current Job Title		Salary Class	FLSA ☐ E ☐ N	MIN. $	MID. $	MAX. $
Proposed Job Title		Salary Class	FLSA ☐ E ☐ N	MIN. $	MID. $	MAX. $

Date of Hire	Date to Current Job	Most Recent Rating and Date	Current Job Performance	Current Attendance	Current Punctuality	Current Overall Rating

Date of Last Increase	Type of Last Increase	Amount of Last Increase $	Current Base Salary $		Current Compa-Ratio $	

		Amount	Percent	Proposed Base Salary	Proposed Compa-Ratio
MERIT INCREASE ▶	$		%		
PROMOTIONAL INCR. ▶	$		%	$	%
COMBINED INCREASE ▶	$		%		

DESCRIPTION OF CURRENT PERFORMANCE AND/OR REASON FOR PROMOTION:

Department	Prepared by: (Supervisor's Name)	Date
APPROVALS	Dept. Manager	Senior Manager	Personnel Department Review For Policy Compliance

Exhibit 10-5
Sample Salary Action Form

Reprinted with the permission of Panel Publishers from the 1993 edition of *Personnel Recordkeeper* by Matthew J. DeLuca © 1993.

NOTIFICATION OF SALARY INCREASE
NAME:
DEPARTMENT:
TITLE:
NEW SALARY:
EFFECTIVE DATE:
AUTHORIZED SIGNATURE

Exhibit 10-6
Sample Notification of Increase From

Reprinted with the permission of Panel Publishers from the 1993 edition of *Personnel Recordkeeper* by Matthew J. DeLuca © 1993.

in the pay statements in a timely and accurate manner. Payroll's task is to try to be of service and to provide on time the pay statements that reflect the new salary levels. In order to accomplish this, it is necessary for the data to be obtained by payroll in sufficient time to be processed and verified. This may be a Herculean task, and many organizations go "down to the wire" in an attempt to meet their deadlines.

Consider the problems that occur if the deadline is missed and the new pay levels do not reflect the salary (wage) increases until after the fact and therefore have to be paid retroactively. The first problem is with the staff members who had been hoping to have that anticipated extra money. Not only will they be disappointed that they will have to wait, but their confidence in the organization will be shaken by the experience—a sad result of an occasion that should be positive for the organization and its staff members.

The second problem is with the payroll unit. They are employees too, so they will be as disappointed as everyone else—if not more so, because they may have additional insight into the reasons for the delay. Payroll employees will have an additional responsibility because they must now resolve the matter by activating the authorized increases and making a retroactive adjustment to correct the discrepancy in pay caused by the lateness of the payment. In addition to the calculation, the payroll unit must consider the impact that the inflated payment (the retroactive portion coupled with the now normally scheduled increase) will have on taxes and other deductions for benefits that are affected by the employee's pay— 401(k) and life insurance premium deductions, for instance.

Anniversary date increases

The second type of salary increase is paid to employees on the anniversary of their hire date. If monthly effective dates are used for salary increases (and they typically are) the payroll unit must meet twelve deadlines each year to ensure that authorized increases are converted into pay each month of the year. This means that there are fewer increases to deal with at one time, but there are twelve opportunities to miss the deadline each and every year.

As with the new employee, payroll has the opportunity to demonstrate the organization's effectiveness to current employees when it comes to the positive practice of including salary increases as soon as they become effective. Doing so accurately and in a timely manner will motivate employees and contribute to the overall effectiveness of the organization.

Processing Transfers

Transfers of employees should be processed in a quick and timely manner by the payroll unit. The problem is that payroll is sometimes the last to know.

A transfer is always a sensitive time for the relocated staff member, because there are certain risks involved and the concept of change can lead to feelings of insecurity.

A fast and effective transfer reflected on the pay statement will not only be appreciated by the transferred employee, who will certainly expect the organization to have his/her pay statement arrive on time, but will also be a signal to the others around him/her that the organization addresses the little details effectively. The organization can increase its credibility with each transfer that occurs.

Processing Promotions

Promotions are another area where it is necessary for you to work with the payroll professional to ensure that the promotion is truly an exciting event. Here again, the promotion should be reflected in the pay statement on the first payday following the effective date of the increase unless the organization has another formal procedure.

As with any other salary increase, any problems with the actual payment will be damaging to the credibility of the organization.

WORKING WITH PAYROLL ON CRITICAL ASPECTS OF THE ROUTINE PAY PERIOD

Working with payroll on issues pertaining to the routine pay period is critical in maintaining an efficient and effective pay program. Following are some of these issues.

Address all employee complaints

Most of the complaints to payroll from employees are about underpayment. Be sensitive to these and all other complaints, even if they seem small or questionable.

Consider the recent case of a major bank that had a pay complaint from one of its employees. It seemed that the employee, in his recalculation of his pay, noticed that he was short one cent each payday. He brought his observation to the attention of both the payroll unit and wage and salary administration.

The first reaction of both payroll and wage and salary administrations was that the claim seemed frivolous. Nonetheless, both the payroll and wage and salary professionals reviewed the documentation and concluded the employee was right. Further investigation within the payroll unit disclosed that someone in systems had created a subprogram to increase his own account by one cent by deducting one cent from several other bank employees. By the time he was caught, he had accumulated almost $20,000, one penny at a time.

Never miss a payday

If there is a routine payday, and the payroll is an exception payroll, care must be given to make the payroll on time at all costs. Any organization that misses a payday has its work cut out for it because of the questions such a situation will raise. No wage and salary administration program will be able to do anything when faced with such a crisis. Mistakes do occur and it is possible for a payday to be missed, but it is far better to avoid the matter in the first place.

Review Pay Frequency on a Regular Basis

Pay frequency is a matter to address that may improve the organization's reputation about pay without putting another dollar in anyone's paycheck. From time to time, payroll and the wage and salary administration units ought to question whether the current pay frequency and payday arrangement is the most appropriate for the organization. Depending on the type of organization and the staff it attracts, the employees may be getting paid once a month, twice a month, biweekly, or weekly. Determine which is most appropriate for your organization.

Paying employees monthly

In the past, executives were expected to budget their personal finances over longer periods in much the same manner that they were to budget their allocations at work. Following this logic, once-a-month paydays were deemed sufficient for them. Lowest-level employees, on the other hand, had weekly paydays because their financial arrangements were considered to be shorter termed. The cash flow depended on the length of the month and the placement of the last working day, the most commonly designated payday. The monthly payday is used less frequently now, as executives see the benefits of more frequent paydays for themselves.

Paying employees semimonthly

The semimonthly payday was introduced as a moderate form of the monthly schedule and is still used frequently. The most popular paydays appear to be the fifteenth and the thirtieth of the month. The problem with this system is that cash flow problems surface twice a month instead of once as in the monthly payday schedule. As a result, undue stress is foisted upon an organization's employees as they calculate the day on which the fifteenth or thirtieth will fall and worry about their cash flow needs until then.

Furthermore, employees commonly prefer to be paid the same day of the week, either every week or every other week because, it is easiest for their planning purposes. It may be helpful to survey the employees if it seems this low-cost effort will be helpful to improve the quality of work life.

Beware though that if the organization decides to change its pay frequency from a monthly or semimonthly format to biweekly or weekly, the employees must be advised of the change long in advance so that they can plan appropriately. The holiday season should be avoided as the time to implement the change because it will add to an already stressful situation for so many people.

Paying employees biweekly

The toughest pay frequency change is from semimonthly to biweekly, because a lot of employees may go into shock when they realize that they will be receiving less pay each payday than before (since the twenty-four pay periods under a semimonthly program is increased to twenty-six biweeklies). It is even tougher to do at the beginning of the year if that is the first payday to reflect any increases in payroll deductions and commencement of FICA (Social Security contributions) for those employees whose pay exceeded the FICA maximum the previous year.

If the organization is on a biweekly basis, in some years, like 1992, will have twenty-seven paydays. Technically if a person is being paid on an annual basis, their annual salary is normally paid out in twenty-six installments. In 1992, however, because of the calendar there is an extra pay period. Some organizations (having been alerted), will divide the annual salary by 27 to determine the biweekly pay rate. There may be a case for this if the employees are all recipients of salary increases on January 1 of that year, but there are many other organizations that, even with calendar year increases, have decided that this is just a quirk of the calendar and will continue to pay their employees as if there were twenty-six pay periods.

Determine the Most Practical Payday

One other question that may be addressed periodically is whether the current day of the week on which payday falls is the most practical and effective. This should not be an opportunity to propose change for the sake of change, but rather to determine what works best for the organization and its employees. A simple factor such as an overcrowded local bank unable to accommodate another Friday payday may influence management to consider moving payday to Thursday, thereby providing a no-cost improvement to the employees' work life.

Determine the Number of Hours in a Workweek

Here the key question is "On what basis are employees paid?" Is it a 40-hour, 37 1/2-hour, or a 35-hour week? Is overtime determined on a daily or weekly basis? Regardless of the findings, eliminate any complicated procedures wherever possible. This low-cost effort will improve the quality of work life in the organization.

Consider this example of a complicated procedure: A well-intentioned company wanted to do its best for its employees and also needed to set high standards to meet its goals. The senior management asked the human resources staff to develop a weekly schedule of hours that would show the employees that it cared for their well-being but at the same time needed their services on a regularly scheduled basis.

The human resources staff developed a policy that they considered innovative. They suggested a 37-1/2 hour workweek of scheduled work and an extra 2 1/2 hours of setup time. An extra half hour of work time each day, consisting of 15 minutes in the morning and 15 minutes at the end of the day, would have to be logged in before overtime would be paid.

In theory it sounded good; in practice it was loaded with problems. First, the first and last 15 minutes was a quickly forgotten procedure. Good employees arrived early to set up and start their day on time. Poor employees did not. Second, supervisors frequently asked staff members to sacrifice 15 minutes of their lunch time. Staff would do it, but when requesting overtime, the supervisor would mention that those 15 minutes should not be entered as overtime because of the 15–15 rule. The employees were angered because they felt the organization was trying to get more work out of them without paying them for it.

Determine Deductions

Payroll may be asked to take at least five types of deductions from employees' paychecks.

Reduction in pay. The worst pay action imposed on an employee is a reduction in pay. This is never an easy decision and one that is difficult for all concerned. For the employee to accept the decision is most difficult of all. Steps should be taken in the wage and salary program to enforce a procedure that any salary decrease requires the affected employee's signature on the salary action form as a guarantee that the employee has been informed of the decrease. No employee should be told of the action by payroll when inquiring about his/her changed pay statement.

Benefits deductions. Care should be taken by the benefits unit to activate deductions when the employee's participation in any plan becomes effective and also to deactivate deductions when plan participation stops. Work with the benefits unit to ensure effective coordination and notification to the employee. Even though this is superficially a benefits issue, any change in pay should be your concern, because the employee may question any change in take-home pay. The fundamental issue here is pay, and you would be well advised to work with the payroll unit to make all managers and supervisors aware of the importance of the pay program and of their contributions to strengthening—or weakening—the credibility of the organization.

Tax changes. Any tax changes that occur to all employees should be explained with a note from either payroll or personnel/human resources. The payroll unit will appreciate the effort because they will immediately notice the reduction in pay inquiry calls.

Garnishments/tax liens. Garnishments are court orders requiring the employer to withhold a portion of an employee's pay and send it to the creditor in payment for a debt. A tax lien is an order to do the same, but the creditor is a governmental entity, usually the Internal Revenue Service.

As with any other pay deduction, the employee must be informed of the action before he/she sees it reflected in his/her paycheck. The personnel/human resources department should establish a policy that will ensure that the affected employee is told before he/she is paid with the garnishment/tax lien deduction present in the pay statement. At the same time, this fact should only be shared with other members of management on a need-to-know basis.

Salary advance deductions. Many organizations have a policy that allows employees a salary advance for specific purposes. The salary advance is frequently used as a management tool to provide staff with a no-cost service. The key to the salary advance is to ensure that a mechanism is in place to keep control over both its use and its payback. Unless the deduction occurs the very next pay period, establish a procedure to ensure that the employee is informed when the advance will be deducted from his/her pay.

Other deductions. The organization and its wage and salary administration unit should be extremely careful about any other deductions from an employee's pay. Not only will it be a cause of concern for the employee affected, but others watching will be concerned for their own pay as well. Before deducting any payments for clothing, lost keys, broken property, or any other matter for which the employer is seeking restitution, the organization ought to seek the advice of counsel.

Optional deductions for payroll savings, U.S. savings bonds, stock purchase plans, or charitable donations (e.g., United Way) should follow the same procedures: Notify the employee in advance of the amount and timing of the deductions he/she has authorized. If appropriate, provide cumulative statements on a periodic basis of amounts deducted to date.

AUDITING PAYROLL TO ENSURE PROPER IMPLEMENTATION OF WAGE AND SALARY ACTIONS

Payroll and wage and salary administration are two separate functions that are interrelated on payday. The decisions made in one area are translated into cash-in-hand in the other. Any audit of wage and salary administration procedures should be done with an eye on the payroll function to compare the output (actual wages and salaries paid) to the input (wage and salary actions taken). The following suggestions will be helpful in building an audit function for the payroll aspects of wage and salary administration.

Perform periodic "face checks." Manage by "wandering around." One of the exercises you can perform when observing units at work is matching names with faces. Outside auditors do this on a spot basis when they conduct their annual review, and it is a good practice for any personnel/human resources professional to perform as well.

Review payroll records regularly. Compare salary action forms and salary cards (or master file if the HRIS environment is automated) with payroll authorization forms to ensure consistency. Regular communication with payroll will identify any discrepancies in payroll records for persons currently on staff.

Match head count. Periodic headcount comparisons should be taken by checking total staff currently active and those on unpaid leave against actual pay statements issued to determine whether there is any discrepancy.

Match dollars. A burdensome but important task is to compare the wage and salary administration's current total estimated base wages and salaries with the actual base figure paid by payroll.

Make sure former employees are off the payroll when they leave the organization. There is one major insurance company that paid a clerk for a full year after the person had resigned: Payroll had continued to send her pay to the branch of her last assignment, and the branch manager had automatically sent her envelope to her home, thinking that "payroll must know what it is doing."

Wage and salary administration should periodically review recent resignations and terminations to ensure that the communication with payroll is timely and complete. Some may argue, as is possible with all the issues raised in this section, that for the most part the items discussed are more payroll than wage and salary administration. However, it is only with the two functions working closely together that the pay program can proceed effectively.

LEGAL ISSUES

There are two major pieces of pay legislation that relate to the interactions of both the wage and salary administration and payroll functions. (For a more detailed discussion of legal issues affecting wage and salary administration, see Chapter 11.)

Fair Labor Standards Act

The Fair Labor Standards Act (FLSA) addresses pay issues in two ways: it establishes the minimum wage and the issue of overtime.

The minimum wage was established by the FLSA and is updated periodically (it started at twenty-five cents per hour in 1938 and had risen to $4.25 per hour by 1991). You must ensure that all pay levels established meet the minimum wage provisions of the FLSA.

The subject of overtime is another matter. When performing job evaluation, make every effort to ensure that exempt (from overtime provisions under the act) and nonexempt determinations are made in a consistent and timely manner. Exhibit 10-7, a sample FLSA exemption test, is a form that may be submitted to line managers and supervisors to assist in this determination.

For its part, payroll ought to monitor overtime sheets in an ongoing dialogue with the wage and salary administration unit to identify problems that might surface from a review of overtime reported. For example, an employee recently promoted to an exempt-level position is no longer eligible for overtime but the time sheets continue to show the overtime that he/she is incurring. Exhibit 10-8 provides a sample weekly overtime hours report, and Exhibit 10-9 provides a sample overtime hours report for weekends and holidays.

Equal Pay Act

The Equal Pay Act is an amendment to the Fair Labor Standards Act and prohibits gender-based wage differentials for work requiring equal skill, effort, and responsibility and which are performed under similar working conditions. Both payroll and wage and salary administration should work together so that there are no differences in payments based on gender differences. For example, are both men and women allowed to take a car service home if they work overtime hours? Are both men and women compensated equally for meal allowances or any other reimbursable expenses that are submitted through payroll?

Name of Staff Member _____

Department _____

Job Title _____

Salary Grade _____

Please respond to each question by checking yes or no in the appropriate box.

Yes　**No**

□　□　1.　Does the staff member customarily and regularly direct the work of two or more staff members, while primarily　managing a section/department?

Yes　**No**

□　□　2.　Does the staff member customarily and regularly exercise discretion and independent judgment in his/her work that is directly related to the management policies or general business operations of the company or its customers?

If you answered yes to questions #1 or #2　　STOP.

If your response was no, answer #3 below.

Yes　**No**

□　□　3.　Does the staff member primarily* do work requiring invention, imagination, or talent in a recognized field of artistic endeavor, or work requiring consistent exercise of discretion and judgment in activities not covered by #2 above?

If #3 is no, check no and STOP.

If #3 is yes, check yes and answer A & B below.

Yes　**No**

□　□　A.　Does the staff member do work primarily* requiring knowledge of an advanced type in a field of science or learning, customarily acquired by a prolonged course of specialized intellectual instruction and study, as distinguished from a general academic education?

Yes　**No**

□　□　B.　Does the staff member do work primarily* concerned with teaching, instructing, or lecturing in the activity of imparting knowledge, and is the staff member employed and engaged in this activity as a teacher by the company?

*Primarily means 50% of the time.

Supervisor's Initials　　　　　Date

_____　　_____

Manager's Initials　　　　　　Date

_____　　_____

Exhibit 10-7
Fair Labor Standards Act Exemption Test

Reprinted with the permission of Panel Publishers from the 1993 edition of *Personnel Recordkeeping* by Matthew J. DeLuca © 1993.

Department _____

Week Ending _____

Minutes are to be entered as a decimal equivalent as shown below:			
08–22 minutes .25	23–37 minutes .50	38–52 minutes .75	53–60 minutes 1.00

Employee Name and Number	OVERTIME HOURS		Total Meal Money	Reason for Overtime
	36–40 Hours Worked Straight Time	Over 40 Hours Worked Time & One-Half		
Grand Total				

Approved by: _____
(Manager)

Exhibit 10-8
Sample Summary Overtime Hours Report

Reprinted with the permission of Panel Publishers from the 1993 edition of *Personnel Recordkeeping* by Matthew J. DeLuca © 1993.

Department _____

Week Ending _____

Minutes are to be entered as a decimal equivalent as shown below:			
08–22 minutes	23–37 minutes	38–52 minutes	53–60 minutes
.25	.50	.75	1.00

Employee Name and Number	Day	In	Out	Less Lunch	Total Hours	Meal Money	Overtime Hours in Decimal Equivalent
	Sat.						
	Sun.						
	Hol.						
	Other						
	Sat.						
	Sun.						
	Hol.						
	Other						
	Sat.						
	Sun.						
	Hol.						
	Other						
	Sat.						
	Sun.						
	Hol.						
	Other						
	Sat.						
	Sun.						
	Hol.						
	Other						
				Grand Total			

Approved By: _____
(Manager)

Exhibit 10-9
Sample Overtime Hours Report: Weekends/Holidays

Reprinted with the permission of Panel Publishers from the 1993 edition of *Personnel Recordkeeping* by Matthew J. DeLuca © 1993.

SUMMARY

Payroll is a unique function and one that is easy to dismiss as important only due to its production aspects. On the other hand, for you, the payroll unit is one whose relationship is worth courting because of the interdependencies involved. In fact, it is difficult to imagine an effective wage and salary administration function without the support, encouragement, and interest of the professional on the payroll side.

Think of the multitude of individual items that constitute the data comprising the payroll of even the smallest organization and one that may pay on an exception basis to boot. (An exception payroll is one where the only entries that must be made for the payroll to be processed are those that represent a change from the last payroll. The only transactions that need to be processed are, for example, a new employee, a termination, a transfer, overtime, or a sick pay docking. This type of pay is in contrast to the type of payroll where all transactions must be initiated for every employee each pay period.)

Consider the myriad of transactions that the payroll professional must perform in an environment where each and every entry must be initiated each pay period. Even with an exception payroll, it is helpful to consider the number of transactions that need to be initiated. Your appreciation of the payroll professional's job will grow as you realize the potential for errors because of the sheer volume of the transactions involved. Consideration for payroll and sensitivity to its relationship to the wage and salary administration function will be time well spent in an effort to be more effective throughout the organization.

chapter eleven _____

COMPLYING WITH THE LAW ON PAY-RELATED ISSUES

The legal aspects of the wage and salary administration function permeate all its activities. Sensitivity to legal aspects of workplace issues should be part of your operational expertise. Anticipate and consider the legal ramifications of any pay-related actions before a final decision is made. At the same time, be mindful that the relevant laws have, in fact, sanctioned certain discriminatory behavior in the workplace as it pertains to work-related performance. You must understand the provisions of the relevant federal, state, and local laws and regulations, in order to anticipate and thus avoid any potential legal action by an employee.

This chapter explains and shows you how to implement the most significant aspects of major federal legislation that impacts the human resources function in general and the wage and salary administration function in particular.

THE CIVIL RIGHTS ACT OF 1991

The Civil Rights Act of 1991 is an attempt by Congress to update the Civil Rights Act of 1964 by strengthening the legal ramifications of discrimination on the basis of sex, religion, race, national origin, or color and by addressing a variety of recent court decisions with some semblance of consistency. Major provisions address the following issues:

- disparate impact
- foreign practices
- race norming
- alternative practices
- motivating factors
- filing charges
- remedies
- retroactivity

Disparate impact

The burden of proof has shifted so that now the employer must show, once a complaint has been filed by an employee, that the disparate impact of the particular employment practice cited in the complaint is required by *business necessity,* that is, "job related for the position in question and consistent with business necessity." Usually the employee who files a complaint will be required to specify the particular business practice that he/she feels has created disparate impact.

Example: A female employee, failing to receive a promotion, files a complaint because the past twenty promotions in the same job category over the past nine months have never included a woman.

Foreign practices

This provision applies Title VII of the Civil Rights Act (as well as the Americans with Disabilities Act) to overseas employment practices by U.S. companies. Under this Act, U.S. citizens working abroad for U.S. companies will be allowed to return to the U.S. to file suit against their employer. The Act also provides that an employer may not be forced to violate the law of the host country in order to be in compliance with the provisions of this Act.

Example: An employee has been relocated back to the United States in spite of his wishes to stay in his overseas post. He files a complaint upon his return citing illegal discrimination on racial grounds against the subsidiary unit where he was assigned overseas.

Race norming

The Civil Rights Act contains a provision which prohibits the adjustment of scores (including different cutoff scores or the alteration of the results of employment-related tests) on the basis of race, religion, sex, or national origin. The practice of *norming* (that is, adjusting the scores of minorities in order to eliminate disparate impact from test results) is used to make referrals from test scores on a *race neutral* basis. *Banding,* by establishing ranges of acceptable scores, or a pass/fail that uses the test for minimum cutoff instead of for selection may be considered permissible. On the other hand, current practice could continue unchanged, regardless of impact, if the employer is able to defend the practice on the basis of business necessity.

Example: A typing test that establishes a minimum of forty words per minute as a minimum cutoff score is permissible under the Act because the 40-words-per-minute standard is applied to all candidates; only if that score is attained will further employment consideration be given. Note that this will not, however, absolve the employer when selection is finally made.

Alternative practices

This aspect of the law addresses previous court decisions which permit the employee filing the complaint to argue against an employment practice where an alternative might have been used instead, even if that practice meets the business necessity test and prevailed in court. This is an area that will certainly be an opportunity for future litigation.

Motivating factors

Under the Act, an employer violates the law if race, sex, religion, or national origin is a *motivating factor* in an employment decision. The employer will be liable for legal expenses and can be subject to an injunction, but can avoid damages by demonstrating that it would have made the same decision notwithstanding the impermissible factor.

Even though the Act has a section which preserves lawful affirmative action, this section poses a threat to affirmative action plans. In this situation, the impact of the law will be felt in any situation (for example, voluntary affirmative action plans and diversity efforts) which encourages race or sex in employment decisions.

Extended filing charges

The Act provides that a seniority system can be challenged either upon its adoption or upon its impact upon an individual—a provision opening up the timing of the filing of a claim.

Remedies

For the first time, jury trials are introduced into employment law to determine liability and compensatory and punitive damages for violations of either this Act or the Americans With Disabilities Act. These damages, however, are remedies for acts of intentional discrimination, not for cases of disparate impact or failure to make a reasonable accommodation where the employer demonstrated good faith.

Retroactivity

There is a question in the courts and at the Equal Employment Opportunity Commission (EEOC) about whether this law will apply to all pending cases as well as to cases involving acts before the Act became effective. Although litigation is expected over this question, the EEOC has taken the position that the law should be applied prospectively.

For you to be effective in the shadow of this law will be a challenge of such magnitude to be exceeded only by the challenges posed by the ADA.

THE AMERICANS WITH DISABILITIES ACT

The Americans With Disabilities Act (ADA) makes it illegal to discriminate toward individuals with disabilities in terms of public accommodation as well in their roles as customers and employees. This law is the most radical piece of legislation to reach the workplace since the Civil Rights Act of 1964 and may even surpass it in terms of impact.

The two sections that affect the workplace are Titles I and V. Title I is the section that addresses the employment issue. The ADA makes it illegal to discriminate against a qualified individual with a disability in employment and imposes an obligation for employers to make "reasonable accommodation" for the disability unless doing so would cause "undue hardship." Title V is an umbrella title, and one of its provisions makes illegal any retaliation against individuals who exercise their rights under the ADA. This title also includes a provision that amends the federal Rehabilitation Act of 1973 to exclude current users of illegal drugs from its protection.

Employers covered under ADA

The employment provisions of the ADA became effective July 26, 1992, two years from the date the act was signed into law, for employers with twenty-five or more employees. Employers with at least fifteen but fewer than twenty-five employees have until July 26, 1994 to take the steps required for compliance.

Defining the Term Disabled

The ADA defines a disabled person in terms comparable to the Rehabilitation Act of 1973, namely, as one who has

"a physical or mental impairment that substantially limits one or more of the major life activities of such individuals; a record of such impairment; or being regarded as having such an impairment."

Under EEOC regulations, a physical or mental impairment includes any physiological disorder or condition, cosmetic disfigurement, or anatomical loss affecting one or more of several body systems, or any mental or psychological disorder. Conditions not considered impairments include environmental, cultural, or economic disadvantages such as poverty or lack of education; a prison record; or traits such as a quick temper or poor judgment (that is, those traits that are not symptoms of a mental or physical disorder.) Similarly, physical characteristics such as hair or eye color, pregnancy, and obesity are not considered impairments.

An impairment must, by definition, "substantially limit" an individual in his/her ability to perform a major life activity that an average person can perform. Major life activities are those basic activities that include caring for oneself, ability to perform manual tasks, walking, sitting, standing, lifting, reaching, seeing, hearing, speaking, breathing, learning, and working.

Temporary or nonchronic impairments such as broken bones, sprains, concussions, appendicitis, and influenza, are not considered substantial limitations on major life activities and are therefore not generally considered disabilities protected by the ADA.

To determine whether a person is substantially limited in a major life activity by an impairment, the EEOC will consider the nature and severity of the impairment, the duration or expected duration of the impairment, and the permanent or long-term impact of, or resulting from, the impairment.

If an individual can show that an employer made an employment decision because of a perception of disability based on myth, fear, or stereotype, the individual will be protected as one who is "regarded as" having a disability.

In the case of disabilities resulting from spinal cord injuries, there are several stages of injury and there are increasing levels of accommodation that are possible and required in order to accommodate the person with the disability.

Major ADA Terms to Keep in Mind

Major terms you need to understand with respect to the ADA are:

- qualified individuals
- essential functions
- reasonable accommodation
- undue hardship

Qualified individuals

The ADA protects only the "qualified" individual with one or more disabilities. A person is not entitled to protection by the ADA simply by being disabled according to its definition. Qualification is a two-step process. First you must determine whether the individual satisfies the prerequisites for the position (for example, technical skills, driver's license). If so, then you must determine what, if anything, the employer must do so that the qualified individual can perform the essential functions of the position with reasonable accommodation that will not result in undue hardship to the employer.

Essential functions

The regulations and interpretive guidelines include specific factors to be considered in determining the essential functions of the position. Some of these factors are:

- The position exists to perform the function.

- There is a limited number of employees available among whom the performance of the job function can be distributed.
- The function is so highly specialized that the person is hired for his/her expertise or ability to perform the particular function.

Factors that provide evidence that these functions are, in fact, essential include:

- The employer's judgment of which functions are essential.
- Written job descriptions prepared before advertising or interviewing applicants.
- The amount of time spent on the job performing the function.
- The consequences of not requiring the incumbent to perform the function.
- The terms of a collective bargaining agreement.
- The current work experience of past incumbents in the job.

Review job descriptions to consider inclusion of those functions considered essential. Keep in mind the EEOC's statement in the guidelines that "inquiry into 'essential functions' is not intended to second-guess an employer's business judgment with regard to production standards."

Reasonable accommodation

Determinations of what constitutes reasonable accommodation must be made on a case-by-case basis. The EEOC highlights three categories of reasonable accommodation:

- Accommodations that are required to ensure equal opportunity in the application process.
- Accommodations that enable the employer's employees with disabilities to perform the essential functions of the position held or desired.
- Accommodations that enable the employer's employees with disabilities to enjoy equal benefits and privileges of employment which are enjoyed by employees without disabilities.

Examples of reasonable accommodation contained in the ADA are:

- Making facilities accessible.

- Restructuring jobs.
- Reassignment to a vacant position.
- Modifying work schedules.
- Acquisition/modification of equipment or devices.
- Changing examinations, training materials, or policies.
- Providing readers or interpreters.

The EEOC suggests a four-step process to determine the appropriate reasonable accommodation:

1. Analyze the job and determine its purpose and essential functions.
2. Consult with the individual with a disability to determine the precise job-related limitations and how those limitations could be overcome with a reasonable accommodation.
3. In consultation with the individual to be accommodated, identify potential accommodations and assess the effectiveness of each.
4. Consider the preference of the individual to be accommodated and select and implement the accommodations that are the most appropriate for the employee and the employer.

Before an employer is required to provide an accommodation, the employee or applicant must inform the employer that an accommodation is needed. Where the need for an accommodation isn't obvious, the employer may ask for proof that one is necessary. While an employer must consider what the employee or applicant prefers as an accommodation, the employer has the right to choose a less expensive accommodation.

Undue hardship

The ADA does not require the employer to make a reasonable accommodation to a qualified individual if the accommodation would "impose an undue hardship to the operation of the business." Just as with reasonable accommodation, determination of what constitutes undue hardship must be made on a case-by-case basis. The law and regulations define undue hardship as anything involving significant difficulty or expense in, or resulting from, the provision of the accommodation and includes any accommodation that would be unduly costly, extensive, substantial, disruptive, or would fundamentally alter the nature or operation of the business.

A determination of what constitutes undue hardship must be made by considering a number of factors, such as:

- The nature and cost of the accommodation needed.
- The overall financial resources of the facility or facilities involved in providing the accommodation, the number of persons working at the facility, and the effect on expenses or resources or the operation of the facility.
- The overall financial resources of the employer, the overall size of the company, and the number, type, and location of its facilities.
- The type of operation or operations of the employer, including the composition, structure, and functions of the workforce of such employer; the geographic separateness and administrative or fiscal relationship of the facility or facility in question to the employer.

The ADA permits the finder of facts to look at the resources of an entire corporation, not just the location involved in the employment decision. Finally, if the disabled candidate obtains outside financing for the accommodation, the provision of the accommodation cannot be claimed as undue hardship by the employer.

FAIR LABOR STANDARDS ACT OF 1938

The Fair Labor Standards Act (FLSA), as amended, is the basic law that addresses pay practices in the workplace and has been in force for more than fifty years. It addresses five major issues:

- minimum wage
- overtime pay
- equal pay (the Equal Pay Act of 1963 is actually an amendment to the Fair Labor Standards Act.)
- recordkeeping requirements
- child labor

The FLSA applies to all employers engaged in interstate commerce.

Minimum wage

The FLSA's minimum wage provisions establish a floor on the amount of base pay an employer may offer to an employee. When the FLSA became effective, the minimum wage was set at $.25 per hour. In 1992, it was $4.25, and several states have raised it higher, thereby taking the initiative away from the federal government. Tips exceeding $30 per month and other "payments," such as the value of a room, board, or other facilities, under certain circumstances, may be considered part of wages when calculating wages paid for minimum wage purposes.

"Working time" is the time for which an employee is entitled to compensation under the FLSA and includes all the time during which the covered employee is required to be on duty on the employer's premises or at a prescribed workplace.

Overtime pay

The overtime provisions define the length of the workweek and specify the amount to be paid for all hours in excess of the normal workweek to be at a rate of 150 percent of base pay. Here it is specified that the workweek is defined as a period of 168 hours during seven consecutive 24-hour periods, with the right retained by the employer to determine the day and hour when the workweek commences.

Overtime pay commences at the completion of the fortieth hour. Overtime pay must be based on the 40-hour workweek (one exception is given to hospitals, which may set up 14-day periods and pay overtime for all hours worked in excess of 80), and compensatory time is not allowed even if the employee prefers it. If an employer put its staff on a week shorter than forty hours, the employer could choose whether to pay overtime for work performed in excess of the normal workweek. Once the employee worked more than forty hours, that person would be entitled to the same time and one half (150 percent) of base pay that he/she would have been entitled to if the workweek was a routinely scheduled 40-hour workweek.

Overtime pay is required by law to those employees determined to be included under the provisions of the law. They are called nonexempt since they are not exempted from its overtime provisions (and therefore must be paid for overtime). All other employees are considered exempt from the provisions of the FLSA, and whether they get paid for overtime is a voluntary decision to be made by the employer.

The FLSA specifies employees, by category, which are to be considered exempt; everyone else is entitled to receive overtime pay. Currently all persons earning less than $13,000 base pay annually are entitled to receive overtime pay regardless of their titles or responsibilities. For example, a major restaurant chain was required to provide overtime payments to its management trainees; although their responsibilities could justify exempt status, their salaries fell below $13,000. There are four categories of exemptions:

- executive
- administrative
- professional
- "outside salesperson"

Once the threshold of $13,000 is reached or surpassed, the burden is on the employer to determine who is and who isn't required to be paid for overtime worked. Guidelines to perform an eligibility test have been promised since the FLSA's introduction and are still coming, so it is indeed difficult to perform a test on each employee. A sample test is provided (see Exhibit 10-7) to determine whether an employee is performing on an exempt level.

Recordkeeping

The FLSA's recordkeeping provisions require an employer to retain the following records regarding each of its employees including:

- name, address, occupation, and gender
- day and hour workweek starts
- total base daily or weekly pay
- total hours worked each workday and each workweek
- hourly pay rate those weeks that overtime is incurred
- total overtime pay by workweek
- wage deductions and additions
- total wages each pay period
- dates of payment and pay period
- special arrangements for tip calculations, room and/or board, and any other arrangements counted as pay

Child labor

The last section of the Act restricts the use of child labor to certain age groups, depending on the type of employment and the degree of hazard unique to the job in question. In addition to prohibiting the shipment of goods produced in an establishment "in or about which oppressive child labor was employed within thirty days prior to the removal of such goods from the producing establishment," the FLSA forbids employing children at ages below those set by the statute or "pertinent regulations for various types of occupations, unless otherwise exempt."

THE EQUAL PAY ACT OF 1963

The Equal Pay Act of 1963 prohibits wage differentials based on gender between men and women employed in the same establishment when they have jobs requiring equal skill, effort, and responsibility, and that are performed under similar working conditions. Employers found to be in violation may not lower pay to correct the violation. There are no exempt employees under the Act.

Comparable worth is not a factor under the provisions of this act. The employer is justified in paying employees different rates if tasks requiring similar effort result in significantly different economic values to the employer.

TITLE VII OF THE CIVIL RIGHTS ACT OF 1964, AS AMENDED

The Civil Rights Act of 1964 is actually the third civil rights law passed in the United States. It was enacted to accomplish what the first and second Civil Rights Acts, passed almost one hundred years earlier, had failed to do.

Title VII of the Civil Rights Act of 1964 forbids discrimination in all areas of the employer–employee relationship when based on race, color, sex, religion, or national origin. Its purpose is to require the removal of artificial, arbitrary, and unnecessary barriers to employment when such impediments operate insidiously to discriminate against individuals on the basis of racial or other impermissible classifications. What makes this law difficult for employers is that the burden of proof rests with the employer. Employees have 180 days after the occurrence of the discriminatory act to file a charge. If within the jurisdiction of a state or locality with its own anti-discrimination law and enforcement agency, the charge must be filed within 300 days after the alleged discriminatory practice occurred (unless the charge has been terminated and then the charge must be filed within thirty days after notification).

The plaintiff in Title VII cases is the employee, and the Supreme Court has ruled that attorney's fees are to be awarded to the prevailing plaintiff in all but "very unusual" cases. Punitive damage awards are generally not available under Title VII, because back pay is considered equitable and compensatory.

The EEOC is charged with the Act's administration and enforcement.

Employers Covered Under Title VII

Every employer "engaged in an industry affecting commerce" falls under the jurisdiction of Title VII if he/she has fifteen or more employees "who have been employed for each working day in each of twenty or more calendar weeks in the current or preceding calendar year."

Title VII provides that it is an unlawful employment practice for an employer to

> "Fail or refuse to hire or to discharge any individual with respect to his or her compensation, terms, conditions, or privileges of employment, because of such individual's race, color, religion, sex, or national origin; or limit, segregate, or classify his or her employees or applicants for employment in any way which would deprive or tend to deprive any individual of employment opportunities or otherwise adversely affect his or her status as an employee, because of such individual's race, color, religion, sex, or national origin."

An employer violates Title VII if he/she discriminates against any employee with respect to wages or benefits because of such employee's race, color, religion, gender, or national origin. For example, it is a violation of Title VII for an employer to pay nonwhite employees of any color less than white employees for work requiring substantially equal skill and responsibility.

On the other hand, an employer is permitted under Title VII to apply different standards of compensation or different terms, conditions, or privileges of employment if he/she is engaging a bona fide performance-based or seniority system, if such differences are not the result of an intention to discriminate against persons protected by the Act.

Employers are required to maintain a working environment free of racial, sex, religious, or ethnic harassment.

Reverse discrimination

Title VII was designed to eliminate all discrimination in employment because of race, color, gender, religion, or national origin. Judicial decisions have introduced the term "reverse discrimination" to address the policy or practice that seems to favor or prefer females or minorities over males or nonminorities. Lawsuits concerned with reverse discrimination have attacked affirmative action policies (the concept of affirmative action is not part of this act) because they in some way provide preferential treatment to females and people of color. The Supreme Court has held that employers and unions in the private sector may voluntarily take affirmative action "to eliminate manifest racial imbalances in traditionally segregated job categories" without violating Title VII.

Comparable worth

Comparable worth may be defined as requiring equal pay for males and females doing dissimilar but comparable work. At first glance it may seem that this issue should be discussed under the discussion of the Equal Pay Act, but that law requires equal pay for similar work and the issue here is equal pay for dissimilar work.

Occasionally, "comparable worth" lawsuits are pursued under Title VII of the Civil Rights Act of 1964. They have generally not been successful, with one major exception: *Gunther* v. *County of Washington,* which was permitted to be pursued under Title VII of the Civil Rights Act of 1964. The courts have narrowly construed the Act's applicability, generally holding it is not up to the courts to evaluate the worth of jobs.

PREGNANCY DISCRIMINATION ACT OF 1978

The Pregnancy Discrimination Act, an amendment to the Civil Rights Act of 1964, requires that women employees "affected by pregnancy, childbirth, or related medical conditions" will be treated the same as other employees for all employment-related purposes. An employer may not discriminate against pregnant employees in providing disability and medical benefits.

THE AGE DISCRIMINATION IN EMPLOYMENT ACT OF 1967

The Age Discrimination in Employment Act of 1967 (ADEA) was enacted with the purpose of promoting employment of older persons (age 40 and up) based on their ability rather than age and prohibiting arbitrary age discrimination in employment. The ADEA makes it unlawful for an employer to:

> "Fail or refuse to hire or to discharge any individual or otherwise discriminate against any individual with respect to his or her compensation, terms, conditions, or privileges of employment because of such individual's age; limit, segregate, or classify his/her employees in any way which would deprive or tend to deprive any individual of employment opportunities or otherwise adversely affect the status of the employee because of age; and reduce the wage rate of any other employee or employees in order to comply with the Act."

The ADEA is enforced through the prescribed procedures available under the Fair Labor Standards Act, not through Title VII.

An exception of particular interest to wage and salary professionals is one that allows employers to adopt a bona fide employee benefit plan which provides lower benefits to older employees "as long as such a plan is not a subterfuge to evade the purposes of the Act." Such a plan, to fall within the employee benefit plan exception, must be of the type or similar to the bona fide plans prescribed in the statute (retirement plans, pension plans, or insurance plans) and must be justified by age-related cost considerations. Moreover the Tax Equity and Fiscal Responsibility Act of 1982 requires employers to provide employees between the ages of 65 and 70 and their dependents with the same group health plan benefits as employees under age 65.

"Bona fide executives" are exempt from the ADEA if they have been employed in an executive or high-level policy-making position for the two-year period immediately preceding his/her retirement, must be entitled to an immediate nonforfeitable annual retirement of at least $44,000 (exclusive of the employee's own contributions or contributions of other employees or social security), and must be between 65 and 69 years of age.

Prohibitions against age discrimination do not apply if the employee is disciplined or discharged for cause, namely poor performance. This does not make the employer immune from charges of discrimination, however, and of late the most common source of illegal discrimination charges has been male white employees who have been forced to take "voluntary retirement."

THE TAX REFORM ACT OF 1986

The Tax Reform Act of 1986 (TEFRA) sets periodic annual limits on the amount of tax-exempt deferred contributions employees can make to a deferred pay plan. TEFRA also put into force provisions to reduce the disparity between benefits provided to highly compensated employees and to all other employees. This law also limits individual contributions to Individual Retirement Accounts (IRA) for employees eligible to participate in corporate-sponsored pension funds.

EXECUTIVE ORDER 11246

Executive Order 11246 specifically prohibits job discrimination based on race, color, religion, sex, and national origin by all federal government contractors and subcontractors who have contracts in excess of $10,000. The Order somewhat parallels the obligations imposed upon private sector employers who fall under the jurisdiction of Title VII of the Civil Rights Act of 1964. Nonconstruction contractors and subcontractors, with federal contracts or subcontracts in excess of $50,000, must develop and maintain written affirmative action programs.

The Secretary of Labor is responsible for the administration of the nondiscriminatory provisions of Executive Order 11246, but much of the responsibility has been delegated to the Office of Federal Contract Compliance Programs (OFCCP).

THE FAMILY AND MEDICAL LEAVE ACT

One of the first pieces of legislation to be passed by Congress after the 1992 presidential election was the Family and Medical Leave Act of 1993. The law applies to all companies with more than 50 employees within a 75-mile radius and to government agencies as well. It requires that all workers (except "key employees, defined as the highest paid 10%) who are employed by organizations covered by the Act be allowed to take leave for the birth or adoption of a child, for an employee's medical condition, or to care for an ill relative. Any employee who takes the leave is guaranteed health benefits at the same level and cost as current employees, and upon his/her return, must be given back his/her original job or an equivalent position at no reduction in pay.

STATE AND LOCAL LAWS AND REGULATIONS

In addition to the federal legislation, it is important to remember that there may be stringent state and local statutes and regulations. You should become familiar with these statutes to ensure that the organization in its local facilities is in compliance with all the laws at all levels of government.

SUMMARY

The more expert you are in the legal aspects of the function, the more effective you will be in the implementation of the wage and salary administration program.

The body of employment law has expanded significantly since the passage of the Fair Labor Standards Act of 1938. It is the responsibility of the wage and salary professional to stay current, not only with the provisions of all the relevant federal, state, and local laws and regulations, but also to be mindful of recent court decisions.

As radical as the passage of Title VII of the Civil Rights Act of 1964 was, the wage and salary administration function will become even more complicated with the enactment of the Americans With Disabilities Act and the Civil Rights Act of 1991. Only by focusing on the purpose and mission of the organization and considering the fact that it makes good business sense to compensate on business-related lines—that is with a bona fide performance management, pay, and reward system—will the organization be able to concentrate on the matter at hand and be competitive in this complicated marketplace. To do otherwise would be myopic at best, and the litigation that will follow will drain needed organization finances, resources and energy into no-win channels.

The legal aspects of the wage and salary administration function are a clear reminder that the old concept of personnel/human resources as a "people" function just doesn't work anymore. The key is to remember that the personnel/human resource function is an information function. The fact is that for you to function effectively and gain credibility, you must demonstrate your willingness to add value to your activities by bringing relevant insights and information to the decision makers throughout the organization. With the volume of court cases coming to trial and the law being interpreted in new decisions, it is especially important that you keep your knowledge current. Though not an attorney, you will be able to deal with current problems and issues with up-to-date information.

chapter twelve _____

AUTOMATING THE WAGE AND SALARY ADMINISTRATION FUNCTION TO INCREASE EFFICIENCY

With the present environment of "doing more with less," an obvious concern is discovering how to be perceived as being on the cutting edge of this new standard. One obvious way to accomplish that is to determine which tasks can be automated, so that those other tasks requiring a "human" touch can be given the time and attention that they require.

In addition to the issues associated with project management, the issue of change must be addressed. Automation is a totally different way of operating and therefore, no matter how gradual the automation process is, there will probably be a major change in daily routines and methods of operation (the very appearance of the office may change). The dynamics of change must be considered alongside the technical aspects of the automation process.

This chapter will first help you determine whether the wage and salary administration function in your organization should be automated, and then, if you decide to automate, how to successfully carry out the project.

THE ROLE OF THE COMPUTER IN WAGE AND SALARY ADMINISTRATION

The wage and salary unit has traditionally been perceived as a logical location for a computer, because everyone expects that a wage and salary unit's

■ Recordkeeping: 　　　Current 　　　Historical ■ Audit ■ Pro Forma: "What if" Exercises ■ Employee Change Updates ■ Policies and Procedures ■ Redundant Typing ■ Presentation Layouts ■ Electronic Communication ■ W & S Program Evaluation ■ Compliance (including adverse impact) ■ Applicant Tracking: 　　　Competitiveness of Salary for 　　　Entry-Level Employees	■ Budgeting ■ Calculations ■ Salary Surveys ■ Job Descriptions ■ Salary Reviews ■ Tickler File ■ Graphic Displays ■ Performance Appraisals ■ Secrecy and Security ■ Organization Charts ■ Survey Compilations ■ Information Exchange: 　　　Bulletin Boards, 　　　E-mail, Databases ■ Incentive/Bonus Plans 　　　Recordkeeping

Exhibit 12-1
Possible Uses for a Personal Computer in the Wage
and Salary Function

job is to compute. The personal computer is an excellent tool for you, but not solely because of the machine's ability to compute. In fact, the personal computer is most effective in its contribution when the design of the automation process places more emphasis on transactional aspects rather than on computation. Consider Exhibit 12-1 for possible uses for computer assistance in wage and salary administration.

The arrival of the personal computer does not, however, automatically mean a radical improvement in performance. In fact, the personal computer may cause problems. The computer, like any other invention or technological innovation, frequently plants the seeds of its own problems: we expect more from it than it can deliver. Internal staff and vendors alike make promises they cannot keep in an attempt to gain approval for the purchase of machines, software, or systems.

The most egregious error is to allow anyone in the organization to approve the request based on the promise that it will reduce headcount. This is an empty promise that will lead to problems when, after the computer's introduction, the headcount fails to fall. In fact, credibility suffers further as the wage and salary administration staff makes every attempt to incorporate the new system into the unit, while still meeting routine maintenance needs from senior management, line managers, and any other staff members.

When considering automating all or a part of the function, be conservative and specific in terms of what the new system will and will not do. Realize from the start that the new system should eventually increase efficiency, but only after a transition period. Until the uncertainties of the transition period have passed, there will be a greater burden on the staff to accomplish "everything." The staff must continue to provide routine services while training on the new system. Many units run parallel systems (both manual and automated) in order to maintain the quality level of services previously provided and to create the new system. Implementing a new automated system involves balancing the following factors:

- inputting data
- formatting standardized reports
- writing new policies and procedures
- reviewing output
- verifying the integrity of the system
- maintaining a parallel system

ANALYZING YOUR PROGRAM TO DETERMINE THE NEED FOR AN AUTOMATED SYSTEM

If you consider only a few of the possible uses for a personal computer in your wage and salary program, the answer may seem obvious. It becomes a little more difficult to make the decision when you consider what the installation of an automated system includes.

To determine the best system for the needs of your wage and salary program, keep in mind that each organization is unique. The system you choose—whether off-the-shelf or customized, internally or externally developed—should reflect the organization's particular needs.

During the initial stages of deciding whether to automate, you must answer a number of questions that will help you assess your needs. Exhibit 12-2 provides a sample needs analysis worksheet that lists some typical points to consider.

Project _____

Date _____Prepared by _____

Department/Division _____

What is the current financial condition of the organization?	
Is the project affordable at this time?	
How does this request relate to other organizational requests/plans under consideration at this time?	
What are the "wish list" requirements of the project?	
What are the "wish list" desirables of the project?	
To what extent is the rest of the organization automated?	
How does this project relate/interface with the organization's overall system?	
To what extent is personnel/human resources already automated? Systems/Departments? New project compatible?	
What other major personnel/human resources projects are pending?	
Is a complete proposal for the project available for presentation?	

Exhibit 12-2
Sample Needs Analysis Worksheet

Other tips to keep in mind in the earliest stages of this project are:

1. **Focus on the desired results.** By identifying the long-term outputs desired or those required and keeping that focus throughout the project, any system change developed will be a strong, result-driven approach.
2. **Seek approval for the project in increments.** When thinking of winning approval to proceed with the project, the more consideration you give to accomplishing the objective in small "chunks," the easier the task and the less time required to get the approval. Because the amount of change required is less, approval and acceptance are more likely.

3. **Treat new hardware or software like a new baby.** Give as much time and attention to learning about this new arrival as you can. The more you grow to understand it (the computer and the software), the more quickly the relationship will grow. To try to do too much too soon will bring frustration and the demise of credibility. Workshops and tutorials are particularly helpful because of the time they force you to commit to becoming familiar with the new product. With discipline, the time may be better spent by first jumping in and trying to make it work. Take the workshop after familiarity with the product is established and you have questions about its use.

4. **Use this opportunity to build relationships.** Relationship building is an important element of any project. Each project gives staff members the opportunity to work closely with others in a different environment. The relationships that develop while working together will be important team-building blocks in the organization's life. The relationship aspects are so important because the project will end but the attitudes developed as a result of working on the project together will linger.

EIGHT STEPS TO IMPLEMENTING CHANGE

The decision to automate represents change in an important way, and therefore consideration must be given to the change process itself. Just as systems are planned, change can also be planned.

Performing a Gap Analysis

Before proceeding with the decision to go ahead, determine the current readiness of the organization to deal with the change that you are considering. Start by performing a gap analysis to determine what specific differences exist between the current way of operating and the desired way. The difference between the two is called the "gap." Do it personally, in writing, to consider whether there is sufficient difference between the desired state and the current state of operation.

Determine how much of a gap there is, and if the gap indicates a strategic or operational discrepancy that may be considered sufficiently important to pursue.

Creating an Environment Conducive to Change

Once you have determined that a gap exists between current and desired levels of performance, and that the gap could be resolved with the introduction of initial or additional computer technology, set about developing a desire for change in others as well. Consider certain elements from a change perspective up front to determine whether the organization is willing to undertake the process of change at this particular time. This exercise needs to be completed to determine whether this project will have the probability of continuing to its desired successful conclusion.

Resistance to change

Before proceeding it may be helpful to consider what causes resistance to change. If you are sensitive to the reasons for resistance, you will be better able to allay those fears and decrease resistance.

Individual sources of resistance to change emerge from basic human characteristics such as personalities, perceptions, and needs. Following are typical reasons for personal resistance:

- Habits: Employees prefer routine and tasks in familiar environments. Particularly in tumultuous times, there is great comfort in unchanging work situations.

- Security: Introduction of new conditions brings uncertainty. In the course of a project, when change is introduced a transitional state exists until the final changed state is achieved. This transitional state can cause anxiety in employees with high security needs.

- Finances: Uncertain economic times heighten employees' fears regarding job security. Changes at the workplace, particularly automation, imply a threat of reduced labor demand. There is a perception that equates automation with a loss in jobs and a loss of financial security.

- Fear of the unknown: Any change presents uncertainty and potentially threatening circumstances. Regardless of how "bad" conditions are at present, employees prefer the "devil they know" to the untested alternative, the "devil they don't know."

- Perceptions: People depend to a great extent on their perceptions. If change causes concern due to their perception of what is really occurring, it will be difficult to change their perception and thus eliminate their concern.

In addition to individual resistance to change, there is another level of resistance to consider: resistance on the organizational level. Resistance on this level can be caused by the following factors:

- Structural inertia: Organizations have built-in mechanisms to inhibit change and encourage stability. To effect change, it is necessary to sacrifice stability by a willingness to do so, because either the change is worth the risk involved or the change will lead to a better level of organizational stability.

- Limited focus of change: A "too small" change will evaporate and will be nullified by the overall system. A change of any size, to succeed, should be intertwined with the fabric of the organization and eventually be assimilated into the system.

- Group inertia: Even when individuals advocate change, groups have internal senses of stability that must be overcome in order to lead to a permanent, new way of doing things. Once that inertia is overcome, the group stability will work for the change and will instill a new pattern of behavior in the environment in conformity with the change.

- Threat to expertise: Any change in an organization may threaten the expertise of certain groups. These groups will continue to opt for the status quo whenever threatened. If care is taken to identify and address their concern and to show the continued need for their expertise within the new system, there is more likelihood that change will be implemented—if not with their support then at least without their resistance.

- Threat to established power relationships/established resource allocations: Any redistribution of information can lead to new power relationships. Any highly visible change and new allocation of resources will send a message that can threaten the established order. By identifying and analyzing those whose "power base" may be perceived as being threatened by the change, attempts can be made to either garner support for the change or to allay concerns.

To bring about change and then successfully make the change part of the new system, it is important throughout the process to identify appropriate strategies for accomplishing this task. Frequently identified tactics and methods that will enhance the change process are:

- Education/communication: Continue to expand on the open, trusting relationship previously in existence. Tell employees what to expect and why changes are important.

- Participation: If managers and employees feel they are part of the change process, support is easier to obtain.

- Facilitation and support: Reassure employees that all will work out. Share with managers thoughts regarding expected impact on employees and ways to cope with the change.

- Negotiation: Great opportunity for staff members trying to cause the change; opportunity to develop a dependent relationship that will increase credibility for both parties in eyes of all in the organization.

Frequently used methods that will impede the change process are:

- Myopic approaches: Manipulation and coercion never seem to work in the long range. Process is as important as the result: relationships are more important than the transactional victory. Delay project until underhanded or damaging tactics are not needed to implement changes.

- Exclusive ownership: The more that the change is perceived as the "baby" of the originator/leader, the more likely a "we/they" situation will develop. The result will be that "they" will have little interest in adopting the change.

- Internalizing: Internal focus of change may be unaware of the dynamics of other changes occurring at the same time. This "head in the sand" attitude is inflexible to seeing situations as they develop differently as expected, as there is no compensating adjustment in the change process.

Establishing the Change Relationship

In this important step, leadership must be taken by the person who is interested in pursuing the change. He/she must make a conscious decision and provide the willingness to take responsibility for the project, including the decision whether to proceed with the project and stay the course.

Diagnosing the Problems of the Current System

Accurate diagnosis is the key element in determining the need for change. The end product or result should be considered in its current and desired states to determine the gap in performance. Then, by analyzing the system that terminated at that point, with the identification of intermediate steps, processes, and end results, there will be a clear understanding of the steps involved in the process from start to finish.

Examining Alternatives and Goals

Once the current system has been examined and current output or results compared with the desired level of output or results, attention can be turned to specific plans to meet those desired results, including consideration of costs and benefits of various approaches and goals and timetables for implementation.

Implementing Action

After the go-ahead decision has been made and the necessary approvals obtained, the difficult process of implementation commences. It is a difficult time in the lifecycle of the project because so much effort and energy has been spent in the earlier stages. Effective implementation is necessary for the project to go to successful completion, and any letdown during this phase may lead to an unsuccessful conclusion: the same situation that existed before this project started with one big difference—less credibility for the plan's originator.

Generalizing and Stabilizing Change

To successfully complete the process, the change must become part of the organization's new fabric, part of its "stabilized" state. Otherwise, the change will fail to assimilate and will evaporate.

Terminating the Change Relationship and Evaluating the Project

In this final project phase, the new system must be evaluated. If it blends well into the organization's structure, it then becomes a part of the current system and its change aspects are ended. Evaluation of the project is important, and reflecting on the recently completed process can be a valuable learning

Project _____

Date _____ Prepared by _____

Department/Division _____

What aspects of the project were particularly effective?	
What aspects could have been improved?	
What improvements are suggested?	
How could the team composition have been improved?	
Were there any particular strengths in the vendor analysis?	
Were there any weaknesses in the vendor analysis?	
Which organizational resources were particularly helpful?	
Why were those resources helpful?	
Which organizational resources were particularly detrimental?	
Why were these resources detrimental?	

Exhibit 12-3
Sample Project Evaluation Worksheet

experience for you. Exhibit 12-3 is a sample project evaluation worksheet that provides questions to consider when evaluating the change process at completion/termination.

ANALYZING THE IMPACT OF CHANGE ON OTHER UNITS IN THE ORGANIZATION

It is of primary importance when considering change to first define the constituencies (or stakeholders) within the organization that interact with the wage and salary administration unit to determine the impact that any change would have on that relationship. This exercise is a two-part process.

First, a list should be made of all the units with whom the wage and salary administration interacts in the course of its activities at the present time. Exhibit 12-4 is a worksheet that can be used for this analysis. In addition to the relationship, note that there is a section to identify, in the course of that relationship, what end products are distributed by the wage and salary administration unit and what end products are received by the wage and salary administration unit.

Second, perform a force field analysis to determine which of those units will represent supportive forces and which will be constraints in the change that is being considered. Exhibit 12-5 is a worksheet that can be used for that analysis.

Time given to this analysis will be helpful in determining at the start what the likelihood for success will be and the organization's readiness to undertake and accept the proposed change.

HOW TO MANAGE A PROJECT FROM IDEA TO IMPLEMENTATION

A key element to the success of any proposal made to an organization is the ability of the person taking responsibility for the project to see the idea through from concept to reality. In order to see a project through from vague idea to completed result, five basic steps are required.

Brainstorming

Make every effort to discuss your idea with other people who could add valuable input. Persons to include regardless of their personal opinions are other members of the wage and salary staff. Bounce your ideas off of colleagues and prospective users. Some will be supportive while others will be resistant, reacting typically to proposed change. In addition to developing the concepts by working with others in a "sounding board" environment, evaluate supportive and resistant forces so that there will be little chance of surprise later when more is at stake. This simple exercise will help you to recognize the accuracy of the force field analysis. A more effective program will develop as a result.

Establishing parameters

Evaluate both the wage and salary function and business needs to determine the organization's readiness and current ability to change. Determine if

List below the various constituencies/stakeholders that you must deal with to accomplish the project in your area of responsibility:	
INTERNAL	**EXTERNAL**

Exhibit 12-4
Sample Stakeholder Analysis

Complete the following steps to recognize the driving and resisting forces in your attempts to accomplish the changes introduced by the project:

1. Identify an important problem that you currently have in the workplace.

   What are the symptoms of the problem?

2. What is your objective in solving the problem?

3. Looking at your problem as the temporary balance between opposing forces, which forces in the situation will help you to accomplish the objective? Driving forces:

4. Which forces act as a barrier to accomplishing your objective? Resisting forces:

5. Assign a priority to each of the forces listed in Steps 3 and 4.

DRIVING FORCES	RESISTING FORCES
1.	1.
2.	2.
3.	3.
4.	4.
5.	5.

6. Restate each of the resistive forces as an objective:

   Objective 1:
   Objective 2:
   Objective 3:
   Objective 4:
   Objective 5:

Exhibit 12-5
Sample Force Field Analysis

7. Develop an action plan for each objective:

Objective 1:
    Task
    Priority
    Person Responsible
    Target Date

Objective 2:
    Task
    Priority
    Person Responsible
    Target Date

Objective 3:
    Task
    Priority
    Person Responsible
    Target Date

Objective 4:
    Task
    Priority
    Person Responsible
    Target Date

Objective 5:
    Task
    Priority
    Person Responsible
    Target Date

Exhibit 12-5 (continued)
Sample Force Field Analysis

this project is in keeping with the organization's philosophy that it must advance technologically in order to continue to grow.

Compare the expense for this project with other projects under current consideration.

Establishing parameters is also a definitive way to identify details in each of the program elements to draw out the specific requirements, needs, and end products that will result from the project under consideration.

Putting together a project team

Selection of team members depends to a great extent on the nature and scope of the project. If the project is a major automation effort, then team members should include systems staff, personnel/human resources staff (including but not limited to wage and salary administration staff), users from the line, and a vendor representative. For smaller projects, the composition should still be comprised of a technological expert, human resources staff (at least one from outside the wage and salary administration unit), and a representative from the line. There should be sufficient size to allow for open discussion and a variety of opinions. Everyone should be a contributor unless, for other reasons (for example, political expediency), it is necessary to have an observer. Team members should be compatible from a workplace perspective, and the project leader should be held accountable for the composition of the project team.

Analyzing current and future output needs

This two-step process is the real work of the project team. The project needs to be focused; the detailed determination of current and future output needs that are not being effectively (if at all) served by the current environment needs to be established.

A "wish list" should be written, containing a detailed description of the desired state, particularly in light of what the present system lacks. The more that current needs are considered, the more specific suggestions will be identified that will address those needs.

Once the subject of current needs is resolved, then the discussion may turn to anticipated future requirements. The process will be the same with each of the project team members attempting to determine what future needs will have to be met that aren't necessary at this time. Include any aspect of human resources and determine whether those issues will have implications for this module. Even though time consuming, the more that future needs are anticipated, the more likely the system undertaken will be effective in the long run. Even though one of the considerations should be the extent to which the system will allow for modifications and adjustments once it is installed, it is much better to include as many future needs as possible from the start, so that the modifications will be kept to a minimum later on.

The next step is to determine what specifically is desired or required to make the proposed system more effective than the current system. Through brainstorming, desirable outputs should be identified with as much detail as possible. As with the exercise conducted in determining needs, there should be no criticism for ideas presented, but all ideas should be described as concretely as possible.

Determining automation needs and system specifications

Once current and future needs and outputs have been determined, the process turns to identifying what system changes, including automation, will help to meet those needs and outputs. Here the process should turn to addressing whether the system will be designed internally (in-house), externally with the assistance of an outside vendor, or purchased "off-the-shelf."

DESIGNING SYSTEMS INTERNALLY

If the system is to be designed internally, then a written "contract" should be drawn up in memo format to provide all the details that will establish the commitment on the part of each of the major participants and the boundaries of the project.

Drafting the Contract for the Automation Project

Include the following key points when drafting an automation project contract for the unit.

- parameters of the project
- project objectives
- statement of the services being sought
- role of both parties (the sender and the recipient of the memo) in the project

- product to be delivered by recipient of the memo
- support required and expected from the recipient of the memo
- project time line
- promise of confidentiality, wherever and whenever appropriate
- periodic meeting schedule for progress reports and coordination
- request for feedback during the project

It is just as important to draft an agreement when seeking a system totally with internal assistance as with vendors outside. Try to draft something that contains little if any "legalese," because it will damage relationships and harm the project. The purpose of a written agreement should be the same as that when engaging outside parties. A written agreement is an opportunity to ensure from the outset that both parties are in complete agreement on the terms and have agreed to go forward. If legal recourse is of major concern, second or third consideration should be given before going ahead with the project.

DESIGNING SYSTEMS EXTERNALLY

When seeking support and assistance from an outside vendor to design a system specifically for one organization, a "Request for Proposal" (RFP) should be the form used to ensure a certain amount of standardization in the proposals received.

Requesting Proposals from Outside Vendors

Five basic elements should be included in all vendor proposals:

1. **Organization description and statement of objectives.** The RFP should provide an overview of the organization and its personnel/ human resources department. There should also be a detailed description of the current state, if any, of the Human Resources Information System (HRIS) in place and of the parameters of this request.
2. **Instructions for submittal.** This part of the RFP should be a brief but explicit description of the form and content of what is being

requested from the vendor. There should be a request that the vendor respond to the system and vendor requirements in the format provided by the requesting organization.

3. **System requirements.** This is the most important section of the RFP and describes what the system must be able to do. Interfaces, report writers, history files, audit trails, and security are issues of particular importance to any system in wage and salary administration. Vendor financial statements, staff profiles, and samples of screens, reports and training course materials should also be requested, together with prices and fees.

   Include a reference to user documentation to let the vendor know from the start that any relationship established will have a clear understanding regarding documentation.

4. **Vendor requirements.** In this section the vendor is expected to provide details regarding training options, acceptance testing, implementation support, and debugging procedures. The vendor will also supply a list of current customers, with telephone numbers, that are comparable in profile to the organization sending the RFP and the system under consideration.

   Details for off-site training are particularly important to avoid the nasty surprise of finding out, after the contract has been signed, that the closest or sole training site is located halfway across the country. The type of on-site support that the system will require after implementation is equally important. In one case, an unhappy customer realized very soon after installation that the frequency and extent of update bulletins required the services of a consultant, which added $100,000 per year to the system's costs.

5. **Administrative Information.** This section will contain the administrative details, including a nondisclosure request, schedule for the proposal process, staff contact name, location, and telephone number, EEO affirmation, and bidder conference information. A disclaimer regarding any proposal development costs and a statement that they will be the responsibility of the bidder should also be included.

PROCESSING AND SYNTHESIZING THE INFORMATION RECEIVED TO DETERMINE THE FEASIBILITY OF THE PROJECT

After reviewing the research findings determine whether to go forward with the project. This determination will be based on both internal and external considerations. Key elements in the decision-making process include:

- the availability of a product that will meet the organization's needs
- the organization's willingness to commit to the project
- the right timing
- the resources needed to allow the project to go to its successful conclusion and then be assimilated by the system currently in place in the organization
- the ability of the personnel/human resources department to absorb the change
- the effort that this change will take in time and effort

All the work that preceded this exercise makes it difficult to say no, but it is better to cut one's losses here than to continue with a project whose proponents have serious doubts.

Selecting the Appropriate Vendor

Once the decision to proceed has been made, then the next big decision is to select the vendor.

The project team should consider all the vendor proposals submitted and narrow the contenders down to no more than three to invite in for a presentation. Consider also a visit to the facility of the finalist to gain an additional appreciation for the vendor about to be selected (to ensure they are not operating out of a telephone booth). The vendor will consider the visit one more sign of the importance your organization is placing on the project.

Your next step is to establish guidelines and procedures to carry the project through to its desired conclusion. There will be a period of time before the project is implemented that you can use to remove the inefficiencies noted during the needs analysis. This is an opportunity for you to have new forms drafted, data flowcharts designed, procedure manuals revised, and redundancies identified and eliminated. Exhibit 12-6 is a sample project checklist that you can use throughout your work on the project to make sure that you have addressed the most important points and issues.

SELECTING THE APPROPRIATE SYSTEM

When choosing a system, always remember that the selection is not expected to last forever. That thought should provide a glimmer of hope and

DESIGN AND DEVELOPMENT

___Develop detailed project plan (milestones).
___Develop user groups.
___Purchase hardware.
___Develop independent focused computer applications.
___Implement independent applications as ready.
___Modify in-house forms.
___Modify/customize initial systems.
___Establish procedures and guidelines to support system.
___Test system and user acceptance.
___Convert data.
___Train HRIS staff and/or project team.

IMPLEMENTATION

___Implement HR core.
___Train other HR users.
___Make system available to HR functional specialists.
___Refine HR core.
___Establish mainframe-micro link.
___Develop/refine user documentation.
___Conduct field analysis.
___Develop procedures for distributed processing.
___Prepare technical documentation.
___Develop/work on other modules.
___Test system and user acceptance.
___Implement additional modules.
___Maintain/enhance.

Exhibit 12-6
Sample Project Checklist

some optimism, too. The selection is important and should be taken with great care. At the same time, you should acknowledge that if something better comes along or if circumstances change (or as you become more knowledgeable), you might have made a different choice.

Don't be like the business school teacher who upon hearing a presentation touting the eventual obsolescence and demise of the personal computer, ran up to the speaker and said, "I am so glad I heard your presentation today. Before it I had been contemplating purchasing one. Now I think I'd better wait."

Be decisive, do the research, find alternatives, determine whether the commitment to change is worth the effort, and then move ahead. The sooner the commencement of the project, the sooner the opportunities to benefit personally and professionally from the change. You will have longer to grow with the new system and will be more ready to determine when the technology chosen has outlived its usefulness and it is time to go through the process again.

There are several ways to begin the selection process:

Go through junk mail

One way to begin selecting a system is by going through your junk mail. Many advertisers use purchased mailing lists to give visibility to their products. By flipping through these notices, pamphlets, and brochures, you can quickly see what the marketplace is offering at the present time. Take advantage of opportunities to send a postcard for further information.

Read professional magazines and journals

Once a year, *HR,* the magazine of the Society for Human Resource Management, has a list of vendors by software category complete with contact information. *Personnel Journal* and *Human Resource Executive* also display automation vendor products and services prominently in each issue.

Contact professional associations

The following are three national organizations with active chapters in many areas that may be supportive in efforts to identify the systems avenues to pursue and alternatives to consider:

Society for Human Resource Management (SHRM) (703)548-3440

Association of Human Resource Systems Professionals (214)661-3727

American Compensation Association (602)951-9191

Take courses at local colleges and universities

Contact local colleges and universities (if you are not on their mailing lists) to request information regarding courses and seminars that address the issue of automation in the personnel/human resources function. The larger the institution the more difficult it might be to track down the appropriate area that handles these programs.

A catalog from a college or university can serve as an informal personal survey of the resources available. The listing of faculty members can provide valuable contacts for information.

Attend public seminars

Public seminar announcements are another source of information for automation systems. Any programs that mention HRIS in the title may be worth pursuing to determine whether attendance will be beneficial.

SHRM and the other professional associations mentioned previously regularly schedule seminars as do the following:

Cornell University (212)340-2870

New York University (212)998-7215

American Management Association (212)903-8270

Local chapters of the United States Chamber of Commerce (800)638-6582

Speak to customers

Customers of your organization are potential contacts, particularly if they have one or more portions of their personnel/human resources function automated currently or under consideration.

Ask vendors/user groups for input

If the organization already has vendors providing other services, consider their organizations as possible sources for information. If the service provided includes user groups, consider the possibility of networking through the user group to obtain information.

Speak to consultants

Major consultants can also be a source for information. Regardless of the outcome, speaking to consultants expands your network of contacts in the field and builds on the base of your experience. It is a small world, and if the organization is not inclined to retain a consultant for one or more phases of the project, the favorable impression received may well be remembered when the organization is in the market for a consultant.

AUTOMATION DETAILS

There are hardware and software decisions to make as soon as the decision to automate is made. The more care given to this process the more likely the result will be successful and effective. Consider the following issues and proceed with caution as you move forward.

Defining Computer Elements

Regardless of equipment selected, there are five components in any computer system. They are: inputs, storage, control, processing, and outputs.

1. **Inputs** relate to those activities concerned with sending data into the automated system for storage and processing. Consider the following data elements as possible inputs for your automated compensation system:
   - Employee number and/or social security number
   - Employee name (last name, first name, middle initial)
   - Employee category
   - Employee status (active, on leave of absence, separated, retired, deceased, or laid off)
   - Hire date
   - Job family
   - Job position/title
   - Inventory of job descriptions
   - Job evaluation updates
   - Job grade
   - International data elements (if the organization operates in more than one country; include citizenship and pay equalization information)
   - External wage and salary rates

2. **Storage** (memory) addresses the retention of data that is available for processing. Here you must determine the data that will be kept as current and data to be retained as history. For current employees a compensation record from their hire date is essential for any organization with a defined benefit pension plan to determine eligibility date and amount. For all other organizations, the data should be stored in an effort to maintain complete but brief records for each employee. For those employees who have departed, essential information is provided to the pension plan's administrator, more often than not an outside organization. For other records establish a retention schedule with advice from counsel. Lawyers tend to be conservative about record retention.

   In any event, periodically purge current files of separated employees and retain separately. Keeping them on the current files will make the files used on a regular basis larger than they should be.

3. **Control** deals with the sequencing of any processing operation. When dealing with the control function, address the issue of the logical order for data inputs so that outputs provide accurate data as well. For payroll and benefit purposes, current salaries will still be used, so be careful not to update files before the new effective date. Part of the audit process should include periodic determinations of proper sequencing of transactions to ensure accuracy in timing of inputs, processing, and outputs.

4. **Processing** addresses the activity that transforms input into altered data. Here consider the tasks that the computer can perform.

   Redundant typing: Avoid errors by setting up tables that will generate data from the input of key words or numbers. When inputting someone's salary, if instructed to do so, the computer will automatically convert the amount provided into the pay rate and compare the submitted salary level with the minimum and maximum for that grade to ensure compliance with current policy. Inputting job code number will also provide title and determine whether current position and staff levels will authorize the inclusion of that person at that level in the particular organizational unit.

   Calculations: The computer is ideal for computations (hence the name!) and there is no place better to accomplish this function than for compensation activities. Compa-ratios, benefit plans that are tied to pay level, job evaluations and pro forma salary planning (that is, projecting actual salary expenses based on a variety of budget assumptions) will be an invaluable and time-effective opportunity for the compensation unit to perform in a strategic manner.

5. **Outputs** are the result of one or more processing operations and are a separate and distinct function from the processing function. With additional directions, the computer will provide sorted and/or computed data on a monitor or as hard copy. These outputs include the following:

- Audit reports (to insure internal and legal compliance)
- Exception reports
- Pro forma exercises
- Graphic representations
- Arrays of data
- Salary surveys and analysis
- Budget data (including salary planning worksheets)
- Salary/performance appraisal ticklers
- "Turnaround" documents for line managers
- Job evaluation reports
- Job tabulation reports
- Salary increase reports
- Unevaluated or outdated job listing reports
- Exceptions reports
- Scatter-grams

Defining data and information

One other issue that deserves upfront attention is the difference between data and information. *Data* can be defined as unstructured facts. Information is organized data or data that have been given structure. Computers process data, but someone must be responsible for taking that data and organizing it so that the information provided is meaningful to the recipient.

Considering Departmental, Organizational, and Personnel/Human Resources Staff Makeup

Consider the following questions in determining the requirements and expectations of the automated system.

Your staff

Consider the composition of your current staff. What is their threshold for change? Their attitude toward automation?

Can they be counted upon to be an active part of the process?

Do they understand that the new system will entail major changes in the way work is done after implementation as well as during the installation process?

Your requirements

Do you have a clear idea of the purposes you want the automation efforts to accomplish? Describe those purposes.

Identify specific instances of redundancies in work flow, opportunities for errors, and report generation that will offer major positive outcomes from an automated process.

What are your professional acquaintances doing in this area and what have their positive and negative experiences been?

Will you be able to avoid their mistakes and problems?

Re-engineering considerations

What efforts have you taken to ensure that departmental work flow has been addressed with current resources in mind?

Has the department already been conditioned to think in terms of continuous improvement so that each staff member will make contributions to work-flow efficiencies that have been resolved without automation until now?

Organizational resources

What resources are present in the organization so that for the automation process in the pay function you may be able to use hardware, software, and technical advice that already resides within the organization?

Customer (i.e., departmental) demands

What demands do customers make of you that are now difficult to provide and that would be more easily done with an automated system?

Are there other services that you may be able to provide with an automated system that you cannot do at this time?

Are you sure that there is a demand for these services?

How flexible will your customers be during the installation phase?

To what extent will they be willing to wait for current needs to be fulfilled if, during the project phase for whatever reason, you are unable to meet their requests in a timely or accurate manner?

Hardware Alternatives

When systems are considered, hardware is the first item addressed more often than not. That may have been necessary when there were no alternatives to mainframe systems (and usually the environment was already decided before HR's priorities even began to be met). Today, however, hardware should be a secondary consideration; it is wiser to select the software first.

The mainframe computer

Some organizations, particularly the larger ones (more than 2,000 employees), frequently still have their personnel data on the mainframe system. The problems, however, are the same as they were in the 1960s and 1970s, when the mainframe was the only machine with which to automate. This alternative continues to put the layperson (nontechnical member) at the total mercy of the technical experts. The result is usually a product delivered late, and a lot of tolerance for the result as well.

A major problem with a mainframe environment is that the equipment must be shared by several users, and therefore the software and expertise must be shared as well. Ongoing support is always required and since HR never seems to have the ability to demonstrate that its needs are most important, it is usually afforded a subordinate level of support. Additionally, in this environment the computer is "off site," that is, housed in its own facility with controlled temperature and humidity levels. Any person requiring access approaches the computer thorough a terminal. These environmental circumstances add to the mystique surrounding the function, thereby distancing the function from the user. Reduced communication and major compromises are the result.

The midrange (mini) computer

In the late 1970s and early 1980s, Digital Equipment Corporation and IBM both brought to the market powerful computers that were not as big or as expensive as mainframes but more than sufficient for human resource needs. These machines are still with us today, but they suffer from a lot of the same problems as the mainframes, in particular the ongoing requirement for technical support that the layperson cannot begin to comprehend. The result is still an unnecessary dependence on the technical side with very little that can be done without ongoing and expensive technical support.

In this environment the computer is usually "on site," that is, physically situated in the department for which it functions. As with the mainframe, any person requiring access approaches the computer through a terminal.

Personal (micro) computers

In the early 1980s, personal computers began to be accepted as more than toys in the work place. Once that happened, the value of the product continued to grow extremely rapidly. The personal computer's successes led to greater and greater successes that led to the next rounds of (sometimes even exponentially) greater successes. Machine power, storage capacity, and increasingly sophisticated (and user-friendly) software were all interrelated determinants in the acceptance of the personal computer in the workplace as a serious and effective tool. With the increasing sophistication of the personal computer, there are two issues to consider when determining the most appropriate approach to automation. These include the environment and operating system alternatives.

When discussing the environment, we are addressing the type of operation in which the computer will be functioning. The personal computer may be used as a stand-alone piece of equipment. In a stand-alone situation, the computer is a self-contained unit and is the repository for a complete set of software and files. In this situation, the computer is located at or near the person's workstation. In some cases, more than one person will share the same machine. Communication may take place with one or more other computers through a modem, that is, a telecommunications line that transmits data.

The alternative to the stand-alone personal computer is a network arrangement. In this situation, several workstations have access to the same files and software. Each person in the network has access to their own computers, onto which they may download any data from the network to perform separate operations. Any person on the network may, with proper access, input or update data for the system.

There are two kinds of networks. The first is a local area network (LAN) and the second is a wide area network (WAN). In the local area network arrangement, several workstations work with the same data through a "host" computer. The wide area network is an expansion of the network to include a broader section of workstations that utilize the same data through one central processing unit.

In any selection of personal computers, operating system alternatives must be considered. The operating system is the software environment that allows any software to function.

- MS-DOS℠ is the extremely popular operating system developed by Microsoft Corporation (hence the MS). DOS is an acronym for disk operating system. It is a relatively unfriendly system and requires some getting used to.
- Windows is an operating system that works "on top of" DOS and was developed in an effort to get nontechnical computer users to be less intimidated. In this environment a mouse and symbols (icons) allow for an environment that is more user-friendly than the DOS operating system. This system was developed by Microsoft as well.
- Macintosh is the operating system developed for the machine of the same name by the Apple Computer Corporation. It is considered the most friendly operating system and is a serious contender, although it is not as popular as DOS or DOS with Windows.
- UNIX is an operating system that is more popular in Europe and with the scientific community in the U.S.

Software Considerations

When deciding to automate, the computer should be selected *after* selecting the software that you wish to use.

Mini or mainframe arrangements

In a mini or mainframe environment, software selection is even more critical due to the ongoing support and dependence on the developer of the product. If you are considering this strategy, then the steps described for managing change earlier in this chapter should be followed extremely carefully because of the time, resources, and money required in the developmental phase of the project and the organizational commitments required during the installation and implementation phases as well.

Personal computer alternatives

Even though the hallmark of the personal computer is that it is an instrument that will allow the user to be truly independent, software selection should include consideration for the level of support the vendor is able and willing to provide. There are two types of software, custom and off-the-shelf.

- Custom software is any software that has been altered specifically for your use. The problem with custom software for the personal computer is the same problem that users have had with custom software for mini and mainframe computers. Namely, the user is totally dependent upon the developer of the software for as long as you use it. Not only is the decision a risky one, it will also invariably be an expensive one. It will always require dependence on the consultant or developer.
- Off-the-shelf software is any software that is purchased directly from the manufacturer or the distributor and is used "as is," without any alterations. You will, of course, input data, manipulate it, and obtain output in a variety of options that you select, but the software remains essentially unchanged.

Off-the-shelf software may be generic or HR-specific. Word Perfect™ Lotus 1-2-3™, and Paradox™ are examples of available word processing, electronic spreadsheet, and database software. Depending on your requirements, any of the three software packages mentioned above may meet the demands you have from an automated system. If you had to select only one of the three, due to the enormous computational demands of any automated system for the pay function, the spreadsheet software package would generally be the most helpful. At the same time, keep in mind that the improved computational and graphics capabilities of database software are making it a much more viable alternative for the compensation professional than it would have been a few years ago.

HR-specific software saves the user the time and effort to make the software specifically useful for the HR function. Usually the software combines all the functions mentioned above, so that you get the most out of the personal computer. The same software package will, for instance, update files for pay changes, recalculate, provide the tickler for the next review date, and issue form letters congratulating staff members for his/her salary increase. Exhibit 12-7 is a sample of a screen that the purchaser can expect from software of this type.

Software vendors

The following vendors are reliable suppliers of HR-specific software.

Abra Cadabra Software
888 Executive Center Drive W, Suite 300
St. Petersburg, Florida 33702-2402
(813) 525-4400

This organization has the most popular software currently in use through-

```
06/28/93                    Z SYSTEMS INC.              Anderson, Cornelia B
                            EMPLOYEE PROFILE

===================== PERSONAL DATA =========================================

EMPNO: 121

FIRST NAME: Cornelia        MI: B        STREET1: 3534 Lemon Tree Dr.
LAST NAME: Anderson                      STREET2:
NICKNAME: Connie                            CITY: Campbell          ST: CA
SALUTATION:                                  ZIP: 98008      CTRY: USA
SSNO: 136-36-3636      AGE: 40            COUNTY:
BIRTH DATE: 11/11/52                  HOME PHONE: (408)358-1652
SEX: F      ETHNIC ID: H
MARRIED: S       SMOKER:              BUS. PHONE: (408)935-1200    EXT:
DISABLED: N      MILITARY: N
VIET VET: N   DISABLED VET: N          ORIG HIRE: 02/10/89   LAST HIRE: 02/10/89
CITIZEN: USA                         ADJ SEN DATE: 02/10/89       YEARS: 4.4
I-9 VERIF: Y  REVERIFY DATE: 06/04/95  RECRUITER:             SOURCE: WANTAD
VISA TYPE:            EXPIRE:  /  /        UNION: MACH      UNION DATE: 03/10/89

TEAM: RED     PARKNG: FA-15       UNIF: MACHINIST              SIZE:    10.00
```

Exhibit 12-7
Sample HR-Specific Software Screen

From ABRA 2000, reprinted with permission of Abra Cadabra, Inc. St. Petersburg, Florida.

out the United States today, part of the reason is its low price and ease of use. In addition to its "2000" product, the company also offers a payroll interface, attendance monitoring, applicant tracking, headcount control, and training packages.

Computing Management Inc. (CMI)
2346 S. Lynhurst Drive, Suite C101
Indianapolis, Indiana 46241
(317) 247-4485

Slightly more expensive than the Abra products, this software has more attractive screens and a basic graphics capability, but won't do scattergrams. Good technical support from a family atmosphere.

Cyborg Systems, Inc.
2 North Riverside Plaza, Suite 1200
Chicago, Illinois 60606-0899
(312) 930-1003

The HR payroll software offered here is more customized than the two mentioned previously. Here the focus is on service for each client. If your organization requires more support because of its size or uniqueness, and if you don't want to rely on telephone support alone, then you might consider this organization—especially if Chicago is not far away, because training is only available there and in-house.

Spectrum Human Resource Systems Corp.
1625 Broadway, Suite 2800
Denver, Colorado 80202
(800) 334-5660

Regional user conferences, more than 100 built-in reports and pop-up windows support this software. (Training is available in their Denver facilities.)

Automatic Data Processing
One ADP Boulevard
Roseland, New Jersey 07068
(800) 225-5237 ext. 443

The product offered here, PC/Personnel, allows for integration with its payroll service. Initially an awkward software package that required a lot of memory, ongoing improvements have substantially improved its reputation, and its popularity has been growing.

Revelation Technologies
Two Park Avenue
New York, New York 10016
(212) 689-1000

This is a popular software package that allows for relatively easy end-user customization. It contains an English language report writer.

For additional information, *HR Magazine,* the monthly magazine of SHRM, *Personnel Journal,* and *HR Executive* all provide periodic listings of vendors, along with descriptions of their products, prices, and contact information. Demonstration disks are frequently available upon request or for a small fee. One more source for information is the Association of Human Resources Systems Professionals, P.O. Box 801646, Dallas, Texas 75380-1646, (214) 661-3727.

Storage Capacity

One issue that requires serious attention is the storage capacity of the hard drive in the personal computer. Here again, the software to be used should be considered at the same time. More sophisticated and user-friendly software usually requires more disk space. You should be encouraged to get as much capacity as you can, because you can always use more.

Security Considerations

Because access to the personal computer is so easy for anyone, security becomes a crucial consideration for all aspects: input, processing, and output. One advantage of specific software is that the security element is built in as part of the program and most of the programs also have different levels of access.

When security is considered, think also about including a tape drive as a backup for the disks that contain data. Backup is an essential part of any automated environment, and a tape drive expedites the process.

The Outsourcing Alternative

There is one last alternative to consider when determining whether automation will be beneficial for your pay function: a service bureau or outsourcing arrangement. In this situation, you retain the services of an outside party to support your automation needs with software, hardware, and staff. A contract is signed and your needs are met without any additional responsibilities to your staff. The effectiveness of the effort depends on the ability of you and your staff to build a helpful relationship at an effective cost.

SUMMARY

This chapter has attempted to provide you with specific ideas to consider when debating the usefulness of automation. By first considering the process as one of major change, then addressing internal and outside constraints, and, last, identifying specific aspects and details, you will have the opportunity to consider both the broad implications and the specific elements in an effort to determine whether—and how—to proceed.

chapter thirteen ────────────────────

FUTURE OF THE WAGE AND SALARY ADMINISTRATION FUNCTION

The traditional method of paying people by placing a heavy emphasis on guaranteed pay with increases for merit, seniority, or for merely showing up doesn't work anymore—if in fact it ever did. Fortunately there are alternatives. A number of organizations committed to excellence now recognize that paying staff members for performance is not only possible but preferable. You can be on the "cutting edge" by helping your organization implement a successful pay-for-performance program that will create a higher level of efficiency and effectiveness at a reasonable cost.

You need to identify, recognize, and consider a few critical issues that will support a pay-for-performance program.

TOTAL COMPENSATION APPROACH

Total compensation is being touted as an innovative approach, yet it is something that might have been considered all along. The premise is basic.

An organization should consider the total cost of all the elements that comprise the employee's compensation package—indirect aspects (benefits, perks, and incentives) as well as cash payments—and not look solely at the direct pay portions.

This is not a difficult thing to do if the organization's compensation and benefit consultants and vendors (such as the designer and/or administrator of the 401 (k) and the provider of the group health insurance plan, for instance) are asked to participate in the exercise. The first step in determining the total compensation expense is to calculate the total of each employee's payouts and related direct expenses for each compensation category. When all the dollars spent are calculated, including all benefit related expenses, then the employer may consider whether the expenses effectively mirror the values the organization wishes to emphasize in its pursuit of its organizational goals.

Exhibit 13-1 is an example of the compensation mix that may result. (This particular chart was produced by the consultants, Hewitt Associates. For several years now, Hewitt has not only assisted in the analysis but also maintains a database to provide competitor comparisons.)

The point of the exercise in calculating total compensation expense is twofold. First, it ensures that the members of senior management are aware of the elements, in addition to wages and salaries, that comprise the compensation package. Second, it initiates discussion of whether the mix is an appropriate one for the organization. Even if the decision is "yes," much is accomplished by going through this exercise because, instead of just allowing the mix to continue to happen, management is reviewing it and proactively determining whether there is a way to compensate more effectively.

There will be ongoing interest in organizations' desire to send a clear signal to their employees that they wish to pay for performance while making employees share more of the risk. Benefits is one area where this has been true. Employers are now asking their employees to bear a greater portion of the cost of their health insurance premiums, for example. Retirement plans are moving with great frequency from the defined benefit plan (where the employer promises to pay whatever the benefit cost when due) to the defined contribution plan. This is one more opportunity for the employer to ask the employee to share the risk. That message is communicated further as the options for investment selection in these retirement plans must be made by the employee as well.

DIRECT PAY FOR PERFORMANCE

One effort now being frequently made is to alter the base pay portion of the compensation package. Here, variable pay and incentives will continue to

XYZ Corporation

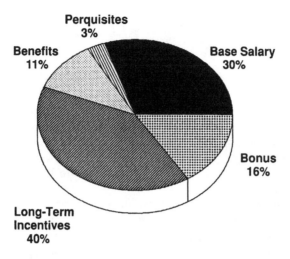

Comparator Group

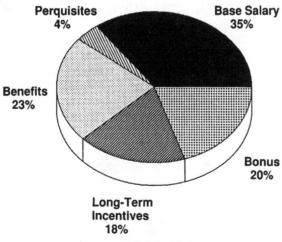

Exhibit 13-1
Compensation Mix*
*Reprinted with permission from Hewitt Associates, Lincolnshire, Illinois.

be popular as part of the organization's effort to send the same consistent message of "pay for performance."

Variable Pay

As far as variable pay is concerned, employers will try to move away from the perception of the guaranteed annual "merit" increase and concentrate on giving increases that will be one-time payments, not annuities. Through this option the organization will accomplish the need to control cost and pay what appears to be a more meaningful incentive because it will be a one-time payment and will cause increases in other elements of the benefits package that are linked to pay.

The real issue here is with implementation. In the past, the merit increase was considered a motivator, particularly because of its security aspects. The problem, though, was not with the concept but with its execution: the merit increases got smaller and smaller because everyone expected and got them.

Incentives

Incentives provide employers with another opportunity to ask employees to share the risk while linking pay to performance. However, effectiveness is often elusive.

In the past, incentive plans have often had lingering problems and this will continue to be true. First, the incentives often elicit behaviors that are not anticipated because the incentive plan was not adequately tested. The "wrong button" was pushed and the result was that employees concentrated on the results for the sake of the incentives but ignored other issues. (New accounts soared, for instance, but customer service suffered because the incentives were directly tied to increases in new customer accounts. Business was great—while it lasted.)

Second, often the organization's incentive plan is just a knock-off of some plan in another organization that may happen to be the market leader. This circumstance calls to mind the old adage, "If stranded on an island, always look to see what the birds eat." This sounds wise, but don't forget to follow the bird to be sure you know what happens to it afterward. There is no substitute for doing research.

Third, incentives are no substitute for good communication. To be effective and perhaps even result in real savings, the staff members affected need to be consulted to determine whether the proposed incentive plan will have the desired effect and whether there are any other suggestions from them. Buy-in to these arrangements makes for a more effective program. Organizations should consider the folly of making no attempt to see if the incentive will "incent" or incense those for whom they are intended.

If organizations consider the strategic aspects of their compensation decisions, there is more likelihood that they will introduce an incentive or other pay plan that will be tied to goals. Such a plan will be properly prepared, compatible with the other elements of the performance management package, and be positioned to deal with these matters on an ongoing basis. The result will be employees who take notice rather than give notice. The links of pay to performance defined by senior management will permeate the organization and will lead to decisions and programs that will be effective for other areas as well.

The alternative is a lose-lose situation. Both the employer and employee will suffer if goals are continuously being missed, if better performers remain unidentified and are lost without notice, and if payout levels don't vary from year to year. Expensive plans that have been around for several years will continue to ignore the question of whether the right performance is being rewarded while poor performers subsidized.

PERFORMANCE MANAGEMENT

One major area for involvement that will provide real opportunity for you is the area of performance management—a simple concept with enormous implications. Performance management can be defined as the comprehensive approach to motivating performance, including performance appraisal, incentives, intrinsic/extrinsic reward opportunities, and disciplinary actions. This is something that will make some ask why this wasn't done sooner; it was just a case of not seeing the forest for the trees.

Performance appraisals that were to accomplish so much were stillborn because they operated in an isolated manner and were given only a cursory opportunity to be a real factor in the life of the organization. In fact, how many companies have their walls—confidential, of course—lined with their superstars destined for senior appointments? Ask if their selections were made on the basis of performance appraisals and a snicker inevitably follows.

Because you are uniquely situated in the area responsible for both pay and performance appraisals, it is just a small step to seize the opportunity to make a real impact in the area of performance management and build a program that will link pay to performance in a permanent way.

CONSIDERATION FOR THE SMALLER ORGANIZATION

The wage and salary professional, regardless of his/her career desires and goals, should take the time and make the effort to share ideas with colleagues from smaller organizations, because the wage and salary issues at those organizations are much more serious. One misstep may lead to the organization's swift and sudden demise.

Smaller organizations lack the structure for sophisticated performance and pay programs, but they also have sound policies and practices that frequently contain elements that will be applicable to your own work situation, regardless of organizational size.

THE CONSULTANT/INTERNAL CUSTOMER SERVICE APPROACH

The wage and salary professional will do well to consider both the consultant aspects and the internal customer service aspects of his/her position. This perspective allows him/her to be more effective by building an organization of stakeholders for the wage and salary administration program. Such an organization will be much more dynamic and effective because there will be a more direct role for employees, who will then more readily see themselves a part of the wage and salary administration program.

LEGAL RAMIFICATIONS

Effective July 26, 1992, for all but the smaller organizations, the Americans With Disabilities Act (ADA) will have an impact on personnel/human resources that is just starting to be felt. As organizations learn to feel their way, they will look to the wage and salary professional for guidance and direction for compliance under the ADA. Job analysis, job evaluations, and job descriptions will have to be examined in a new light, with a new vocabulary of "qualified individuals," "reasonable accommodation," "essential functions," and "undue hardship" brought to the table. Salary actions and promotions will need to be monitored and audited. Performance management will add one more aspect to the process.

SUMMARY

There is much to learn about human behavior and the effect that pay has in motivating performance. With the challenges coming from global competition, changing technology, and the increasing visible legal environment, this is a challenging time for the wage and salary professional. The business environment continues to change at such a rapid pace, and yesterday's solutions will continue to pose challenges in every organization's attempts to meet tomorrows needs. You are uniquely positioned to work through those changes with skill and effectiveness, if you are ready to face the task.

The intellectual curiosity, demonstrated ability and expertise, solid communication skills, and a consultative orientation will prepare you to support the organization's mission while you work to ensure that it is the organization that will pull it all together.

appendix a ———————————

WAGE AND SALARY ADMINISTRATION PROGRAM REVIEW

ORGANIZATIONAL ISSUES:	Yes	No	Comments
What is the organization's mission?			
What is the organizational structure?			
Is there an organization chart?			
Obtain a current copy of the organization chart.			
How old is the chart?			
Date of last reorganization:			
List of job titles			
What is the organization's pay policy?			
Is there a written statement?			
Date of statement:			
Are there incentives?			
Describe.			
Bonuses?			
Describe.			
Benefits?			
Describe.			
Perquisites?			
Describe.			

ORGANIZATIONAL ISSUES: (Continued)	Yes	No	Comments
What is the basis for salary increases?			
What is the basis for promotions?			
For demotions?			
Is there a severance policy?			
Describe.			
What is the basis for periodic salary reviews:			
Calendar?			
Anniversary?			
Are salary increases given on time?			
Is there a performance appraisal system?			
Describe.			
Obtain copy of the form(s).			
Identify and describe.			
What function/position is responsible?			
How long in use?			
What levels participate?			
Where is the documentation kept?			
Is there a review procedure?			
Linked to salary/wage increase?			
Linked to salary/wage decrease?			

ORGANIZATIONAL ISSUES: (Continued)	Yes	No	Comments
What is the organization's attitude towards pay decreases? Demotions?			
Terminations?			
Are there any bonuses, awards, or recognition programs (not identified elsewhere) that employees are eligible for?			
Is there a separate compensation program for part-time employees?			
Describe.			
Has there been an analysis of compensation components?			
Date:			
Obtain copy.			
What is the organization's attitude towards unemployment insurance claims?			
What matters are currently under consideration that might affect wage and salary administration practices (for example, open staff requisitions, outstanding hire offers)?			
Does the organization have a budget?			
Is wage and salary administration part of the budget?			
Is there a staffing budget?			
Obtain a copy of current budget(s)			

ORGANIZATION REPUTATION:	Yes	No	Comments
What does the current staff think of the organization's:			
Pay practices?			
Senior management?			
Middle management?			
Supervisors?			
Nonexempt employees?			
Personnel/human resources department?			
Wage and salary administration function?			
How is the organization's compensation policy viewed by:			
Other personnel/HR professionals?			
Other compensation professionals?			
Other organizations/competition?			
COMMUNICATION:			
What is communicated to employees about the organization's pay policies?			
Do supervisors/managers have a personnel/human resources procedures manual?			
Last revision/update:			
Obtain a current copy.			
Do employees get a handbook?			
Last revision/update:			

COMMUNICATION: (Continued)	Yes	No	Comments
Obtain a current copy.			
Is there a staff orientation?			
What function is responsible?			
What are employees told about the pay program?			
Are offer letters given to job applicants?			
What mention, if any, is made of pay?			
Is there a written sexual harassment policy?			
Obtain a copy.			
Is there a written policy regarding employees with disabilities?			
Obtain a copy.			
Is there a tracking program?			
Are exit interviews conducted?			
Is there an "open-door" policy for employees?			
Is there a formal grievance procedure?			
Describe.			
Is there an active suggestion system?			
Describe.			
Are any employees required to sign a confidentiality agreement?			
Obtain copy.			
For what positions?			
Is there any drug testing?			

COMMUNICATION: (Continued)	Yes	No	Comments
Describe procedure.			
Is there a job posting program?			
Describe.			
DISCRIMINATORY PAY PRACTICES:			
Are there any gender-based titles (for example, hostess, foreman, maintenance man)?			
Are there any positions where all incumbents are solely male?			
Solely female?			
Within positions, are there instances of discriminatory pay practices (for example, are women in a position paid at a lower rate than men)?			
Average age of men in the organization?			
Average age of women in the organization?			
Average length of service for men?			
Average length of service for women?			
COMPLIANCE:			
What issues are currently pending?			
Has the organization ever been audited/investigated by			
Department of Labor?			
Any civil rights agency?			
Have any complaints been filed within last 5 years by employees/former employees?			
Outcome/pending?			

SURVEYS:	Yes	No	Comments
What surveys has the organization initiated during the past year?			
What surveys has the organization participated in during the past year?			
What surveys has the organization purchased during the past year?			
PAYROLL MATTERS: How are employees paid?			
Cash?			
Check?			
Direct Deposit?			
Frequency of payment?			
What is overtime policy?			
What is a "normal" scheduled work week?			
How many hours?			
Are there shift differentials?			
Are there other payments made to employees (meals, uniforms, travel allowances)?			
On what basis?			
What is the procedure for determining FLSA status?			
What is the relationship of payroll to personnel/HR?			
To wage and salary administration?			
What reports are generated by payroll?			
Schedule/frequency?			

AUTOMATION/HRIS:	Yes	No	Comments
Is the unit automated?			
Type of system(s)?			
When automated?			
What functions are automated?			
Online or batch?			
Any proposals currently pending?			
Is it an integrated system (payroll/personnel)?			
If not automated, why?			
What reports are available?			
Schedule/frequency of reports?			
JOB DESCRIPTIONS:			
Are there any currently in place?			
How old are they (months or years)?			
What is their status?			
List each for an inventory.			
Is there one for each person?			
What are they used for:			
Training?			
Recruiting?			
Compensation?			

JOB DESCRIPTIONS: (Continued)	Yes	No	Comments
Performance Appraisal?			
All of the above?			
JOB GRADES:			
Are there job grades?			
List them.			
Is each position graded?			
Date last revision.			
Which were changed?			
Reasons for changes:			
SALARY RANGES:			
Are there ranges?			
List them.			
Is each graded position within the salary range for that position?			
Date of last revision.			
Reason for changes:			

appendix b

WAGE AND SALARY ADMINISTRATION POLICY AND PROCEDURES–DRAFT DOCUMENT

ORGANIZATIONAL POLICY

(Name of organization) provides salaries (wages) that are equitable throughout the organization and are competitive with the salaries (wages) paid by other organizations in our industry.

Or, the organization may choose one of the following policy statements:

Our organization's pay philosophy is to pay employees competitively. Employees earn higher rates of pay primarily through merit increases based on performance appraisals.

* *

The organization's policy is to ensure that all employees are paid a fair salary (wages) for the work they do. Every employee's salary (wage) will be established, reviewed, and adjusted using the same standards. To accomplish this, each position in the organization is assigned a salary (wage) grade and range and appropriate programs have been established.

* *

The (name of organization) pays salaries (wages) which are based upon the nature of the job performed and are competitive with the rates being paid for similar work by other employers in the community.

Each position is evaluated in terms of the knowledge and skill required and the organization's viability. A salary (wage) class is established for each job classification. The salary (wage) class makes it possible to reward an employee as skill and experience are gained on the job, while maintaining a fair relationship among the salary (wage) ranges for different jobs.

The Wage and Salary Administration unit of the Personnel/Human Resources Department continually monitors the conditions of the job market and, when appropriate and necessary, makes recommendations to the Personnel/Human Resources Committee so as to retain the competitiveness of our salary (wage) classes.

For an organization with locations in many geographic areas:

The Organization's Wage and Salary Administration program is designed to provide salaries (wages) which are competitive with those paid in the local community. Staff members' salaries (wages) are directly related to their level of job performance and the amount of skill and responsibility required by their jobs.

ORGANIZATIONAL GUIDELINES

Each position is assigned a salary (wage) grade and range. Salary (wage) grades are based upon a comparison of each position with similar jobs both inside and outside (name of organization). Salary (wage) ranges within the grade are designed to keep compensation levels competitive and to reflect *individual* experience and performance.

The timing and amount of salary increase depend upon:

the salary level of the position held;

the employee's salary within the range; and,

the employee's performance.

SUPERVISORY GUIDELINES

Supervisors should:

• Make sure that each staff member is classified correctly according to job title, job code, and salary (wage) class.

- Notify the staff member of any changes in salary (wage) class.
- Evaluate the performance of each staff member and conduct salary (wage) reviews.
- Consult with the unit manager when new jobs are created or when major changes occur in either a job or the job market.
- Be familiar with the wage and salary administration program so that staff members' questions can be answered.

JOB DESCRIPTIONS

Job descriptions are written by the line manager and reviewed by the wage and salary administration unit. New job descriptions should be written whenever job content or responsibilities change significantly.

Some organizations prefer to add:

Job descriptions for certain jobs the organization has in common with other organizations in the same industry or any other companies are available in the wage and salary administration unit and are broadly worded, general descriptions of the responsibilities of the jobs. If managers wish to write job descriptions for the specific, day-to-day job responsibilities for jobs in their unit, they may get assistance from the wage and salary administration unit.

CHANGES IN JOB DESCRIPTIONS

Supervisors are responsible for promptly consulting the unit manager when new jobs are created or substantial changes in a job occur. The manager should then request that the wage and salary administration unit analyze the new job description and assign an appropriate salary (wage) class. This will ensure that each job description is current and accurately reflects the content and level of the work being performed.

JOB EVALUATION

Using the information provided in the job description, the wage and salary administration unit assigns each job to a salary (wage) grade based upon:

- the complexity of the job,
- how it compares with other jobs within the department and throughout (name of organization), and
- average salaries (wages) paid for similar jobs.

Each of these considerations is covered in a step:

1. Supervisors update job descriptions, write new job descriptions for each job function in the unit, and annually review such descriptions. After updated descriptions are approved by the manager in charge, they are forwarded to the wage and salary administration unit of the personnel (human resources) department with a recommended salary grade. In the course of the annual review (if there is one), it is important that new descriptions be written whenever job content or responsibility has changed significantly.

2. The wage and salary administration unit reviews each job description and evaluates it, comparing it to similar jobs within the organization and, where possible, outside as well. Based on this analysis an appropriate salary (wage) grade is assigned. Since the effort is a joint effort between a department and the wage and salary administration unit, another review may be requested if a department feels any position has been evaluated incorrectly. Although every grade determination should be mutually acceptable, the wage and salary administration unit has final approval authority.

3. To ensure salary levels are competitive, the organization participates in surveys and studies of salaries (wages) paid by other organizations in the same industry as well as by those in other industries. Throughout the year, salaries (wages) paid for specific jobs are carefully analyzed; the overall salary structure of each organization participating in any survey is compared to the organization's. In this manner, the organization's salary (wage) grades remain competitive with those of other employers in similar areas of business.

To ensure that salary levels are competitive, (name of organization) participates in salary (wage) market surveys and studies.

If a line manager believes that the wage and salary unit has evaluated a position incorrectly, a review may be requested. Every grade determination should be acceptable to both the manager and the wage and salary unit. The wage and salary unit however has final approval.

SALARY (WAGE) GRADES

Jobs at (name of organization)—with the exception of top executive jobs—are assigned a salary (wage) grade by the wage and salary administration unit. Salary (wage) grades are determined through a process of job evaluation.

Salary (wage) grades for each job are based on a comparison of each position with others in the organization and with comparable jobs outside the organization.

There are _____ salary grades.

They are grade _____ through grade _____.

If the organization decides it wants it, this statement may be added:

Employees should know the salary (wage) grade of their own job and may know the salary (wage) grade of other jobs for career planning purposes.

SALARY (WAGE) RANGES

Each salary (wage) grade has a salary (wage) range which represents the range of competitive pay rates for positions in that salary grade. Salary ranges are reviewed regularly by the compensation department and adjusted, if appropriate, to assure that they remain competitive. Employees should know the salary range for their job and may have a copy of the organization's current ranges.

Salary ranges consist of a **minimum, midpoint,** and **maximum** salary rate.

Minimum

Employees must be paid at least the minimum of the assigned salary range for their jobs. If an employee's salary is below the minimum rate, he/she should be given an equity increase to raise the salary to the minimum rate. Any exceptions to this policy must be approved in writing by the manager of the compensation department.

Midpoint

Once an employee's salary exceeds the midpoint of the salary range, merit increase percentages are smaller than they are for salaries below the midpoint.

Maximum

Employees whose salary is at or above the maximum of the salary range are not eligible for merit increases. Any exceptions to this policy must be approved by the group head of the employee's organization and by the manager of the compensation department.

Transfers of staff members from one regional area to another are handled as follows:

Staff who transfer to an area with a **higher** range scale may receive a salary (wage) adjustment bringing them to the minimum of the range upon transfer (an equity increase). This does not affect the review date of the staff member.

Salaries (wages) of staff who transfer to an area with a **lower** range scale are not reduced. However, future salary (wages) increases depend on the range in effect in the new area and may, therefore, be limited.

APPROVALS

All job descriptions, job titles, job codes, and salary classes must be agreed upon and approved by the unit manager and wage and salary administration unit before they can be considered effective.

BUDGET MATTERS

Each year a merit increase, headcount, and promotion budget for all employees is set based upon economic and competitive trends in the marketplace. It is communicated to managers by the wage and salary administration unit and is expressed as a percentage of base salaries (wages).

Managers are responsible for operating within their merit increase budget when awarding merit increases for their employees.

In the annual guidelines for merit increase, a range of increase percentages is given for each level of performance. Managers should consider this range of possible percentages when proposing merit increases for employees.

Even within one performance rating, there may be differences in performance and salary (wage) of employees which make different percent increases appropriate. For instance, an employee with a salary that is very low in the range, but who is a strong performer may be given a larger increase than another employee with similar performance but a salary (wage) that is higher in the salary (wage) range.

NEW HIRE SALARIES

The salary (wage) rate of new hires is determined by the hiring manager in coordination with the personnel (human resources) department. Factors that are considered are the applicant's previous experience and pay, the salary (wage) range for the position, and what other employees in similar jobs inside the organization are paid.

Or this may be considered, especially if the organization tends to hire most staff at the entry level:

Starting salaries (wages) of prospective staff members in entry-level jobs such as general clerk, stenographer, etc. are established by the wage and salary administration unit. For most other jobs, the unit manager determines the starting salary (wage) using the following information to guide the decision: the salary (wage) range for the job, salaries (wages) of other staff members who have the same job title and salary (wage) class as the prospective staff member, and qualifications of the individual.

A prospective staff member is usually hired at a salary between the minimum and the midpoint of the salary (wage) range.

SALARY ACTION PROCEDURES: PAY INCREASES, OTHER ADJUSTMENTS, AND DEFERRALS

Annual Salary Review

Each staff member's salary (wage) is reviewed at least once a year. The result of the review is either a recommendation for a salary (wage) increase or a decision to defer a salary (wage) increase to a specified future time.

Supervisors should:

- Be aware of staff members' salary (wage) review dates.
- Be familiar with the wage and salary administration program so that staff members' questions can be answered.
- Consider staff members' job performance and positions within the range when deciding on amounts for increases.
- Process the salary action according to the procedure below.
- Discuss the salary action with the staff member only after it has been approved by necessary parties and written notification has been returned to your area.

Each month the wage and salary unit sends the unit manager a listing of staff members who are scheduled for salary (wage) reviews two months later. The following steps should be followed:

- Make a salary recommendation (increase or deferral) in writing on form (insert the form number from the organization).
- Enter the salary (wage) amount and the month it is to be effective.
- Attach the latest performance appraisal form (where applicable).
- Explain all salary actions fully. Recommendations for promotional increases or reclassifications must include specific responsibilities of the individual and be fully explained in writing.
- Complete, sign, and date the written recommendation by the first of the month preceding the effective date of the increase.
- When the recommendation is approved, the supervisor will be informed in writing. This is the official notice of approval. The salary action may be discussed with the affected staff member at this point.

MERIT INCREASES

OVERVIEW

A merit increase is monetary recognition for meeting or exceeding job requirements. Merit increases are considered annually for all employees and are based upon:

- the employee's performance rating

- the position of the employee's salary within the salary (wage) range
- the merit increase budget (if there is one) and guidelines issued by the company (organization) for that year
- how the employee's performance and salary (wage) compare to those of other employees in the department.

TIMING OF MERIT INCREASES

In general, merit increase reviews are given annually.

MERIT INCREASE GUIDELINES

Guidelines for merit increases are issued annually by the wage and salary administration unit. These guidelines include recommended ranges of merit increases for each performance rating. The recommended increases are higher for salaries (wages) below the midpoint than for salaries (wages) above the midpoint.

PROMOTION INCREASES

REASONS FOR PROMOTION INCREASES

Promotional increases are given only in the following situations:

- The employee has taken on significantly higher-level responsibilities, resulting in the job changing into an already established, higher-graded job.
- The employee has been selected to fill a vacant higher-graded position within a department or in another department.

Promotional increases are not appropriate when:

- The duties and/or title of the job have changed, but the changes have not added significantly higher-level responsibilities.
- A job is reevaluated by the wage and salary administration unit and the grade of the job is increased organization-wide. This may happen as the result of comparison to industry surveys and is considered a job reclassification only. In this situation, managers should consider individually the salary of each affected employee. If an employee's salary (wage) seems too low in the new salary (wage) range in comparison to other employees' salaries (wages) and performance, an equity increase may be appropriate.

A promotion increase should bring the staff member to at least the minimum of the new salary (wage) range. To accomplish this, an increase of up to 20 percent may be given. If a 20 percent increase is not sufficient to bring the staff member to the minimum of the new range, an accelerated merit increase will be scheduled for six months later.

EQUITY INCREASES

Equity increases are used when a merit or promotional increase is either not appropriate, or not sufficient to increase an employee's salary (wage) as needed.

An equity increase may also be one that raises a staff member's salary (wage) to the minimum of the salary (wage) range. This type of increase is granted to those individuals whose performance rating is at least satisfactory. (An equity increase does not change the date of the staff member's next scheduled review.)

REASONS FOR EQUITY INCREASES

Equity increases are given only for the reasons listed below:

- to adjust an employee's pay rate to the salary (wage) range minimum
- to create an appropriate differential between the salaries (wages) of a supervisor and subordinate

- to maintain a proper relationship among the salaries (wages) of peers, taking into account experience and performance
- to respond to changes in competitive rates based on surveys or other data available to the organization.

PROPOSING AN EQUITY INCREASE

Managers wishing to propose an equity increase should summarize the facts in a memo (the facts should support one or more of the reasons listed above) and contact the wage and salary administration unit.

OTHER SALARY ACTIONS

ACCELERATED MERIT

An accelerated merit increase is a result of a review scheduled on a six-month basis. These review schedules for certain jobs, and grades vary from the annual review schedule in order to meet competitive market conditions. In addition, any staff member below the minimum of his/her range is eligible to receive an accelerated review every six months until the minimum range is reached.

SPECIAL MERIT

A special merit increase recognizes outstanding performance. A minimum of six months since the last increase must elapse before a special merit increase can be considered. The employee must be rated outstanding. The next regular review date is one year from the increase.

RIPPLE

A ripple increase is designed to remove salary (wage) inequities caused by range adjustments and subsequent equalization increases. Ripple increases *are* generally reserved for those circumstances where employees are in the lower portion of their salary (wage) range, with the amount of each ripple increase depending on the individual's performance. A ripple increase does not change the date of the affected employee's next scheduled salary (wage) review.

ADJUSTMENT

This is an increase made that is due to a processing error.

DEFERRAL

Deferral is an instance in which the scheduled review results in no salary (wage) increase. The supervisor indicates, in writing on the salary action form provided, the new review date (usually three to six months later), the reason for the deferral, and a statement, preferably signed by the employee, to the effect that the employee has been told about the decision.

EXCEPTIONS TO POLICY

The wage and salary administration unit (or committee) reviews increase recommendations for compliance with organization policy. If appropriate, the recommended increase is processed. If an increase is not within salary (wage) increase guidelines or if the documentation is insufficient, a member of the wage and salary unit will contact the area.

Salary (wage) recommendations which clearly exceed policy guidelines require additional written documentation and substantiation. They are individually reviewed by the wage and salary administration unit (and/or committee) and if necessary, presented to the president/CEO (or another designated individual of the organization) for approval.

appendix c ——————————————

POSITION ANALYSIS QUESTIONNAIRE*

Your Position Title:	Date:

Department:	Employee Status:
	Full-time_____ Part-time_____

Your Supervisor's Name and Title:

Please complete this questionnaire, which is designed to obtain information about your job as it currently exists. This information will be reviewed by your supervisor and the Human Resources Department and, with their appropriate input, will be used for a number of purposes including: recruiting, training, career counseling, compensation and performance appraisal.

PART I: BASIC FUNCTION

Summarize the overall purpose of your position.

PART II: ORGANIZATIONAL RELATIONSHIPS

To the extent possible, draw an organization chart for your department or unit.

*Reprinted here with permission from Towers Perrin, New York City.

POSITION ANALYSIS QUESTIONNAIRE (Continued)

PART III: POSITION ACCOUNTABILITIES

Please list — in order of importance — the major outputs/results of your job; i.e., what are you expected to produce as a result of your efforts?

1. Accountability/Expected Results: _____
    _____

    a. What standards of performance do you use to determine if you have achieved these results?
        _____
        _____

    b. List the key tasks that you must perform to accomplish the above results:

        1. _____
        2. _____
        3. _____
        4. _____
        5. _____
        6. _____

2. Accountability/Expected Results: _____
    _____

    a. What standards of performance do you use to determine if you have achieved these results?
        _____
        _____

    b. List the key tasks that you must perform to accomplish the above results:

        1. _____
        2. _____
        3. _____
        4. _____
        5. _____
        6. _____

POSITION ANALYSIS QUESTIONNAIRE (Continued)

PART III: POSITION ACCOUNTABILITIES (continued)

3. Accountability/Expected Results: _____

_____

   a. What standards of performance do you use to determine if you have achieved these results?

     _____

     _____

   b. List the key tasks that you must perform to accomplish the above results:

     1. _____

     2. _____

     3. _____

     4. _____

     5. _____

     6. _____

4. Accountability/Expected Results: _____

_____

   a. What standards of performance do you use to determine if you have achieved these results?

     _____

     _____

   b. List the key tasks that you must perform to accomplish the above results:

     1. _____

     2. _____

     3. _____

     4. _____

     5. _____

     6. _____

POSITION ANALYSIS QUESTIONNAIRE (Continued)

PART III: POSITION ACCOUNTABILITIES (continued)

5. **Accountability/Expected Results:** _____

    _____

    a. **What standards of performance do you use to determine if you have achieved these results?**

        _____

        _____

    b. **List the key tasks that you must perform to accomplish the above results:**

        1. _____

        2. _____

        3. _____

        4. _____

        5. _____

        6. _____

PART IV: POSITION SPECIFICATIONS

1. **Technical Skills**

    a. **List the knowledge and basic office/trade skills required to successfully achieve the major results that you described on pages 2 through 4.**

        Describe each knowledge and skill by denoting `R` **if it is required to do your job or** `N` **if it is not required but would significantly enhance performance.**

        _____   [____]

        _____   [____]

        _____   [____]

        _____   [____]

        _____   [____]

        _____   [____]

POSITION ANALYSIS QUESTIONNAIRE (Continued)

PART IV: POSITION SPECIFICATIONS (continued)

    b. What professional licenses, degrees, certificates or on-the-job apprenticeships are <u>required</u> for someone to achieve the results you listed on pages 2 through 4?

_____

_____

_____

_____

2. <u>Analytical Skills</u>

Describe several of the more difficult problems you must solve to obtain expected results. Include situations which are a constant challenge or "headache. " Also include situations which require judgment and time to consider alternative solutions before problems can be resolved. Following each problem, indicate whether you make recommendations ☐ R or make final decisions ☐ D in solving these problems.

1. _____ ☐

    _____

2. _____ ☐

    _____

3. _____ ☐

    _____

3. <u>Management Skills</u>

    a. What is the <u>scope</u> of your position's supervisory responsibilities? (Check one, please.)

       _____ 1. Has <u>no</u> supervisory or management responsibility.

       _____ 2. Provides work direction, training and technical assistance to lower-level employees.

       _____ 3. Has performance review and other supervisory responsibilities. May recommend, but does not make final hiring and firing decisions.

       _____ 4. Has supervisory responsibilities, which include final hiring and firing decisions.

    b. If you have supervisory responsibilities, please complete 3b, c, and d on the next page. If you do not, please go on to 3e.

POSITION ANALYSIS QUESTIONNAIRE (Continued)

PART IV: POSITION SPECIFICATIONS (continued)

Title(s) of Position(s) Reporting Directly to You	Number of Incumbents	Number of Employees Supervised by Position(s) Reporting to You	
		Exempt*	Nonexempt*
_____	___	___	___
_____	___	___	___
_____	___	___	___
_____	___	___	___
_____	___	___	___
_____	___	___	___
_____	___	___	___

*Exempt or nonexempt from overtime requirements.

c. How much of your time is spent on work similar to work of employees you direct (express as a percentage).

[___ %]

d. What is the total annual operating budget for your position?

$ _____

e. Identify any resources not described in 3a through 3d that you must control to meet your position's accountabilities. Describe your authority to obtain, organize and monitor these resources.

_____

_____

_____

_____

POSITION ANALYSIS QUESTIONNAIRE (Continued)

4. Communications Skills

In the table below, identify the primary contacts you have with individuals inside and outside the Company. (Do not include your immediate supervisor or subordinates). For each audience, enter the letter that corresponds to the frequency of the contact:

| F | Frequently (daily)

| R | Regularly (weekly)

| P | Periodically (monthly)

| O | Occasionally (quarterly to annually)

Also indicate the reason for the communications with these contacts as follows:

| I | Inform

| E | Explain

| P | Persuade

Primary Contact	Frequency	Reason
1. _____		
2. _____		
3. _____		

POSITION ANALYSIS QUESTIONNAIRE (Continued)

PART V

Sign and date the questionnaire below when it is completed. Then return it to your supervisor for review.

_____   _____
Your Signature   Date Completed

_____   _____
Supervisor's Signature   Date Reviewed

_____   _____
Human Resources Department   Date Reviewed

appendix d ──────────────────

AUDIT AND REVIEW WORKSHEET

DATA TO EXAMINE:	ANNUAL BASE PAY		STAFF LEVELS	
	yes	no	yes	no
ACTUAL PAYROLL EXPENSES:				
Variance current month vs. last month?				
Variances explained by:				
Staff increases?				
new positions?				
replacements?				
documentation consistent with grade, range, starting date?				
Staff decreases?				
termination:				
employer initiated?				
employee initiated?				
layoff?				
retirement?				
BUDGET:				
Variance of actual to budget?				

DATA TO EXAMINE:	ANNUAL BASE PAY		STAFF LEVELS	
	yes	no	yes	no
SCHEDULED SALARY ACTIONS:				
Documentation authorized and complete?				
Processed as scheduled?				
Follow-up noted?				
Notification date?				
Review status of missing/unprocessed salary actions?				
Review delayed salary actions?				
Process/further action?				
PERFORMANCE APPRAISALS:				
Consistent with salary action(s)?				
JOB CLASSIFICATIONS:				
Consistent with:				
organization structure?				
similar jobs within organization?				
similar jobs in other organizations?				
Changes:				
Authorized documentation?				
Consistent with Daily Change Log?				

DATA TO EXAMINE:	ANNUAL BASE PAY		STAFF LEVELS	
	yes	no	yes	no
NEW HIRES:				
Authorized Salary Action Card?				
Salary between minimum and midpoint?				
Consistent with Daily Change Log?				
TERMINATIONS/RETIREMENTS/LEAVES OF ABSENCE:				
Authorized Salary Action Form?				
Consistent with Daily Change Log?				
ALTERATIONS TO SALARIES:				
Within range for grade?				
Comply with budget guidelines?				
Consistent with organizational policies and practices?				
Comply with legal requirements?				
Authorized Salary Action Form?				
Consistent with Daily Change Log?				
JOB DESCRIPTIONS:				
Comply with all legal requirements as to discrimination?				
Consistent with other jobs established?				
New job descriptions reviewed for FLSA determination?				

DATA TO EXAMINE:	ANNUAL BASE PAY		STAFF LEVELS	
	yes	no	yes	no
Jobs targeted for updated job descriptions?				
SALARY SURVEYS:				
Review recent surveys:				
actions taken/recommended?				
Surveys scheduled:				
initiate?				
participate in?				
purchase?				
EXIT INTERVIEWS:				
Review reasons stated by employee for leaving?				
Review new position accepted by exiting employee?				
Review new compensation package?				
Final evaluation received?				
TRAINING:				
Programs scheduled for wage and salary professionals?				
Programs scheduled for staff regarding wage and salary issues/procedures?				

appendix e _____

SAMPLE PERFORMANCE APPRAISAL USING GRAPHIC RATING SCALE

BEHAVIOR CRITERIA-BASED PERFORMANCE APPRAISAL*

Secretary/Typist	
Employee Name	**Department**
Job Title	**Date of Last Review**
Reviewer's Name	**Time in Position**

Preparing the Report

This report is designed to help managers appraise each employee based on particular and distinct characteristics of each position.

To be most effective, the report must be prepared in a careful and thorough manner. To serve this end, here are some suggestions.

- Consider only one item at a time.

- Base your ratings on direct knowledge and employee performance on the job.

- Have the rating reflect typical current performance. At the same time avoid being influenced by recent instances of success or failure which are not typical or by past performance which has now changed.

- Concentrate on evaluating specific, observable behavior that directly affects job performance.

- If possible, have some other manager in your area prepare an independent report and compare the two appraisals.

- Completion of this report will be an occasion for discussing job progress with each employee. You should show the report to the employee. You may find it of great value to give the employee a blank report for a self-evaluation. Both you and the employee will benefit by comparing and discussing the evaluations.

- Use the Comments section on the last page for amplification, additions, or explanations.

Reprinted with the permission of Panel Publishers from the 1993 edition of *Personnel Recordkeeper* by Matthew J. DeLuca © 1993.

Performance Appraisal Form page 2

Below is a list of categories specifically relevant to the secretary/typist positions. Determine the weight appropriate for each category and then multiply that weight by the rating given for the incumbent's performance during the time period for the appraisal. Keep in mind total weight for all categories selected should equal 100.

The rating for each category is on a scale of 0 to 5. Each level is established with a numerical value in the column on the left hand side of the page. For each category where the lowest level of performance is indicated, written documentation is required. The highest possible score is 400 points. Ratings are as follows: Outstanding: 352–400; Commendable: 278–350; Competent: 212–276; Minimal/Acceptable: 152–210; Unsatisfactory: 0–150.

I. Knowledge of Department Functions (Secretaries only) | Rating × Weight =

0 Work falls below minimum acceptable performance. (document)
1 Knows basic functions of most sections in department. Routine calls and inquiries promptly directed.
2 Understands functions of each section in department and can refer customers and calls to proper areas. Can identify applications for opening various services. Uses files to locate customer information.
3 Knowledge of most department services and procedures. Able to use available resources to resolve customer requests.
4 Answers questions on all services. Calls and inquiries never misdirected. Able to handle basic questions if boss or other employee is unavailable.

II. Dictation (Secretaries only) | Rating × Weight =

0 Work falls below minimum acceptable performance. (document)
1 Dictation inadequate for routine assignments. Speed is below organization standard.
2 Dictation skills are acceptable for routine work. Speed equals organization standard (80–90 wpm).
3 Takes dictation of a more complex nature. Work consistently accurate. Speed clearly above organization standard.
4 Demonstrates proficient dictation skills superior to organization standard.

III. Customer Service | Rating × Weight =

0 Work falls below minimum acceptable performance. (document)
1 Courteous to customers. Answers questions if asked. Does not always screen telephone calls or customers. Recognizes only a few regular customers.
2 Serves as a central information point for customers. Answers questions in a polite, friendly manner. Recognizes regular customers. Generally demonstrates good telephone techniques. Comes to the assistance of waiting customers.
3 Courteous to customers both in person and by phone even during difficult situations. Customers rarely kept waiting.
4 Promotes the organization and its services. Recognizes major accounts and their principals.

Performance Appraisal Form	page 3
IV. Quantity 0 Work falls below minimum acceptable performance. (document) 1 Output below expected level. Has occasional difficulty completing tasks within the same day. Frequently misses deadlines. Usually some work backlogged. 2 Output approximately equal to expected levels. Completes all tasks within the same day. 3 Output clearly above the expected levels. Completes work within deadlines. Able to assist others in duties. 4 Output far superior to expected levels. Consistently has time to develop customer service, or to assist as needed in other areas.	Rating × Weight = ☐
V. Typing & Correspondence 0 Work falls below minimum acceptable performance. (document) 1 Completed tasks are occasionally without proper format or neatness. Proofreads work. Some work is returned for correction. Deadlines sometimes missed. Typing is less than organization standard. 2 Work is completed in proper format and is neat. Proofreads all assignments. Work is rarely returned for correction. Meets deadlines. Typing speed equals organization standard. 3 Work is thoroughly prepared and submitted correctly. Completes tasks well within deadline. Typing skills above organization standard. 4 Completed tasks consistently error free. Demonstrates proficient typing skills superior to organization standards.	Rating × Weight = ☐
VI. Business English 0 Work falls below minimum acceptable performance. (document) 1 Has difficulty applying proper use of the English language and its rules (spelling, grammar, vocabulary, punctuation). 2 Demonstrates adequate use of the English language and grammatical rules. 3 Has good command of the English language. Demonstrates proficient editing skills. 4 When required, composes original correspondence.	Rating × Weight = ☐
VII. Cooperation 0 Work falls below minimum acceptable performance. (document) 1 Reluctant to take on new tasks or assist in usual situations. Often has excuses when asked to help. 2 Cooperates when called upon. 3 Always available to assist department or co-workers in any situation. 4 Exhibits a spirit of teamwork and assumes leadership in promoting cooperation. Able to resolve conflict without assistance.	Rating × Weight = ☐

Performance Appraisal Form	page 4

VIII. Attendance & Punctuality (Recorded from Employee Attendance Record. Be sure to review accuracy of the Attendance Record.)

Rating × Weight =

Attendance

	Total Incidents (Chargeable)	Total Days (Chargeable)
0	6 or more	12 or more
1	4–5	8–11
2	2–3	5–7
3	1	1–4
4	0	0

Punctuality

Rating × Weight =

	Total Lost Time:
	Tardiness Incidents
0	31 or more
1	21–30
2	11–20
3	1–10
4	0

Total Points:

Comments (Use extra sheets if necessary)

Prepared by _____ Date _____

Reviewed by _____ Date _____

Employee Remarks (Use extra sheets if necessary)

Employee Signature _____ Date _____

appendix f

Sample Performance Appraisal Using Graphic Rating Scale

Performance Appraisal*

(May be useful for the evaluation of management or technical/professional employees.)

Employee Name	**Employee No.**
Job Title	**Cost Center No.**
Date of Previous Performance Appraisal	

INTRODUCTION

Performance Evaluation is the process that ensures an employee's performance against standards/expectations set for the job. Its purpose is to recognize and reward contributions and to improve performance for the benefit of the employee. This performance appraisal document is an integral part of the Performance Evaluation process.

In preparing for the performance appraisal you should:

1. Ensure that the employee's job description is up-to-date and that the employee has a copy.
2. Determine the standards of performance for each performance criterion job responsibility, and the relative importance of each criterion and responsibility. These standards then represent the expected levels of performance that have been determined for each job.
3. Review facts concerning the employee's performance since the last appraisal. Measure the employee's performance against the standards for the entire review period. It may be helpful to review the employee's most recent Performance Appraisal.

INSTRUCTIONS:

Consider the degree to which the employee meets expectations in applying sound methods and effectively utilizing skills to meet job responsibilities.

- Review the criteria listed below under the categories of Job Knowledge, Productivity, and Organizational Skills.
- Place a checkmark in the box to the left of the criteria which are applicable to the job.
- Rate the selected criteria by checking the degree to which the employee meets the supervisor's expectations.
- Space is provided for specific comments or pertinent examples under the assessment scale for each evaluated criteria.
- Determine a summary evaluation for each category based upon the ratings given on those criteria used. Weight the ratings given to each criteria according to their importance.
- Space is provided for a plan of action for each major category. The plan of action should include specific ways in which the employee can improve: job knowledge, productivity, and organizational skills. Where appropriate, outline further on-the-job experience and other training which have been recommended to the employee.

Base your assessment upon the entire review period and not upon isolated incidents alone. Be objective. Rate each criterion independently.

JOB KNOWLEDGE CATEGORY					
CRITERIA	**ASSESSMENT**				
☐ **KNOWLEDGE OF JOB RELATED PRINCIPLES AND PRACTICES:** Has sufficient knowledge, acquired through experience or training, to perform duties of the job.	☐ Clearly Outstanding	☐ Exceeds Expectations	☐ Meets Expectations	☐ Below Expectations	☐ Unacceptable
	Comments:				
☐ **APPLICATION OF KNOWLEDGE TO PRACTICAL SITUATIONS:** Applies sound judgement, makes recommendations or decisions that are timely and reflect consideration of alteratives.	☐ Clearly Outstanding	☐ Exceeds Expectations	☐ Meets Expectations	☐ Below Expectations	☐ Unacceptable
	Comments:				
☐ **UNDERSTANDING OF WORK RELATIONSHIPS:** Understands the general relationship of own work activities to the activities of the primary work group, department, or other departments.	☐ Clearly Outstanding	☐ Exceeds Expectations	☐ Meets Expectations	☐ Below Expectations	☐ Unacceptable
	Comments:				
ASSESSMENT SUMMARY - JOB KNOWLEDGE	☐ Clearly Outstanding	☐ Exceeds Expectations	☐ Meets Expectations	☐ Below Expectations	☐ Unacceptable

PLAN OF ACTION - JOB KNOWLEDGE (Outline specific training if necessary)

_____

_____

_____

_____

PRODUCTIVITY CATEGORY					
CRITERIA	**ASSESSMENT**				
☐ **QUALITY OF WORK:** Produces work that is accurate and completed according to instructions.	☐ Clearly Outstanding	☐ Exceeds Expectations	☐ Meets Expectations	☐ Below Expectations	☐ Unacceptable
	Comments:				
☐ **QUANTITY OF WORK:** Produces an acceptable volume of work.	☐ Clearly Outstanding	☐ Exceeds Expectations	☐ Meets Expectations	☐ Below Expectations	☐ Unacceptable
	Comments:				

TIMELINESS OF WORK OUTPUT: Completes assignments within established time limits.	☐ Clearly Outstanding	☐ Exceeds Expectations	☐ Meets Expectations	☐ Below Expectations	☐ Unacceptable
	Comments:				

ATTENDANCE:	☐ Clearly Outstanding	☐ Exceeds Expectations	☐ Meets Expectations	☐ Below Expectations	☐ Unacceptable
PUNCTUALITY: Include days absent or late as basis for assessment. Note significant improvement or consistently high performance as defined in policy #1026	☐ Clearly Outstanding	☐ Exceeds Expectations	☐ Meets Expectations	☐ Below Expectations	☐ Unacceptable
	Comments:				

ASSESSMENT SUMMARY - PRODUCTIVITY	☐ Clearly Outstanding	☐ Exceeds Expectations	☐ Meets Expectations	☐ Below Expectations	☐ Unacceptable

PLAN OF ACTION - PRODUCTIVITY (Outline specific training if necessary)

ORGANIZATIONAL SKILLS CATEGORY

CRITERIA	ASSESSMENT				
ORGANIZATION OF WORK: Schedules and plans work assignments to effectively meet job responsibilities.	☐ Clearly Outstanding	☐ Exceeds Expectations	☐ Meets Expectations	☐ Below Expectations	☐ Unacceptable
	Comments:				
ADAPTABILITY: Adjusts to changes in priorities and procedures, and normal day-to-day job demands.	☐ Clearly Outstanding	☐ Exceeds Expectations	☐ Meets Expectations	☐ Below Expectations	☐ Unacceptable
	Comments:				
INNOVATION: Recommends changes to existing systems, policies and/or equipment which result in improvements.	☐ Clearly Outstanding	☐ Exceeds Expectations	☐ Meets Expectations	☐ Below Expectations	☐ Unacceptable
	Comments:				

☐ **DECISION - MAKING:** Makes decisions to meet job responsibilities by considering the pertinent facts, issues and alternatives.	☐ Clearly Outstanding	☐ Exceeds Expectations	☐ Meets Expectations	☐ Below Expectations	☐ Unacceptable
	Comments:				

☐ **IMPROVEMENT OF JOB PERFORMANCE:** Accepts and follows through on recommendations for improved job performance.	☐ Clearly Outstanding	☐ Exceeds Expectations	☐ Meets Expectations	☐ Below Expectations	☐ Unacceptable
	Comments:				

☐ **COMMUNICATION OF NECESSARY INFORMATION:** Provides information regarding work progress and problems to supervisor, co-workers, and other employees and departments.	☐ Clearly Outstanding	☐ Exceeds Expectations	☐ Meets Expectations	☐ Below Expectations	☐ Unacceptable
	Comments:				

☐ **ABILITY TO WORK WITH OTHERS:** Cooperates with and obtains the cooperation of others to meet job responsibilities.	☐ Clearly Outstanding	☐ Exceeds Expectations	☐ Meets Expectations	☐ Below Expectations	☐ Unacceptable
	Comments:				

☐ **ORAL COMMUNICATION SKILLS:**	☐ Clearly Outstanding	☐ Exceeds Expectations	☐ Meets Expectations	☐ Below Expectations	☐ Unacceptable
☐ **WRITTEN COMMUNICATION SKILLS:**	☐ Clearly Outstanding	☐ Exceeds Expectations	☐ Meets Expectations	☐ Below Expectations	☐ Unacceptable
Communicates information orally and/or in writing in a clear and understandable manner.	Comments:				

ASSESSMENT SUMMARY - ORGANIZATIONAL SKILLS	☐ Clearly Outstanding	☐ Exceeds Expectations	☐ Meets Expectations	☐ Below Expectations	☐ Unacceptable

PLAN OF ACTION - PRODUCTIVITY (Outline specific training if necessary)

THE FOLLOWING CRITERIA MAY BE USEFUL FOR EVALUATING MANAGEMENT & TECHNICAL SKILLS

CRITERIA	ASSESSMENT				
ABILITY TO PLAN AND ANALYZE: Identifies needs, specifies required activities, and sets priorities to improve departmental performance.	☐ Clearly Outstanding	☐ Exceeds Expectations	☐ Meets Expectations	☐ Below Expectations	☐ Unacceptable
	Comments:				
ABSENCE CONTROL: Monitors employee attendance and provides appropriate feedback according to the Center's Attendance Policy; rewards employees and takes disciplinary action when necessary.	☐ Clearly Outstanding	☐ Exceeds Expectations	☐ Meets Expectations	☐ Below Expectations	☐ Unacceptable
	Comments:				
CONTROLLING AND MEASURING: Monitoring department's activities by establishing standards and developing systematic and efficient methods.	☐ Clearly Outstanding	☐ Exceeds Expectations	☐ Meets Expectations	☐ Below Expectations	☐ Unacceptable
	Comments:				
DELEGATION OF WORK: Utilizes staff effectively through the assignment of work and responsibilities.	☐ Clearly Outstanding	☐ Exceeds Expectations	☐ Meets Expectations	☐ Below Expectations	☐ Unacceptable
	Comments:				
SUPERVISION: Orients and directs others in the performance of their work assignments.	☐ Clearly Outstanding	☐ Exceeds Expectations	☐ Meets Expectations	☐ Below Expectations	☐ Unacceptable
	Comments:				
EVALUATION AND DEVELOPMENT OF EMPLOYEES: Evaluates employees objectively; uses evaluation results to improve employee performance and encourage development.	☐ Clearly Outstanding	☐ Exceeds Expectations	☐ Meets Expectations	☐ Below Expectations	☐ Unacceptable
	Comments:				
ASSESSMENT SUMMARY - MANAGEMENT SKILLS	☐ Clearly Outstanding	☐ Exceeds Expectations	☐ Meets Expectations	☐ Below Expectations	☐ Unacceptable

PLAN OF ACTION - MANAGEMENT SKILLS (Outline specific training if necessary)

_____

_____

_____

PERFORMANCE PROFILE

PERFORMANCE SUMMARY

Review the preceeding sections of the form that you have completed and indicate below your overall evaluation of the employee.

SUMMARY	☐ Clearly Outstanding	☐ Exceeds Expectations	☐ Meets Expectations	☐ Below Expectations	☐ Unacceptable

State below developmental needs that have not been previously discussed:

List the employee's strongest points:

COMMENTARY ON EVALUATION

Employee comments on the evaluation and the evaluation discussion:

Supervisor's comments on evaluation discussion:

Signature of Reviewer:	Date Signed:
Signature of Reviewer's Supervisor:	Date Signed:
Signature of Employee Reviewed:	Date Signed:

Reprinted with the permission of Panel Publishers from the 1993 edition of *Personnel Recordkeeper* by Matthew J. DeLuca © 1993.

appendix g ───────────────

RESULTS/OUTCOME-BASED PERFORMANCE APPRAISAL

Performance Planning and Review Worksheet

Name
Title
Department
Employment Date
Date Assigned
Period Covered
Date Discussed with Employee
Prepared by

RESULTS/OUTCOME-BASED PERFORMANCE APPRAISAL (Continued)

I—PERFORMANCE PLAN

The Performance Plan should focus on the 6 to 8 significant objectives planned for the year. Indicate target date for completion and note how performance will be measured. Assign a weight to each objective. Additional work relating to ongoing responsibilities should be summarized in one objective which should be assigned a weight of not more than 15%. Total weight of all objectives should equal 100%. List objectives in descending order of importance based on the assigned weight.

No.	Objectives	Weight

Employee's Signature		Date	100%
Signature & Title of Employee's Immediate Supervisor		Date	
Signature & Title Next Level of Supervision		Date	

RESULTS/OUTCOME-BASED PERFORMANCE APPRAISAL (Continued)

	II—PROGRESS REVIEW	
	Record any additions or changes to the Performance Plan (Section I). Indicate any changes in the weighting of the objectives. Review and document employee's progress to date toward attaining each objective.	
No.	**Objectives**	**Weight**

100%

Date of mid-year Progress Review: _____

RESULTS/OUTCOME-BASED PERFORMANCE APPRAISAL (Continued)

III—PERFORMANCE REVIEW
Indicate what results were achieved during the year, being as specific as possible. Where objectives were not met, note the specific reason. Include a review of all significant work, whether or not it was planned.

RESULTS/OUTCOME-BASED PERFORMANCE APPRAISAL (Continued)

IV—MANAGEMENT SKILLS

How did the individual accomplish results? Comment on this person's demonstration of important managerial skills, being specific about why a particular assessment is made. Note areas where skills are well developed, as well as those needing improvement. Refer to "Management Skills" in the Guidelines when completing this section.

V—PERFORMANCE IMPROVEMENT AND DEVELOPMENT PLAN

Describe what should be done in the coming year to improve performance in the current job and/ or to further develop skills that will help prepare the individual for other positions. Consider experience on the job as well as formal training/education programs. Also, consider what the manager can do to help the development of this individual through activities such as coaching and counseling, frequent feedback, and delegation. Be specific—e.g., what training program, coaching in what skill.

Action to be taken	By Whom	When Completed

RESULTS/OUTCOME-BASED PERFORMANCE APPRAISAL (Continued)

VI—OVERALL RATING OF PERFORMANCE

☐ Accomplishments in all areas far exceeded expectations for position, both in terms of results and the manner in which they were achieved. This rating should be reserved for truly exceptional performance.

☐ Accomplishments exceeded expectations for position in most areas and fully met the requirements in all others. Work performed in a highly effective manner.

☐ Performance fully met expectations for position in most areas and exceeded expectations in some others. Employee is effective both in achieving results and in demonstrating a competent level of management skills.

☐ Overall results achieved met the basic expectations for the position. While performance in one or two areas may have fallen slightly below expectations, this was balanced by performance above expectations in others.

☐ Performance falls short of fully meeting expectations for position in several areas. Attention required to bring performance up to an acceptable level.

☐ Does not meet minimum expectations for position. If performance does not improve within the time specified and discussed with the employee, the employee should be moved out of the position.

VII—SIGNATURES AND COMMENTS

Appraiser: Your signature indicates that you have discussed this review with your employee.

Signature _____ Date _____

Employee: Your signature indicates that you have read this form and that your manager has reviewed your performance with you. It does not necessarily indicate your agreement with everything that was written or discussed. Use the space below for additional comments.

Signature _____ Date _____

Appraiser's Manager: Your signature indicates that you have reviewed and concur with this appraisal.

Signature _____ Date _____

Comments:

appendix h _____

Wage and Salary Survey *

NAME OF PERSON(S) INTERVIEWED AND TITLES:

_____   _____
            NAME   NAME

_____   _____
            TITLE   TITLE

TOTAL STAFF

A. How many staff members are employed as of __/__/__ in the category of "Exempt Staff"? _____

B. How many staff members are employed as of __/__/__ in the category of "Nonexempt Staff"? _____

---

1. PAY STRUCTURE
   A. How often are your wage or salary scales revised?
      EXEMPT STAFF _____
      NONEXEMPT STAFF _____
   B. On what basis are these revisions paid?

	EXEMPT	NONEXEMPT
1. Movement of salary or wage index	Yes/No	Yes/No
2. Basis of various surveys	Yes/No	Yes/No
3. Executive Decision	Yes/No	Yes/No
4. Wage Salary Meeting	Yes/No	Yes/No
5. Combination or other than above	Yes/No	Yes/No

   If Yes, please explain _____

   _____

   C. What was your last revision and amount?
      EXEMPT (date) _____   _____ % or $ _____
      NONEXEMPT (date) _____   _____ % or $ _____
   D. Can you provide copies of current salary ranges?
      EXEMPT . . . Yes/No   NONEXEMPT . . . Yes/No
   E. Do you have a job evaluation system? . . . . Yes/No
   F. Can you provide job descriptions for corresponding jobs surveyed?
      EXEMPT . . . Yes/No   NONEXEMPT . . . Yes/No
   G. Do you have an Official Salary Program?
      EXEMPT . . . Yes/No   NONEXEMPT . . . Yes/No
   H. How often is an employee's salary increased?
      EXEMPT   6 Months __   NONEXEMPT   6 Months __
                1 Year   __   1 Year   __
                18 Mos.   __   18 Mos.   __
                Other*   __   Other*   __
   *If Other, please explain: _____   *If Other, please explain: _____

   _____   _____

341

WAGE AND SALARY SURVEY (Continued)

2. <u>BENEFITS</u>

   A. Upon employment, what is the waiting period, if any, for an employee to become eligible for various plans? (Please fill in the appropriate amounts or percentages in each column, as well as the waiting period before benefits begin.)

	EXEMPT	COMPANY	WAITING PERIOD	NONEXEMPT	COMPANY	WAITING PERIOD
Group Life Ins.						
Pension Plan						
Medical Insurance Indiv. Plan						
Family Plan						
Dental Insurance Indiv. Plan						
Family Plan						
Workman's Comp.						
Long Term Disabil.						
Unemployment Ins.						

   B. Do you provide the following benefits?

	EXEMPT	NONEXEMPT
1. Year-End Bonus/Award	YES/NO ___% OR $___	YES/NO ___% OR $___
2. Profit Sharing	YES/NO ___% OR $___	YES/NO ___% OR $___
3. Payroll Savings Plan	YES/NO ___% OR $___	YES/NO ___% OR $___
4. Seniority/Long Service Award	YES/NO ___% OR $___	YES/NO ___% OR $___
5. IRA via Payroll Deductions	YES/NO ___% OR $___	YES/NO ___% OR $___
6. OTHER _____	YES/NO ___% OR $___	YES/NO ___% OR $___

3. <u>WORKING HOURS AND LEAVES</u>

   A. What is the basic working day, excluding lunch breaks? ____ hrs. per day

   B. How many vacation days do you grant?

	EXEMPT	NONEXEMPT
After 1 year of service	____ working days	____ working days
____completed years of service	____ working days	____ working days
____completed years of service	____ working days	____ working days
____completed years of service	____ working days	____ working days

   C. Do you grant personal days? If so, how many based on length of service:

EXEMPT	NONEXEMPT
____ days after ____ months	____ days after ____ months
____ days after ____ year(s)	____ days after ____ year(s)

   D. Do you grant special days off, e.g., for birth of child, marriage, death of relative, jury duty? (Please list and briefly explain policy)

   _____

   _____

   _____

   E. Do you provide paid sick days?   YES/NO

                   EXEMPT _____ Days Paid   NONEXEMPT _____ Days Paid

   F. Do you provide paid maternity leave?   YES/NO

           If yes, please indicate amount of paid leave _____

WAGE AND SALARY SURVEY (Continued)

G. OVERTIME—WHAT ARE YOUR PROVISIONS?

1. Work in excess of __ hrs per week—paid as __% of base salary

2. Work in excess of __ hrs per day —paid as __% of base salary

3. Work in excess of __ hrs per shift —paid as __% of base salary

4. for Saturdays   —paid as __% of base salary

5. for Sundays   —paid as __% of base salary

6. for Holidays   —paid as __% of base salary

7. Outside normal working hours, do you pay for:

Meal Money—YES/NO ___% OR $___ Transportation—YES/NO ___% OR $___

H. What additional compensation, if any, do employees receive if and when they are required to work:

a) At night as part of their regular shift?   _____%
b) At night beyond their regular scheduled shift?   _____%
c) Shifts which include weekends?   _____%
d) Can they receive shift & night differential simultaneously? YES/NO
   If Yes, please indicate   _____%

I. How many Holidays do you grant?   _____

J. Do you have a policy for "Early Departures" before Holidays?   YES/NO
   If yes, briefly explain policy _____
   _____

4. TUITION ASSISTANCE

Do you give financial assistance to an employee for outside study?

YES/NO

a) towards a primary degree   YES/NO
b) towards a secondary degree   YES/NO
c) towards nonacademic work-related study   YES/NO
   (PLEASE EXPLAIN WORK-RELATED)

_____
_____
_____

5. OTHER

A. Do you hire part-time help on a regular basis?   YES/NO

B. Do you hire "cooperative" students?   YES/NO

C. Do you have a mandatory retirement age?   YES/NO
   If yes, please indicate age _____

D. Do you offer special functions to all employees?   YES/NO
   (e.g., company picnics, year-end dinner dances)

IF YES, please list and indicate whether these functions are paid by the company, employees or both.

FUNCTION	COMPANY	EMPLOYEES	BOTH

WAGE AND SALARY SURVEY (Continued)

JOB TITLE	NUMBER OF INCUMBENTS	AVR. BASE SAL. (ANNUALLY)	SALARY RANGES			COMMENTS (if any)
			MIN.	MID.	MAX.	

WAGE AND SALARY SURVEY (Continued)

ESSENTIAL FUNCTIONS ANALYSIS FORM

List below, in order of importance, the major functions of the job	Incumbent performs function? Y/N	Function is prime reason for job? Y/N	Function requires special skill or expertise? Y/N	% of time spent on function %	What happens if the function is not performed? Scale 1-5	Other employees perform function in department? Y/N, #	Conclusion: Is this function essential? Y/N
1							
2							
3							
4							
5							
6							
7							
8							

What are the essential physical and/or mental requirement for the job?

_____

_____

_____

WAGE AND SALARY SURVEY (Continued)
ESSENTIAL FUNCTIONS ANALYSIS

Job Title:_____	Department/location:_____
Job Code:_____	EEO-1 Category:_____
Exempt/nonexempt:_____	
Analysis prepared by:_____	Date:_____
Approved by:_____	Date:_____

INSTRUCTIONS: On the attached form, provide the following information.

1. Using the current Job Description, combine appropriate functions and rank them in accordance of importance, with #1 being the most important and #8 being the least important. List these functions in the left hand column of form.

2. Complete each of the questions in the top row for each of the functions as follows:

    A. Employee currently in position performs the function. If the job description specifies a function, does the incumbent actually perform the function?

    B. The function is the prime reason why this job exists. For example, a person is hired to proofread documents. The ability to proofread is essential for that is the reason for the job.

    C. The function requires a special expertise or skill. If a license, degree or certification is required to perform the function, this would be an indication of an essential function.

    D. Percentage of time spent on the function. A percent of the time actually spent by the employee doing the function would be an indicator of the essential nature of the function.

    E. Consequences of not performing the function. Rate #1 through #5 the seriousness of the consequences if the function were eliminated. A police officer may actually only spend a small portion of his/her time making arrests, but eliminating this function would rate a #1 for "very

WAGE AND SALARY SURVEY (Continued)

serious consequences if eliminated". Less serious consequences would rate a #4 or #5.

F. Are there other employees within the department performing the function? If a function cannot be distributed due to small number of employees or fluctuating business cycles, it may be an essential function. If it can be distributed, state the number of employees who could perform the function if redistributed.

F. You consider the function essential. Based on the foregoing answers, a decision is reached as to the essential nature of each ranked function.

3.What are the essential physical and mental requirements for the job? List the types and frequency of physical effort and mental concentration needed by citing results or outcome expected. For example, the ability to learn information may be the mental requirement, not merely the ability to read. The ability to lift and carry specific weights of materials a specified distance or frequency may be an example of a physical requirement. Other skills or conditions which should be considered are eye-hand coordination; extended sitting, bending, talking or moving; working closely with others or working under stress; manual dexterity; and the ability to follow orders.

GLOSSARY

ability to pay
the ability of an organization to meet its pay commitments and remain financially healthy; a frequent issue in contract negotiations with unions.

accidental death and dismemberment insurance (AD&D)
insurance coverage providing benefits in the event of loss of life, limbs, or eyesight as the result of an accident.

across-the-board increase
a flat increase given to everyone in a particular category (or categories) regardless of level of performance.

actual hours worked
the actual number of hours worked during a pay period by an employee.

administrator
the person or organization (frequently the sponsor) specifically designated by the terms of the instrument under which a pension welfare or other retirement plan operates to implement and oversee the plan.

Age Discrimination in Employment Act of 1967, (ADEA)   as amended in 1978—the federal law that makes it illegal for employers to discriminate against persons 40 years of age and over in the terms and conditions of employment. Executives and college faculty members may be considered exempt.

annual bonus   usually a lump-sum payment given to an employee in addition to normal salary or wages.

annualized increase percentage   the increase percentage expressed as an annual rate of increase by dividing the actual percentage increase by the number of months since the last increase and dividing by twelve.

annuity   periodic payment made over a fixed period of time (for example merit increases become annuities for the duration of employment). The term is normally used when talking about pensions when the retired employee is paid a fixed sum monthly for the duration of his life unless he/she chose to take a lump-sum distribution instead.

annuity, joint and survivor   also called a contingent annuity, payable as long as the pensioner lives and continued after his/her death to a named survivor or contingent annuitant until his/her death.

area wage surveys   wage surveys conducted by the Bureau of Labor Statistics in local labor markets. They serve as a useful reference point for wage and salary professionals.

base wage   wage provided to employee before any add-ons such as shift differential, performance bonus, clothing allowance, or overtime.

benchmark job   one used in wage surveys and job evaluation. They should vary in job requirements, exist in most organizations surveyed, represent a wide spectrum of salary levels in the organization and be technologically stable.

benefits   that portion of the compensation package that is provided in the same terms to all the employees of the same group, regardless of performance. The three types of benefits are: pay for time not worked, health and welfare, and free or reduced-cost services.

bonus   any direct lump-sum cash payment given in addition to base pay on either a discretionary or formula basis.

cafeteria benefits program see *flexible benefits program*

classifica-tion method a job evaluation technique that determines the relative value of each job by comparing its several compensable factors to a standard outside the organization. The Federal Government's Directory of Occupational Classifications may be used as a reference point; a helpful approach for marketplace comparisons of similar jobs in a variety of organizations in a wide range of industries.

closed pay system one in which information regarding the organization's pay system is closely held, if disclosed at all.

COLA cost of living adjustment; used for pay increase determinations; usually tied to rises in the Consumer Price Index.

commission a payment directly tied to results achieved; usually provided to sales personnel as a percentage of sales; intended to reduce or eliminate the base salary portion of the compensation package.

compa-ratio the ratio of actual salary of an incumbent to the midpoint of the salary range in which the position is located. The spread is usually from .8 (or 80 percent) to 1.20 (120 percent). The midpoint, 1.0, is the price the market will pay for the job.

comparable worth a concept that proposes that jobs have an inherent value (worth) that may be determined even when they have little or no relation to each other (librarian and construction worker for example); if they have the same value, they should be paid the same.

compensa-ble factor any factor used to provide a basis for determining job value. Usually four or five in number, the most common include responsibility, skills, effort, and working conditions.

compensa-tion the sum total of payments, direct and indirect that an employee is given in exchange for service provided. There may be as many as five elements, including: base pay, short-term incentives, long-term incentives, benefits, and perquisites.

compensa-tion planning a strategic process that commences with the determination of the organization's philosophy toward the sum total of payments to be made to employees; for maximum effectiveness the compensation program and policies established from the definition of the organization's philosophy toward pay are then linked to the organization's mission and objectives.

competitive compa-ratio	the ratio of the organization's standing on the compra-ratio scale for a position versus the market.
cost of living adjustment	see *COLA*
cost reduction program	performance bonus plans tied to improvements in production, for example, lower scrap totals, less downtime on the assembly line, fewer returns or rejects.
earnings	total wages due to an employee, including base pay, shift differentials, and bonuses.
employee benefits	see *benefits*
Employee Retirement Income Security Act of 1974 (ERISA)	a federal law primarily intended to protect employee pension plans; has been extended to other employee health and welfare plans as well.
employee stock owner-ship plan (ESOP)	an employee benefit in which the organization contributes its stock, usually in the form of profit sharing, to an employee trust.
Equal Employ-ment Opportunity Commission	an agency of the federal government charged with enforcing the Civil Rights Acts of 1964 and 1991, as well as the Equal Pay Act of 1963.
equity	anything of value on a par with something else of different but equivalent value.
ESOP	see *employee stock ownership plan*
exception payroll	a payroll that is automatically processed each pay period unless a specific exception is made. This is in contrast to a payroll where each pay period for every pay must be entered each time.
exempt job	a job not subject to the provisions of the Fair Labor Standards Act with respect to minimum wage and overtime. These jobs include professional, management, and administrative positions.

external equity a measure of equal value that an employer tries to use when comparing positions inside the organization to the perception of the market outside.

ERISA see *Employment Returement Income Security Act of 1974*

factor comparison a quantitative method of job evaluation that measures the same factors in different jobs to determine their value in relation to each other.

Fair Labor Standards Act of 1938 (FLSA) a federal law governing minimum wage, overtime pay, equal pay for men and women in the same type of job, child labor, and recordkeeping requirements.

Federal Insurance Contributions Act (FICA) the federal law passed in 1935 authorizing the withholding of pay for social security purposes. Since its inception there has been a portion withheld from the employee's pay and an additional tax paid by the employer.

FICA see *Federal Insurance Contributions Act*

flexible benefits program a benefits program in which employees are able to select the benefits they wish to receive within the established parameters. Usually a common core (life insurance and pension) is offered with a group of elective programs from which the employee may select depending on appropriateness and affordability.

fringe benefits see *benefits*

garnishment a court order requiring the employer of a debtor to deduct a portion of the debtor's pay and deliver it to the creditor.

green-circle the name given to the practice of identifying an employee who has a salary below the minimum for the position.

Hay system a popular, customized, quantitative job evaluation system (developed by the Hay Group, a management consulting firm) that determines a job's worth based on an analysis of three compensable factors; know-how, problem-solving, and accountability.

human resource information system (HRIS) an organized process for gathering, storing, manipulating, analyzing, retrieving, and distributing relevant timely and accurate data and information regarding the staff of an organization, for both organizational effectiveness and legal compliance.

individual equity   criteria established for pay level based on individual considerations.

industry wage surveys   wage surveys conducted by the Bureau of Labor Statistics in more than seventy industries.

internal equity   a measure of value that an employer tries to use when comparing positions inside the organization to each other.

job analysis   a systematic process of describing the purpose of a job along with its activities, skills required, and conditions under which it is performed.

job code   an arbitrary number assigned by the wage and salary administration unit so that each authorized job title in the organization can be located by its number instead.

job content   elements of a job that include: the specific activities that have to be performed; the responsibilities and accountabilities of the incumbent; and the expected results, mission, or outcome of the completed tasks.

job context   consideration for the job with attention given to the job's position in the organization's structure and its relationship to others in the organization. Analysis on this basis includes: the environment within which the activities are performed; the physical conditions of the work area where the job being analyzed is located; any required physical demands; work location; nature and extent of supervision provided to incumbent; visibility of the job in the organization; its relationship to the rest of the jobs in the unit.

job evaluation   the formal process by which an organization assigns relative weights to jobs according to the method established for determining the hierarchy of jobs inside the organization.

job family   a group of jobs clustered together for job evaluation, wage and salary administration, and other Personnel/Human Resources purposes on the basis of similar skills, occupational qualifications, workplace conditions and other organizational and external environmental factors.

job grade   an organizationally determined number that is given by the Wage and Salary Administration unit to each job so that the organization may identify for pay purposes each job by the salary range in which it has been located.

key job   see **benchmark job**

labor demand the highest price (wage) an employer is willing to pay for a given level of employment or number of employees.

labor market the place where labor is provided in exchange for wages; the market is affected by a complex combination of factors including: geography, technology, and experience.

labor supply the lowest price (wage) necessary for an employer to pay for a given level of employment or number of employees.

lag policy an organizational decision, made for a defined period, to pay lower than the market for a job or group of jobs in the organization.

lead policy an organizational decision, made for a defined period, to pay higher than the market for a job or group of jobs in the organization.

marginal revenue product (MRP) defines the highest wage an employer is willing to pay for additional labor and is used as a vehicle by economists to define the maximum wage that an employer is willing to pay for additional labor. The MRP may also be considered as the additional output furnished by another unit of labor at a price that the employer can sell the additional item generated as a result.

maturity curve wage trends for professionals that are affected by years of experience in the profession.

merit increase a periodic increase to wages based on seniority, performance, or some other individually determined basis.

minimum wage the lowest wage to be paid for a particular position. Usually applied specifically to jobs as they are affected by the Fair Labor Standards Act of 1938. When the FLSA was passed the minimum was set at $.25; in 1992 it was $4.25. State laws take precedence if their minimum wage is higher, and in some states it is.

nonexempt job any job subject to the minimum wage and overtime provisions of the FLSA.

open pay system one in which information about the organization's pay program is shared openly with its employees; in some extreme situations, individual wage and salary levels are shared along with wage ranges.

overtime time worked in excess of that expected in return for the base pay rate or wages; as defined by FLSA, the time worked in excess of 40 hours that must be compensated by a rate at least one and one half times the regular rate.

PAQ   see *position analysis questionnaire*

pay compression   a pay level discrepancy that exists as a result of either later hires being paid a higher wage due to external factors (as during periods of high inflation or increased demand for certain skills) or internal factors such as organizational discrepancies (for example, a subordinate being paid at a higher level than a supervisor).

Pension Benefit Guarantee Corporation   a unit of the U.S. Department of Labor which guarantees the vested retirement plan rights that an employer promises its employees; mandatory insurance premiums paid by the employer fund the program.

performance appraisal   a program to evaluate a person's job performance during a specified period of time, usually a year; frequently tied to the process of determining merit pay increases.

perquisite   a benefit tied to a specific job and usually tied to the services the person performs for the organization in his/her capacity as an employee.

point factor comparison method of job evaluation   the most commonly used method of determining the value of jobs both for internal and external comparison; uses a few compensable factors, usually four or five, that have universal characteristics and relative characteristics (compared to other jobs in the hierarchy).

position analysis questionnaire (PAQ)   a job analysis technique that compares questionnaire results against wage survey data to determine values for various job characteristics.

prevailing wage   the wage for a job in a geographical area, determined by the U.S. Department of Labor, which is determined to be the standard; usually the union rate paid in that area.

profit sharing   a program in which a portion of profits is given to employees as a reward for performance.

range   see *wage range*

range overlap   the degree to which two adjacent pay ranges coincide.

ranking method of job evaluation   the simplest form of job evaluation that compares one job to another; job descriptions not required.

red circle   the term given to a pay rate that is frozen because the incumbent is being paid at a rate that exceeds the maximum value of the range; the wage/salary will be held at that level until the range is adjusted to such an extent that the pay level for this person falls below the top of the range in which the job is located.

Scanlon plan   an incentive program that links cost savings obtained by employees with bonus payments that are tied to the savings obtained by a specified formula.

shift differential   extra wages given to employees who work periods other than the normal work week (Monday through Friday; nine in the morning to five in the afternoon) to compensate them for an inconvenience and encourage them to work the off hours; there is frequently a two-tier differential; one is half the other and coincides with approximately half the time spent in and half outside the normal shift.

Social Security   a federal insurance program designed to provide supplementary income for the retired and payments to disabled people.

take-home pay   gross earnings less deductions; the cash in the pay envelope or cash direct deposit for the pay period.

unemployment insurance   government sponsored, partial income payments for a limited time provided to those who have lost their jobs without choice.

vesting   the process of acquiring ownership of a pension plan sponsored by an employer; under ERISA the vesting schedule must be five years or earlier under a cliff vesting arrangement or seven years or less if a graded schedule is used instead.

wage range   a minimum and maximum level of value set for a group of jobs evaluated to possess the same relative weight.

workers' compensation   state insurance programs designed to compensate any employee or his/her beneficiary who is the victim of a disease or accident tied to employment that results in wages lost and/or out-of-pocket expenses.

bibliography ───────────────────────────────

SUGGESTED READINGS

Below are two lists of books for your reference. The first is a compendium of recent works. The second are books that continue to survive in the absence of updates and revisions.

I. CURRENT TOPICAL WORKS

Calzon, Jan. *Moments of Truth.* New York: Harper & Row, 1989.

Cascio, Wayne F. *Costing Human Resources: The Financial Impact of Behavior in Organizations* (Third Edition). Boston: PWS-Kent, 1991.

Cascio, Wayne F., ed. *Human Resource Planning, Employment & Placement.* Washington, D.C.: Bureau of National Affairs, 1989.

Ceriello, Vincent R., with Christine Freeman. *Human Resource Management Systems.* Lexington, Massachusetts: D.C. Heath, 1991.

Clifford Donald K. Jr., and Richard E. Cavanaugh. *The Winning Performance.* Toronto: Bantam, 1988.

Crocker, Olga L., Syril Charney, and Johnny Sik Leung Chiu. *Quality Circles.* New York: New American Library, 1984.

Crystal, Graef S. *In Search of Excess.* New York: W. W. Norton, 1991.

DeLuca, Matthew J. *Cost Containment in Human Resources.* Greenvale, New York: Panel, 1987.

DeLuca, Matthew J. *Personnel Recordkeeper.* New York: Panel, 1993.

Drucker, Peter F. *Innovation & Entrepreneurship.* New York: Harper and Row, 1985.

Fine, S. A. *Functional Job Analysis Scales: A Desk Aid.* rev. ed. Milwaukee: Sidney A. Fine Associates, 1989.

Fisher, Roger, and William Ury; Bruce Patton, ed. *Getting to Yes.* 2d ed. New York: Penguin, 1991.

Fitz-enz, Jac. *How to Measure Human Resources Management.* New York: McGraw-Hill, 1984.

Gomez-Mejia, Luis R., ed. *Compensation and Benefits.* Washington, D.C.: Bureau of National Affairs, 1989.

Ginzberg, Eli, ed. *Executive Talent.* New York: John Wiley, 1988.

Grove, Andrew S. *High Output Management.* New York: Random House, 1983.

Handy, Charles. *The Age of Unreason.* Boston: Harvard Business School Press, 1990.

Iacocca, Lee, with William Novak. *Iacocca.* New York: Bantam Books, 1984.

Kanter, Rosabeth Moss. *The Change Masters.* New York: Simon & Schuster, 1984.

Kavanagh, Michael J., Hal G. Guental, and Scott I. Tannenbaum. *Human Resource Information Systems: Development and Application.* Boston: PWS-Kent, 1991.

Lawler, Edward E. III. *High Involvement Management.* San Francisco: Jossey-Bass, 1988.

Lawler, Edward E. III. *Strategic Pay.* San Francisco: Jossey-Bass, 1990.

Levering, Robert, Milton Moskowitz, and Michael Katz. *The 100 Best Companies to Work For in America.* 2d ed. Reading, Mass: Addison-Wesley, 1993.

Levering, Robert. *A Great Place to Work.* New York: Random House, 1988.

Manzini, Andrew O., and John D. Gridley. *Integrating Human Resources and Strategic Business Planning.* New York: Amacom, 1986.

Mohrman, Allan M. Jr., Susan M. Resnik-West and Edward E. Lawler III. *Designing Performance Appraisal Systems.* San Francisco: Jossey-Bass, 1989.

Naisbitt, John, and Patricia Aburdene. *Reinventing the Corporation*. New York: Warner, 1985.

Patten, Thomas H. Jr. *Fair Pay: The Managerial Challenge of Comparable Worth and Job Evaluation*. San Francisco: Jossey-Bass, 1988.

Peters, Tom. *Liberation Management*. New York: Alfred A. Knopf, 1992.

Peters, Tom. *Thriving on Chaos*. New York: Alfred A. Knopf, 1987.

Peters, Tom, and Nancy Austin. *A Passion for Excellence*. New York: Random House, 1985.

Pinchot, Gifford III. *Intrapreneuring*. New York: Harper & Row, 1985.

Rock, Milton L., and Lance A. Berger, eds. *The Compensation Handbook*. New York: McGraw-Hill, 1991.

Schuler, Randall S., and Vandra L. Huber. *Personnel and Human Resource Management*. 4th ed. St. Paul, Minnesota: West, 1990.

Senge, Peter M. *The Fifth Discipline*. New York: Doubleday, 1990.

Tarrant, John. *Perks and Parachutes*. New York: Linden Press, 1985.

U.S. Department of Labor. *Opportunity 2000: Creating Affirmative Action Strategies for a Changing Workforce*. Washington, D.C.: Government Printing Office, 1988.

Wallace, Marc J. Jr., and Charles H. Fay. *Compensation Theory and Practice*. Boston: Kent, 1983.

Wolfson, Jay, and Peter J. Levin. *Managing Employee Health Benefits*. Homewood, Illinois: Dow Jones–Irwin, 1985.

Zuboff, Shoshana. *In the Age of the Smart Machine*. Basic Books: New York, 1988.

II. EARLIER BOOKS THAT CONTINUE
TO HOLD THEIR OWN

Alpander, Guvenc G. *Human Resources Management Planning*. New York: Amacom, 1982.

Baehler, James R. *Book of Perks*. New York: St. Martin's Press, 1983.

Belcher, David W. *Wage and Salary Administration*. Englewood Cliffs, New Jersey: Prentice Hall, 1978.

Bennis, Stephen E., Ann Belenky, and Dee A. Soder. *Job Analysis: An Effective Management Tool*. Washington, D.C.: Bureau of National Affairs, 1983.

Berg, J. Gary. *Managing Compensation.* New York: Amacom, 1976.

Blanchard, Kenneth, Ph.D., and Spencer Johnson, M.D. *The One Minute Manager.* New York: William Morrow, 1982.

Chon, I., and Lundberg, R.A. *Compensating Key Executives in the Small Company.* New York: Amacom, 1979.

Deal, Terrence E., and Allan A. Kennedy. *Corporate Cultures.* Reading, Massachusetts: Addison-Wesley, 1982.

Ellig, Bruce R. *Executive Compensation: A Total Pay Perspective.* New York: McGraw-Hill, 1982.

Foulkes, Fred K. *Personnel Policies in Large Non-Union Companies.* Englewood Cliffs, New Jersey: Prentice Hall, 1978.

French, W.L., and C.H. Bell Jr. *Organization Development.* 2d ed. Englewood Cliffs, New Jersey: Prentice Hall, 1978.

Gellerman, Saul W. *Motivation and Productivity.* New York: Amacom, 1963.

Henderson, Richard I., and Kitty L. Clarke. *Job Pay for Job Worth: Designing and Managing an Equitable Job Classification and Pay System.* research monograph 86. Atlanta: Georgia State University, 1981.

Hersey, P., and K.H. Blanchard. *Management of Organizational Behavior: Utilizing Human Resources.* 3d ed. Englewood Cliffs, New Jersey: Prentice Hall, 1978.

Herzberg, R., E. Mausner, and B.B. Snyderman. *The Motivation to Work.* 2d ed. New York: Wiley, 1959.

Korda, Michael. *Power! How to Get It / How to Use It.* New York: Random House, 1975.

Latham, Gary P., and Kenneth N. Wexley. *Increasing Productivity Through Performance Appraisal.* Reading, Massachusetts: Addison-Wesley, 1981.

Lawler, Edward E. III. *Pay and Organization Development.* Reading, Massachusetts: Addison-Wesley, 1981.

Levinson, Harry. *The Exceptional Executive: A Psychological Conception.* Cambridge, Massachusetts: Harvard University Press, 1981.

Levinson, Harry. *Organization Dynamics.* Cambridge, Massachusetts: Harvard University Press, 1972.

Likert, Rensis. *New Patterns of Management.* New York: McGraw-Hill, 1971.

Maccoby, Michael. *The Gamesman.* New York: Simon & Schuster, 1976.

Maslow, Abraham H. *Motivation and Personality.* New York: Hayes, 1954.

McCaffery, Robert M. *Managing the Employee Benefits Program.* rev. ed. New York: Amacom, 1983.

McGregor, Douglas. *The Human Side of Enterprise.* New York: McGraw-Hill, 1967.

Odiorne, George S. *How Managers Make Things Happen.* Englewood Cliffs, New Jersey: Prentice Hall, 1961.

Odiorne, George S. *Management by Objectives.* New York: Pittman, 1965.

Ouchi, William G. *Theory Z.* New York: Avon Books, 1982.

Pascale, Richard Tanner, and Anthony G. Athos. *The Art of Japanese Management.* New York: Warner, 1981.

Peters, Thomas J., and Robert H. Waterman. *In Search of Excellence.* New York: Harper & Row, 1982.

Schein, Edgar H. *Process Consultation: Its Role in Organization Development.* Reading, Massachusetts: Addison-Wesley, 1969.

Sibson, Robert E. *Compensation.* New York: Amacom, 1960.

Simon, H.A., and Herbert A. Nevall. *Human Problem Solving.* Englewood Cliffs, New Jersey: Prentice Hall, 1971.

Sloane, Alfred Jr. *My Years With General Motors.* ed. John McDonald with Catherine Stevens. Garden City, New York: Anchor Books, 1963.

Whyte, William H. Jr. *The Organization Man.* New York: Simon & Schuster, 1956.

INDEX